INTERPERSONAL COMMUNICATION

INTERPERSONAL COMMUNICATION
A Question of Needs

MICHAEL D. SCOTT
West Virginia University

WILLIAM G. POWERS
University of Missouri, Columbia

HOUGHTON MIFFLIN COMPANY   BOSTON
Dallas   Geneva, Illinois   Hopewell, New Jersey   Palo Alto   London

Printed in the U.S.A.

Library of Congress Catalog Card Number: 77-76342

ISBN: 0-395-25055-2

To Randi Susan, Lois, and Scott

WE NEED TO FEEL MORE

we need to feel more
to understand others.
we need to love more
to be loved back.
we need to cry more
to cleanse ourselves
we need to laugh more
to enjoy ourselves.
we need to see more
other than our own little fantasies.
we need to hear more
and listen to the needs of others.
we need to give more
and take less.
we need to share more
and own less.
we need to look more
and realize that we are not so
    different from one another.
we need to create a world where
everyone can peacefully live
    the life they choose.

Susan Polis Schutz

CONTENTS

As the title of this book implies, the pages that follow are predicated on three principles inherent in the notion that interpersonal communication and human needs are fundamentally interdependent. The first principle suggests that people communicate because communication with living things is a need every bit as important to our psychological well-being as food and water are to our physical well-being. The second principle suggests that people not only communicate because communication is a human need, but also because communication is the medium through which many of our human needs are satisfied. The final principle, which we believe embodies the spirit in which this book was written, suggests that our interpersonal communication skills are not measured solely by the degree to which our communication behaviors assist us in satisfying the needs we feel, but also by the degree to which these same behaviors assist others in satisfying the needs that they feel.

In order to facilitate the acquisition of interpersonal communication skills, our text provides students with two sets of opportunities. First students are provided with opportunities to thoroughly come to grips with the relationship between what they say and what they feel; opportunities to think about how they got to be who they are and how that affects what they say and feel; and opportunities to thoroughly acquaint themselves with interpersonal communication as it affects the process by which people meet, become involved, and all too frequently grow apart. Secondly, we also provide students with opportunities to test their interpersonal communication skills in a variety of situations.

With respect to the first set of opportunities, this text consists of three parts: Human Communication and the Question of Needs; Interpersonal Communication and Identity; and Interpersonal Communication in Process. Part 1 provides students with information about the relationship between what they say and what they feel, discusses the human communication transaction in its most general sense, and then details the human communication transaction in its more specific, interpersonal sense. The second section of the book begins with commentary on the origins and nature of identity, emphasizes the fact that each and every identity is unique, and provides students with a framework from which they can view their own identity systems, as well as the identity systems of others. Following this, the section focuses on how communication reflects the interaction of our identities with our environment and, among other things, discusses perceptual processes, human expectancies, and communication strategies frequently exercised when expectancies are violated by what people say and do. The final section of the book then applies the framework provided in the preceding sections to the interpersonal communication process itself. This section approaches interpersonal communication from a relational perspective, suggesting that interpersonal communication basically concerns the meeting and merging of human identities. The section begins with a discussion of self-disclosure and other facets of communication that affect people as they meet and begin to explore their respective identities. This section next sees this process through, detailing how interpersonal communication changes as people become acquainted, achieve solidarity, become intimate, and sometimes come apart. This final section concludes with speculation about the peculiar demands that may be made on us by interpersonal communication in the future.

We have tried to create hypothetical situations that will enable students and teachers to test and, we hope, refine their interpersonal communication skills. We have tried to avoid being overly prescriptive, because we believe a book, for all its worth, is no substitute for what takes place in the classroom. We do not want to write a cookbook of interpersonal communication skills, with a list of do's and don'ts for each and every situation in which students are likely to find themselves. Such an approach demands that authors be in a position where they can learn about and observe the special needs of the students exposed to the information and advice supplied in their book, which we are not. To contend that the information and advice this book does offer is applicable to each and every student would be pretentious, if not absurd.

We have tried to provide students with opportunities to apply what they have learned from this book in the presence of the people who are most qualified to offer tailored advice—their teachers. Specifically, each chapter in this book is followed by three hypothetical interpersonal settings: educational, organizational, and relational. These hypothetical situations typically pose problems that students are likely to face in one of these three settings, and ask students how they would approach these interpersonal communication problems after reading a given chapter or chapters. Whether students discuss how they would approach these problems in a communication diary or in the presence of the teacher, the situations provide both students and teachers with an opportunity to assess interpersonal communication skills. Thus, we not only believe these situations are valuable pedagogical tools for students, but also believe they protect the rightful role of their teachers.

Finally, there is one other thing about this book that we believe distinguishes it from other books about interpersonal communication. For reasons both good and bad, our relationships with people sometimes come apart at the seams. As we see it one reason this happens is that the parties in a relationship frequently are unaware of both the signs of relational decay and the communication strategies in which they might engage to prevent further decay.

Therefore, we have included in this book a chapter that (1) describes how relational deterioration occurs and how it can be prevented, (2) provides students with information which will enable them to make intelligent decisions once they perceive a relationship is in trouble, and (3) suggests some ways students can constructively communicate this perception to their relational partners.

In closing, we hope the information presented here gives you a flavor of what this book is about and the approach it takes. We need only add that we, too, have tried to communicate to the student reader, in a personal manner, examples that will make much of what we say in this book come alive, and we hope that it will enrich your classes.

M. D. S.
W. G. P.

ACKNOWLEDGMENTS

Like any other project of this magnitude, the pages of this book reflect the thinking of people other than Mike Scott and Will Powers. Therefore, we would like to extend our heartfelt thanks to some people who made this book much more than we had originally envisioned. First of all, we would like to thank the people who took time from their already hectic schedules to review this book in its various stages, especially Eldon Baker (University of Montana), John Boyd, Roy Berko, Lorain County Community College, Larry Chase (California State, Sacramento), Dick Cheatham (Texas Tech.), Isa Engleberg (Prince George's Community College), Wayne Hensley (University of Wisconsin, Milwaukee), Lynn Phelps (Miami University of Ohio), George Rodman (University of New Hampshire), and Janice Rushing (UCLA).

Also, we would like to extend our appreciation to our friends and colleagues in the departments where we work, and give special thanks to Buddy Wheeless and Max Black for directing us to theory and research which we might have overlooked.

M. D. S.
W. G. P.

A PERSONAL NOTE TO STUDENTS:
THE PEOPLE WHO MAKE IT ALL WORTHWHILE

We would like to explain a few things about this book. First of all, the book is divided into three major sections: (1) Human Communication and the Question of Needs, (2) Interpersonal Communication and Identity, and (3) Interpersonal Communication in Process. This developmental sequence reflects our belief that in the effort to become a more skilled interpersonal communicator you need to understand the nature of the relationship between needs and communication behaviors, individual identities and their impact on our interpersonal communication behaviors, and the evolutionary nature of interpersonal communication as our relationships become more involved.

Secondly, each chapter within these three sections begins with something called "Shop Talk" and ends with something called "Think About It."

SHOP TALK

As you probably know all too well, most scholarly disciplines have a language of their own. Human Communication is no different. For example, in the area of nonverbal communication, touch is called naptics, time is called chronemics, and smell—get this—is called olfactics. While we could have thrown such jargon out of the book, part and parcel, we felt it would be a disservice to students who may major in communication and who, therefore, may need to be familiar with these terms. As a result, each chapter begins with Shop Talk, which lists and defines jargonistic words commonly used by people in our discipline. Prior to reading a specific chapter, you might find it useful to familiarize yourself with these words and their appropriate definition. If you do, we believe these words will not get in the way of the content that really counts.

THINK ABOUT IT

We have included a special feature called, "Think About It" at the end of each chapter. Here, you will find a set of tasks in which you are asked to apply the information in each chapter generally and also to apply it specifically in three communication contexts: (1) The educational environment, (2) the organizational environment, and (3) your present relationships. Exactly how you use the Think About It sections depends on your individual needs and those of your teacher. We suggest, however, that you may want to discuss the tasks in class, which would enable the teacher to observe and instruct you in the ways you approach interpersonal communication situations, or you may want to use some of these tasks as the focal point for a communication diary that details your day-to-day interpersonal communication encounters. Whatever you and your teacher decide, we hope you will use the tasks described in the Think About It sections to make the material discussed in each chapter come alive as it relates to you and the people in your life.

To sum up, then, we think the study and practice of communicating interpersonally should be a lifetime process. It is our sincere hope, moreover, that the material in this book leads you to a like conclusion.

INTERPERSONAL COMMUNICATION

Part One
Human Communication
and the Question of Needs

What meaning do you have for the word *need*? Do you think of a need as something you want or desire? Or do you think of a need as something essential to your physical and psychological well being?

Are physical needs the same as psychological needs? Are personal needs the same as interpersonal needs? Are the needs you feel or experience while attending classes anything like the needs you feel or experience while spending time with friends or while working?

What does communication have to do with the question of needs? Is communication in itself a need? Or is communication just a convenient device that assists you in satisfying needs? Do you communicate the same way to satisfy all the needs you feel or experience? Or do you communicate in different ways in the attempt to satisfy the different needs you feel, depending on the people you are with and the situation in which you find yourself?

These are a few of the questions we will consider in the first three chapters. In Chapter 1 we examine some of the major characteristics of the needs all of us experience, discuss two need systems developed by Abraham Maslow and William Schutz, and conclude with an analysis of the relationship between human needs and human communication. Chapter 2 builds on this foundation by detailing communication in terms of what it is and what it involves. Finally, Chapter 3 extends the information provided in the initial two chapters to the specific area of interpersonal communication.

Chapter One
Human Communication and
Human Needs: An Overview

Needs Physical and psychological feelings that give rise to discomfort and motivate us to behave in such a way that we can overcome the discomfort.

Hierarchy A sequence of principles that usually are arranged on the basis of importance.

Biological needs Food, water, and air.

Safety needs Freedom from fear or the threat of physical harm, as well as order and structure in our lives.

Self-esteem The need to feel that you are significant and worthwhile.

Social esteem The need to feel that others share your belief that you are significant and worthwhile.

Self-actualization The need to find out what you are uniquely suited to be as a person.

Knowing and understanding The need to know and understand one's own existence in relationship to the universe.

Aesthetic need The need to embellish or to correct imperfections that we perceive in nature and ourselves.

Social inclusion An interpersonal need concerned with one's ability to interact and associate with people.

Behavior control An interpersonal need concerned with one's ability to make and accept decisions affecting behavior.

Affection An interpersonal need concerned with one's ability to give and receive affection.

In this age of winning through intimidation and looking out for number one, we sometimes forget that how we treat other people will go a long way in determining how they treat us. We all have problems and hang-ups. And we realize how difficult it sometimes is to manage our own lives, much less assist other people in the management of their lives.

But when you think about it, can we really afford to ignore the people with whom we come in contact, for example, the brother-in-law who bores us to tears, the person who pesters us about lecture notes after skipping class, or the person at work who can't seem to relate to coworkers? Can we really afford to shut ourselves off completely from their problems, their weaknesses, or their needs? Before you make up your mind, consider the following excerpt taken from an article written by Sally Quinn, a former newscaster and current reporter for the *Washington Post*. The excerpt is not intended to depress you but rather to point out what can happen when people have difficulties in communicating what they feel or when other people fail to realize the importance of their attempts to communicate what they feel.

> Sarasota, FL — Christine Chubbuck flicked her long dark hair back away from her face, swallowed, twitched her lips only slightly and reached with her left hand to turn the next page of her script. Looking down on

the anchor desk she began to read: "In keeping with Channel 40's policy of bringing you the latest in" — she looked up from the script, directly into the camera and smiled a tentative smile. Her voice took on a sarcastic tone as she emphasized "blood and guts . . . and in living color." She looked back down at her script, her left hand shook almost unnoticeably.

Her right arm stiffened. "We bring you another first." Her voice was steady. She looked up again into the camera. Her eyes were dark, direct and challenging. "An attempted suicide." Her right hand came up from under the anchor desk. In it was a .38 caliber revolver. She pointed it at the lower back of her head and pulled the trigger. A loud crack was heard. A puff of smoke blew out from the gun and her hair flew up around her face as though a sudden gust of wind had caught it. Her face took on a fierce, contorted look, her mouth wrenched downward, her head shook. Then her body fell forward with a resounding thud and slowly slipped out of sight.

Hours later at the hospital, shortly before Christine Chubbuck died, her mother was interviewed by a local reporter.

"She was terribly, terribly, terribly depressed. She had a job that she loved. She said constantly that if it ended tomorrow she would still be glad she had had it. But she had nothing else in her social life.

"No close friends, no romantic attachments or prospects of any. She was a spinster at 29 and it bothered her. She couldn't register with people. That's the main thing. She was very sensitive and she tried and she would reach out, you know, 'Hi, how are you, won't you come have a cup of coffee with me,' and you say 'no,' but you don't say 'Won't you come have a cup of coffee with me,' that sort of thing, in her personal people realtionships, and it really got to her. She'd been very depressed. She'd been seeing a psychiatrist who really didn't feel that she was that serious about not wanting to live. She felt if you've tried as hard as you can, you've prepared yourself, you work hard, you reach your hand out to people and nobody takes it, then there's something wrong with your drumbeat, and she really felt she couldn't register with anyone except her family. And at 29, that's sad."[1]

While we do not believe Christine Chubbuck's suicide was solely the result of her inability to register with people, we can't help but wonder whether her death could have been prevented had she or the people around her been able to express and cope with the needs she felt. Here was a young woman who was articulate, attractive, and making it in a profession that for too long has been dominated by men. She was a young woman who, on the surface, appeared to be the prototype of the modern female.

[1]Sally Quinn, "Christine Chubbuck: 29, Good-Looking, Educated. A Television Personality. Dead. Live and in Color," in *Writing in Style,* ed. Laura Longley Babb, Houghton Mifflin Company, Boston, 1975, pp. 123–134. Copyright © The Washington Post.

In spite of everything she apparently had going for her, Christine could not accomplish what most of us take for granted. As evidenced in the words of Sally Quinn, she could neither communicate the needs she felt nor relate to the needs of other people:

> She had no real friends. She was a strange combination of someone who at once wanted, needed desperately, the support and friendship of others and in another way rejected others out of a sense of defensive pride. Her initial image was one of a self-confident, totally contained, together young woman. She would seem haughty, distant, standoffish really. Yet when people began to know her she evidenced such a crying need for a completely committed relationship that it drove them away.

Christine Chubbuck was obviously plagued by severe psychological problems. But in a way, she was really no different from any of us. We all try to attract and not repulse people through what we say and do. The satisfaction of our needs is dependent on how well we communicate the needs *we experience* and how well we assist other people in satisfying the needs *they experience*.

In this opening chapter we discuss this function of communication and the fact that when we ignore the needs of others we diminish the quality of our own lives. Before doing so, though, you may be wondering why we have decided to use needs as a focal point for a book about interpersonal communication. As you will learn in class, communication performs many important functions, for example, maximizing the rewards and minimizing the punishments in our environment, establishing affinity with others, and making predictions about human behavior, to name just a few. Why then did we decide to restrict our focus to the relationship between human needs and human communication? Based on our own experiences with students in our interpersonal communication courses, we have found that students not only can relate to the idea that communication is the medium by which a majority of our needs are satisfied but also can apply it in their day-to-day interpersonal communication experiences. With this in mind, let's begin our discussion of human communication and the question of needs by examining the very nature of the needs we all experience.

HUMAN NEEDS AND HUMAN BEHAVIOR

During the course of a given day we experience a number of needs. Some are physical, like hunger and thirst, while others are psychological, like love and affection. Although we experience these needs regularly, few of us are in the habit of thinking about them or their effects on our day-to-day behaviors.

NEED DEFINED

A *need* is really nothing more than a drive-producing state or condition.[2] By *drive-producing,* we mean a state or condition that causes us to feel discomfort, which in turn motivates us to engage in behavior that will assist us in overcoming the discomfort. Hunger is exactly the kind of state or condition we are talking about. When we are hungry, we feel some discomfort. In the effort to overcome this discomfort, we normally engage in behaviors that will satisfy our need for food. Failure to satisfy even a simple need like hunger may detract from our ability to function successfully. If you've ever had a class scheduled at the time you normally eat lunch, you know what we mean. While an instructor's comments about westward expansion may be important for an upcoming exam, they may take a backseat to your hunger pains and their embarrassing growl.

The point to be made, then, is that needs tend to consume us when we experience them, because they motivate us to take action to satisfy them. And it is only after these needs have been taken care of that we can go about conducting our day-to-day communication activities in an efficient and effective manner.

CHARACTERISTICS OF NEEDS

Like people, needs are different. Physical needs are not identical to psychological needs. Certainly they are less complex and more easily understood. With the exception of sex, which we believe is a psychological as well as physical need, physical needs also are easier to satisfy. Hunger or thirst are easily understood and can be satisfied more or less at any one of the thousands of McDonalds that dot the landscape of this nation. But can the same be said for psychological needs? We think not.

Recognizing Needs One of the primary differences between physiological and psychological needs is that we can more easily recognize the physiological needs we experience. While you may not dwell on a physiological need like thirst, you normally are well aware of what is causing your throat to feel dry or your mouth to feel as if it were made of cotton. Because you recognize the source of your discomfort, you can plan a course of action that will dispel the discomfort almost immediately.

But it's not so simple with our psychological needs, because we are not always aware of experiencing them. Often, we cannot identify the source of our

[2]William Schutz, *The Interpersonal Underworld*, Science and Behavior Books, Palo Alto, 1968, pp. 1–15.

discomfort nor associate that source with behavior that will lead to its disappearance. How many times, for example, have you felt that something in your life was missing, but you couldn't put your finger on exactly what that something was? Maybe more often than you care to remember. Such an experience is hardly uncommon. Furthermore, most of us have experienced the frustration of not being able to identify the source of a feeling or pinpoint the behavior we engage in that is attributable to the feeling. Actually much of our behavior during the course of the day is not consciously thought about and decided on. This is why we sometimes "wake up" and ask ourselves questions like "Why in the world did I act like that?" While a large percentage of unconscious behavior is habit, many habits are associated directly with the needs we experience but are unable to recognize on a conscious level.

Thus, one of the primary distinctions between physiological and psychological needs concerns how easily they are recognized. While we can recognize and even explain a physiological need, we are not always aware of our psychological needs. As a result, psychological needs sometimes place us in the position of not being able to explain the "why" and "what for" of much of our communication behavior.

Personal and Interpersonal A majority of the physiological needs that we experience can be satisfied without the benefit of direct contact with other people. We do not always need to talk with other people in the effort to satisfy our need for food or to quench our thirst. To this extent, our physiological needs are personal and do not demand involvement with other people.

Whether personal or interpersonal, however, our psychological needs demand at least some involvement with other people if they are to be satisfied. Whereas we can satisfy a physiological need like thirst without becoming involved with someone, most of us would be hard pressed to satisfy a need like self-esteem or affection without becoming involved with someone. Thus, a second distinction that can be drawn between physiological and psychological needs is that the satisfaction of our psychological needs demands at least minimum involvement with people.

Relational Levels Physiological needs also tend to remain constant across our relationships with other people. We use the word *tend* here because there are exceptions like sex. In contrast to the relative stability of physiological needs, our psychological needs vary depending on the people we are with and the situation in which we find ourselves.

In a romantic relationship and under romantic circumstances, a psychological need like affection may dominate your feelings and characterize your relationship. At school, however, a psychological need like the need to know and understand may dominate your feelings and characterize your relationships with classmates. Finally, a psychological need like feeling that others consider you competent and responsible may be the most dominant need you experience at work and while involved with coworkers.

The point is a simple one. The psychological needs that dominate our feelings will vary depending on the people with whom we are involved and the situation in which we find ourselves. As you may guess, the degree to which our psychological needs vary also will affect the ways we communicate with people.

Importance The final characteristic of psychological needs that we shall discuss is also a characteristic of physiological needs. We prefer to dwell on this characteristic as it relates to psychological needs, however, because they are most important to our communication transactions and interpersonal relationships. With this in mind, why do you think some people periodically enjoy solitude, while others shudder at the slightest hint that they will soon be without company? We believe it is partially attributable to the fact that some of our psychological needs are much more important than others. A person who occasionally enjoys solitude, for example, may not need to be constantly surrounded by people. The reverse may be true for the person who can't stand to be isolated from other people. For this type of person, isolation may mean anxiety or depression — two states most of us would judge to be extremely unpleasant. As a result, social inclusion may be the most important need this person experiences.

Whether or not a need is perceived to be an important motivational force is usually a function of how often the need has been satisfied.[3] As a general rule, psychological needs that have typically gone unsatisfied are much more potent motivational forces than psychological needs that have seldom gone unsatisfied.[4] Thus, adults who had little difficulty surrounding themselves with friends during childhood may not need the attention of others as much as the adult who had extreme difficulties in this regard as a child.

So what have we said thus far in our discussion of needs? To begin with, we have said that needs are motivational in the sense that when we feel one we behave in a manner which is targeted at satisfying the need. Also, we have indicated that our psychological needs are more complex and not as easily recognized as our physiological needs. Finally, we have said that our psychological needs may be personal or interpersonal, may vary depending on people and situations, and also may vary in terms of importance. Now that we

[3]Abraham H. Maslow, *Toward a Psychology of Being,* 2nd ed., Van Nostrand, New York, 1968.
[4]Abraham H. Maslow, *Toward a Psychology of Being.*

have discussed the basic nature of the needs we experience, we would like to focus on two perspectives concerning how our needs affect our individual orientations and our personal and interpersonal communications.

NEED SYSTEMS

The viewpoint that human behavior is often the outgrowth of human needs has served observers of the human condition ranging from Aristotle to Lenny Bruce. The perspectives of two such observers, Abraham Maslow and William Schutz, are particularly well suited to the purpose of this chapter and the chapters that follow. Although some would disagree, we do not necessarily see these perspectives as competing with one another. Rather, we present Maslow's work to provide an overall view of the physical and psychological needs humans experience, and Schutz's work to provide a specific view of a set of interpersonal psychological needs.

MASLOW'S HIERARCHICAL SYSTEM

Few twentieth-century thinkers have had as much impact on the study of human behavior as the late Abraham Maslow. The impact of his thinking was first felt in 1943 when his article "Theory of Human Motivation" was published.[5] His influence has continued with his other works, notably *Motivation and Personality* (1954), *Toward a Psychology of Being* (1968), and *The Farther Reaches of Human Nature* (1971).

Central to Maslow's theory of human motivation is the concept that human beings experience two sets of needs: deficiency and growth needs. Maslow believed that people engage in behaviors designed to satisfy deficiency needs so that they can move on to the task of satisfying their more pleasurable growth needs. Maslow also believed that our deficiency needs are prepotent. By this, he meant that deficiency needs must be satisfied prior to the satisfaction of growth needs. Thus, from Maslow's perspective our needs are satisfied in a sequential fashion. We have illustrated this sequence in Figure 1-1.

Deficiency Needs As illustrated in Figure 1-1, there are four sets of deficiency needs. The first consists of biological needs like food to eat, water to drink, and clean air to breathe. Maslow believed these biological needs serve as the foundation of all other human needs. To illustrate this point, think back to a time when you were not just merely hungry but were famished. Were you

---

[5]Abraham H. Maslow, "A Theory of Human Motivation," *Psychological Review*, 50 (1943), 370–396.

FIGURE 1-1
MASLOW'S HIERARCHY OF NEEDS

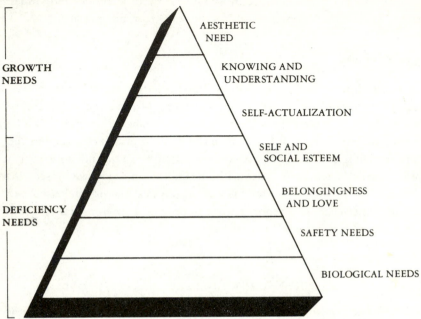

Data (for diagram) based on Hierarchy of Needs in "A Theory of Human Motivation" in *Motivation and Personality,* 2nd Edition by Abraham H. Maslow. Copyright © 1970 by Abraham H. Maslow. By permission of Harper & Row, Publishers, Inc.

concerned with your need for self-esteem, affection, or knowledge? Probably not. Imagine, then, what it would be like if you were a member of an emerging nation where famine is the rule rather than the exception. In such nations, food, not self-worth, love, or knowledge is the primary need and the primary determinant of human behavior. Until that need is satisfied routinely, the complex psychological needs that we experience are not likely to emerge.

As can be seen in Figure 1-1, the second set of deficiency needs you experience concern your safety. Safety needs refer to things like protection from physical harm or the threat of physical harm, freedom from fear, and order as well as the need for structure in our lives. Maslow contended that these safety needs become important once we feel secure that our biological needs are being satisfied. We seriously doubt that you are preoccupied with questions or fears about your own safety or the safety of those with whom you are involved. If you were, however, needs like social esteem, belongingness and love, or self-actualization probably would be suppressed until you were assured of your continued safety. People who live in constant fear of being mugged, raped, or murdered in their beds will concern themselves with little else, as evidenced by the fact that record numbers of handguns, locks, and guard dogs were sold in Los Angeles the day after Charles Manson's family brutally murdered Sharon Tate, Abigail Folger, Jay Sebring, Voytek Frykowski, and Steven Parent.

Once we can satisfy our biological and safety needs routinely, we are in a position to confront our more complex deficiency needs. As in the two preceding instances, these more complex deficiency needs must be satisfied in a sequential fashion. The first set of needs in this regard pertains to belongingness and love which are essential to our psychological well-being. Many case studies have demonstrated that a child's intelligence and ability to adapt to his or her environment is tremendously influenced by parental affection. Sally Quinn's portrait of Christine Chubbuck illustrates how important belongingness and love needs really are to a person's psychological well-being. This example also serves to make another point. People who like themselves seldom take their own lives. The satisfaction of belongingness and love needs bears directly on the degree to which people can look into a mirror and tell themselves they like what they see.

This brings up the final set of deficiency needs. Maslow believed that once we have satisfied our belongingness and love needs we are in a position to confront two esteem needs: self-esteem and social esteem. Self-esteem is basically the need to believe that you are significant and worthwhile. Social esteem is the need to believe that the people you come in contact with share this belief about you. The relationship between the needs for self-esteem and social esteem is a reciprocal one, and both needs are satisfied through communication. To a large extent, the satisfaction of our need for self-esteem occurs as a function of others interacting with us and sharing their affection. By the same token, the satisfaction of our need for social esteem depends a great deal on what we think of ourselves. Children who feel that they belong and are loved and who have been reinforced for communicating are more likely to satisfy their need for self-esteem than children who have not been so treated. Children with self-esteem, then, will be less fearful about communicating in the attempt to make friends or establish relationships.

At this point, let's quickly review what we've said regarding deficiency needs. First, we must be able to satisfy deficiency needs routinely prior to confronting our growth needs. Second, deficiency needs must be satisfied sequentially, that is, beginning with our biological needs and ending with our esteem needs. Keep these points in mind as we discuss what Maslow believed are the most complex and most difficult needs to satisfy.

Growth Needs When people feel secure about the routine satisfaction of their deficiency needs, their growth needs begin to emerge. These needs are not as much concerned with establishing relationships with other people as they are with maximizing an individual's potential. The first growth need described by Maslow is *self-actualization.*

Once you reach the need to self-actualize, you must look inward and begin to question the very fabric of which you are made, for self-actualization is really the need to find out what you and only you are uniquely suited to be. Examples of truly self-actualized people are rare. According to Maslow, though, such people do exist. What distinguishes them from others is the way they behave toward themselves and the people with whom they come in contact. They accept more readily themselves and others, they are oriented toward problems outside their own, and they are keenly sensitive to the needs of others. The self-actualized person, in other words, is what most of us would like to be but are not.

Difficult as self-actualization is to achieve, it is not the pinnacle of Maslow's hierarchy. There are two levels of needs beyond it. The first level concerns what Maslow called *the need to know and understand.* This need to question and challenge existing thought is not idle curiosity. It is concerned with our abilities to know and understand ourselves in relationship to the order of the universe. And if it is safe to assume that self-actualization is rarely achieved, it is even safer to assume that only a few of us ever satisfy the need to know and understand ourselves.

Lastly, Maslow believed that there is an *aesthetic need* that is unique to humans. Evidence of this need to embellish or to correct the imperfections that we perceive in nature and in ourselves can be found in the caves of southern France and northern Spain, the Gothic cathedrals — Notre Dame and St. Denis — and the words of Homer and Robert Frost. While few of us ever become artists in the true sense of the word, most of us experience at some time in our lives the need to leave behind us some trace of beauty that will transcend our mortality. We may be able to satisfy this aesthetic need through the people we touch. That is to say, we may be able to leave a trace of beauty in the lives of the people who remember and still find pleasure in their experiences with us.

Concluding Remarks on Maslow   One of the great strengths of Maslow's hierarchial approach is its use as an explanatory base for a full range of our communication behavior. For example, most of us could explain at least some of our communications on the basis of our need to achieve structure in our lives, to attain a sense of security, or to free ourselves from the fear of physical harm — all of which are safety needs. We might also explain our desire to communicate with certain types of people on the grounds that such people are genuinely affectionate toward us (belongingness and love) or contribute to our sense of self-worth (esteem).

Perhaps the best indicator of the social utility of Maslow's hierarchy is the fact that the seventies have become what in a recent essay Tom Wolfe called "The Me Decade." Although Wolfe never refers to Maslow, he argues that widespread economic security has resulted in a search by many people for "the real me." No doubt Maslow had something different from "The Me Decade" in mind when he conceived his need system and theory of motivation. The sad truth is, though, that people are now paying groups like TM International and est to learn how to self-actualize.

SCHUTZ'S INTERPERSONAL PERSPECTIVES

In 1958 Schutz introduced his model of fundamental interpersonal relations orientation.[6] Since that time, the model has undergone extensive research in laboratory settings and has been used widely in real-life settings by people interested in studying the behavior of organizational personnel.

Schutz's interpersonal need system presents three needs with which each of us can identify, and it describes behaviors in which we have engaged or that we have seen others exhibit. From his perspective, an interpersonal need is one that may be satisfied only through the development of a satisfactory relationship with another person or other persons. Schutz establishes three primary interpersonal needs, which he calls inclusion, control, and affection, and these are outlined in Table 1-1. If these needs go unsatisfied, Schutz contends, the individual may experience extreme anxiety and exhibit abnormal behavior.

TABLE 1-1
SCHUTZ'S INTERPERSONAL SYSTEM

INTERPERSONAL NEED	DEFINITION	TYPES OF BEHAVIOR
Social inclusion	Successful interactions and associations with people	Oversocial Undersocial Ideal social
Behavior control	To feel competent and worthwhile with respect to decision making; the ability to accept as well as make decisions	Abdicrat Autocrat Democrat
Affection	The ability to both give and receive affection	Overpersonal Underpersonal Ideal personal

[6]William Schutz, *FIRO: Fundamental Interpersonal Relations Orientation*, Holt, Rinehart, and Winston, 1958.

SOCIAL INCLUSION

Basically, social inclusion is the need to establish and maintain rewarding interpersonal relationships that are comfortable to the persons involved with respect to the type of association and level of interaction that characterize their relationship. Thus, a rewarding interpersonal relationship in this sense could range from two coworkers who enjoy working on a mutual task to a social group consisting of people with similar interests.

On an individual level, the interpersonal need for inclusion is roughly equivalent to the need to feel significant and worthwhile, and this need becomes evident in one of three ways: (1) undersocial behavior, (2) oversocial behavior, and (3) ideal social behavior.

Undersocial Behavior No matter how hard they try, some people consistently meet with failure in their attempts to satisfy their need for social inclusion. If you search hard and long enough into your past, you will probably recall some painful reminders of this fact. Maybe it was the kid in elementary school whose physical appearance was the focus of every cruel joke at recess time. Perhaps in junior high school it was the student with the severe speech impediment, or maybe it was the dateless young man or woman who spent prom night watching television.

Such people must compensate for their inability to satisfy the need for inclusion. The compensation may take the form of withdrawal, which means a disassociation or disengagement from other people in order to protect oneself from being hurt. In effect, they say to themselves, "Since no one really cares about me, I won't let them have the opportunity to prove the point."

Undersocial people who withdraw usually become self-indulgent in the sense that they create shells around themselves. The shell actually consists of a pattern of behavior designed to defend their self-concept from the abuses of other people. This behavior communicates things like, "I don't need other people" or "I'm strong enough to go it alone." But such shells are typically quite thin and easy to see through. Ultimately, the people who come into contact with the shell houses of undersocial people will see them for what they really are — facades.

Undersocial people are not undersocial by choice. Like Christine Chubbuck, they become undersocial to compensate for the succession of failures they have met with in the attempt to satisfy their need for inclusion. They act as if "they don't give a damn about other people" because they perceive that no one "gives a damn about them."

Oversocial Behavior People who are overly social suffer from the same perception as people who are undersocial. They too feel that people are uninterested in them. But people who are overly social behave much differently from people who are undersocial. Instead of withdrawing, they assert themselves and engage in attention-getting behavior. Ultimately such people may pay a high price for their efforts to hide their insecurities. Marilyn Monroe, Lenny Bruce, and Judy Garland are a few cases in point. If we are to believe their biographers, each of these personalities was extremely insecure and perceived that few, if any, of the people they came in contact with were seriously concerned with their well-being. Their private image of themselves, in other words, was the opposite of the overly social image that they presented to the public.

Yet, we needn't turn to the famous or notorious to find people who are overly social. In the classroom, some people try to dominate discussions in the effort to prove that they are significant and worthwile. On the job, some people may constantly boast about their contributions to the organization in an effort to demonstrate their significance.

Needless to say, it's very easy for us to condemn people when they appear to be overly social. We can judge them to be pushy, loudmouthed, vulgar, conceited, or obnoxious. But what we should do is try to be sensitive to the fact that such people behave as if they are pushy or obnoxious for a reason: they have continuously failed to satisfy an interpersonal need that is extremely important — to be liked and accepted by the people with whom they come in contact.

Ideal Social Behavior People who experience little or no difficulty in associating and interacting with other people seldom exhibit behavior that can be labeled as undersocial or oversocial. For one thing, such people consistently satisfy their need for inclusion, and they experience none of the insecurities characteristic of undersocial and oversocial people. Generally, people exhibiting what Schutz calls ideal social behavior think well of themselves, see some sense of purpose in their lives, and express genuine interest in other people. Unlike those who are undersocial, people who exhibit ideal social behavior are not afraid to involve themselves with others or make a commitment to others. Unlike overly social people, they are not compelled to surround themselves with others at all times or try to prove their significance. Put simply, people who have had little difficulty in satisfying their need for inclusion can discriminate between advantageous and disadvantageous relationships with other people; that is, they can distinguish relationships that hold some promise for mutual reward from relationships that do not.

For the most part, people who exhibit ideal social behavior seem to be highly skilled in communicating. It is not that such people simply know the right thing to say or how to say it eloquently, but rather that they seem to be able to interpret accurately and respond appropriately to the communication behavior of other people. Thus, their ability to satisfy their own need for social inclusion may be tied to the fact that they assist other people in satisfying their need for social inclusion.

BEHAVIOR CONTROL

A second interpersonal need that Schutz recognizes is the need for behavior control. This is the need to establish and maintain rewarding interpersonal relationships that enable the persons involved to feel comfortable with the degree of control and power they exert over each other. A rewarding interpersonal relationship in this mode could range from two people who exert equal control and power over each other to a relationship where one person has most of the control and power over the other. It simply would depend on whether the parties in the relationship felt comfortable.

From the perspective of the individual, the interpersonal need for behavior control is the need to feel competent and responsible. To put it another way, it is the need to feel that people trust your judgments about matters which have direct bearing on their behavior. As was the case with the interpersonal need for inclusion, people try to cope with their interpersonal need for behavior control by adopting one of three behavioral postures: (1) the abdicrat, (2) the autocrat, and (3) the democrat.

The Abdicrat People who have met with one failure after another in their attempt to be perceived as competent and responsible soon come to think of themselves as being incapable of making decisions or taking on responsibilities. Schutz refers to such people as *abdicrats.* Abdicrats are always submissive when it comes to power and responsibility. In fact, abdicrats shirk power and responsibility even when the situation requires it. Humphrey Bogart's portrayal of Captain Queeg in *The Caine Mutiny* courtmartial exemplifies the behavior of the abdicrat. After failing to properly command his ship and crew during maneuvers and then during an actual landing invasion, Captain Queeg ascribed blame and responsibility for his failures to officers of lesser rank rather than recognize his own ineptitude. Finally, he failed to take control and command of his ship when it was about to capsize in a typhoon.

Abdicrats also resent and distrust people who fail to assist them in carrying out their responsibilities. Again, Bogart's portrayal of Captain Queeg illustrates this fact. Unable to carry out his responsibilities and faced with a doubting crew, Queeg became so suspicious and distrustful of his crew that he appeared paranoid. Ultimately, the first officer relieved Queeg as captain on the grounds that he had become a textbook example of paranoia.

Because they have been unable to satisfy their need for behavior control in the past, abdicrats assume submissive postures and usually seek out positions that do not require leadership. Such people also attempt to shirk their responsibilities to others and become resentful or even hostile toward those who fail to assist them in carrying them out.

The Autocrat People who become autocrats attempt to dominate every person and every situation in which they are involved. Whereas the abdicrat is meek, the autocrat is aggressive with respect to control and power. Interestingly enough, autocrats believe that other people think they can't make decisions or assume responsibility. It is this perception that gives rise to their desire to dominate. Schutz describes the unconscious attitude of an autocrat: "No one thinks I can make decisions for myself, but I'll show them. I'm going to make all the decisions for everyone, always."[7]

History has provided us with numerous examples of the autocrat. Among the most notorious are Julius Caesar, Napoleon Bonaparte, Adolph Hitler, and Richard Nixon. Each of these historical figures gravitated toward power, harbored deep-seated suspicions of those who doubted their decision-making abilities, and surrounded themselves with people who unhesitatingly accepted their decisions to be the only decisions.

The Democrat As children, we sometimes found it difficult to understand why we couldn't always be at the head of the recess line, couldn't always be the quarterback or pitcher, or couldn't always have the lead in the holiday season pageant. As we mature, however, we begin to understand and cope with this reality. For those of us who do learn to understand and cope in this regard, the satisfaction of our interpersonal need for behavior control will be routine rather than problematic. Instead of becoming submissive or domineering with all people in all situations, we learn to cope, and we understand that life requires us to take orders and accept decisions as well as give orders and make decisions.

Schutz calls people who exhibit this kind of flexibility *democrats*. Such people, he asserts, suffer from none of the fears about their competencies or sense of responsibility that are characteristic of the abdicrat and the autocrat. Democrats believe in their own capabilities and, therefore, need not shirk responsibility nor demand it to an excessive extent. In short, they are realistic about their abilities to influence and control as well as to be influenced and controlled by others. As was the case with people who exhibit ideal social behavior, democrats seem to have acquired the ability to accurately interpret and appropriately respond to the messages of other people. This is evident in that they can communicate their own wishes with respect to behavior control, but at the same time they can respect and weigh what is communicated by others regarding behavior control.

[7]William Schutz, *The Interpersonal Underworld*, Science and Behavior Books, Palo Alto, 1966, p. 29.

AFFECTION

The final interpersonal need in Schutz's perspective is the need to establish and maintain a rewarding interpersonal relationship of love and affection. Such a relationship would be one in which the persons involved feel psychologically comfortable about their emotional attachment to each other. The range can extend from the relation of parent and child to boy friend and girl friend. In these relationships, the individual has the need to be perceived as worthy of receiving affection and as capable of giving affection. Schutz believes that people try to satisfy or cope with the interpersonal need for affection by engaging in one of three types of behavior: (1) underpersonal, (2) overpersonal, and (3) ideal personal.

Underpersonal Behavior Few experiences in adolescence are as painful as those involving our first attempts to establish a mutually affectionate relationship. Yet the pain that inheres in this experience is not nearly as great as the pain in one of its potential consequences—having our affection rejected by the object of our affection. Most of us can recall at least one time in our lives when we agonized for days on end over the person who remained untouched by our amorous advances. But most of us got over the fact that "you can't always get what you want." That is to say, we learned to cope with the fact that our attempts to gain affection do not always succeed. People who are characteristically underpersonal are unable to make this kind of adjustment. They cannot come to grips with the knowledge that the rejection of affection is as much a part of life as the acceptance of affection. Instead, such people view rejection as a personal indictment against their lovability.

Unable to cope with the rejection of affection, people who are underpersonal tend to adopt one of two patterns of behavior. The first and most obvious pattern is one in which the person's life is void of close, interpersonal ties. He or she is likely to establish and maintain relationships that can be best described as superficial, distant, and simplistic. The second pattern of behavior that underpersonal people may exhibit is less obvious. On the surface it would appear that the person has many close, personal ties, but this is misleading. Such a person will often embrace a number of people in superficial interpersonal relationships to avoid becoming intimate with or committed to only one person in one relationship.

The behaviors of people who are underpersonal have the same motivational base as the behavior exhibited by undersocial people. Whereas undersocial people perceive themselves as insignificant and not worthwhile, underpersonal people perceive themselves as unlovable. Rather than avoid people, however, the underpersonal individual simply avoids getting very close to them.

Overpersonal Behavior Sometimes, people who have consistently failed to satisfy their interpersonal need for affection will overreact. To compensate for their early failures in establishing mutual affection, such people are likely to try to initiate close and intimate interpersonal relationships with most of the people with whom they come in contact or to dominate the relationships in which they are already involved.

Neither of these patterns of behavior is all that uncommon. For instance, most of us have come in contact with people who appear to be abnormally personable or affectionate even with the most casual acquaintances. Very often such people also seem to disclose intimate information about themselves to people they hardly know. Just as most of us have met people who are overly personal, most of us also have come in contact with people who try to dominate the relationships in which they are already involved. For example, we can recall people from our graduate school days who discouraged their friends from initiating new relationships or ridiculed them when they actually made new acquaintances.

Neither of these behavior patterns is likely to lead to satisfying the need for affection. For one thing, close interpersonal ties do not come about overnight. People need time to feel each other out and weigh the advantages against the disadvantages of becoming involved. Most of us are well aware of this fact. So, when a person we meet immediately begins to unload his or her internal feelings on us, our suspicion rather than our affection is more likely to be elicited. For another thing, most of us enjoy a variety of relationships with a variety of people. We also attach some measure of value to such relationships. It stands to reason, then, that when one person we are involved with begins to malign or ridicule our other relationships, we will most probably devalue our relationship with this individual.

In summary, people who are overly personal suffer from the same perception as underpersonal people. They harbor deep-seated anxieties about their abilities to satisfy their interpersonal need for affection. To compensate for their self-doubts, they become overly personal with other people.

The Ideal Personal As we pointed out in our discussion of people who are underpersonal, most of us learn to cope with the fact that not everyone is going to love or even like us. Most of us also learn that when a person appears to dislike us, it does not mean that everyone dislikes us. The ability to discriminate in this way approaches what Schutz might call *ideal personal behavior*. People who exhibit ideal personal behavior are psychologically comfortable with relationships that are close and intimate. But even more importantly, such people are capable of understanding and coping with a situation in which they become the object of someone's dislike. People who exhibit ideal personal behavior appear to be able to relate to others and understand them on a symbolic level. By this we mean that such people can both accurately communicate what they feel and relate to the feelings communicated by other people.

Concluding Remarks on Schutz   As you've probably noticed, there are a number of similarities between Abraham Maslow's hierarchy of needs and William Schutz's interpersonal needs perspective. What Maslow calls belongingness and love needs, for example, are much the same as what Schutz calls the interpersonal needs for inclusion and affection. Also, Maslow's esteem needs are related to Schutz's interpersonal need for inclusion because esteem and inclusion needs are satisfied in a similar fashion. What Schutz does that Maslow doesn't, however, is emphasize the fact that few of our needs — whether they're interpersonal or not — can be satisfied without the benefit of rewarding interpersonal relationships. From the standpoint of interpersonal communication, such a perspective is crucial because one of the characteristics of interpersonal communication is that it very often concerns communication between people who are attempting to satisfy needs that cannot be satisfied outside the human relationship.

Before moving on, we caution you about unfairly stereotyping people on the basis of the preceding information. To begin with, at times, each of us has engaged in behavior that is, for example, overly social. Does it mean that characteristically we have failed to satisfy an interpersonal need? Probably not! What this should suggest to you, then, is that stereotyping a person as overly social or personal on the basis of a single meeting would be grossly unfair. Judgments about people are more accurate when we have had sufficient time to get to know them.

HUMAN COMMUNICATION AND HUMAN NEEDS

What has communication got to do with human needs? The answer is everything. Human communication and human needs are inextricably tied to each other. Not only is human communication a need as basic and as essential to a person's psychological development and well-being as any of the needs previously discussed but also it is the very means by which human needs are identified and satisfied.

COMMUNICATION AS A HUMAN NEED

To begin with, human communication is requisite to normal, psychological development, and two case studies will illustrate this fact.[8] The first case study concerns a six-year-old girl named Anna who, in 1937, was discovered bound to a straight, high-back chair in a second-story room of a house in rural Illinois. Her discoverers were later to learn that Anna had been confined and isolated in this manner since almost infancy.

As you might expect, Anna's confinement had an appalling affect on her

[8]Roger Brown, *Words and Things,* Free Press, New York, 1958, pp. 191–192.

physical condition. Denied proper food and hygienic care, she was suffering from severe malnutrition, and her physical appearance was deplorable. But Anna's confinement had less of an impact on her development than her total isolation. Denied both the verbal and nonverbal stimulation that children normally experience, she had failed to progress psychologically beyond infancy. Unable to relate to herself or to others, she was diagnosed a congenital idiot and placed in an institution where she died four years later.

The second case study involves a young girl in Ohio who was discovered at about the same time as Anna. Isabelle was the illegitimate child of a deaf mute, and she was also about six years of age. She and her mother had been ostracized from the rest of the family and forced to live in a shabby room devoid of both sunlight and sound. When discovered, Isabelle was suffering from rickets. Her legs were so bowed that the soles of her shoes were nearly parallel to one another when she stood. She did not walk but hurried about in a skittering gait. She made gutteral, animal-like sounds and cowered when approached by other humans.

Initially, Isabelle was also diagnosed a congenital idiot. But Dr. Marie K. Mason disagreed with this diagnosis and took Isabelle into her charge. She began to teach her to communicate. Isabelle not only learned to communicate but also learned at an accelerated rate all those things expected of a normal child. By the time she reached eight-and-one-half years of age, she exhibited a normal intelligence quotient (IQ) and appeared similar to children of the same age who had been reared in a normal home environment.

More significant than the fact that Isabelle learned to communicate is the fact that Isabelle received tactile stimulation from her mother. Most likely, this enabled Isabelle to develop the ability to communicate. Tactile stimulation or touching is such an extremely important form of nonverbal communication that many developmental psychologists have come to regard it as a precursor of all the psychological skills we now associate with normal human development. What ultimately distinguishes Isabelle's case from that of Anna's, then, is that Isabelle's early environment was not totally void of human communication.

In addition to being necessary to our psychological development, communication is also necessary to our psychological well-being. On one level, communication is a pleasurable and rewarding activity, and when we are denied this activity, we purposely seek it out. For instance, we strike up a conversation with the stranger seated next to us in an airplane, the person seated next to us on the first day of class, or a coworker when taking a break on the job. But communication is more than a pleasurable and rewarding experience. It is also the medium by which people assist each other in satisfying the needs they feel. If we accept the idea that the satisfaction of needs — like affection and inclusion — is necessary to our psychological well-being, then it must follow that the medium by which we satisfy them also is necessary.

COMMUNICATION AND NEED IDENTIFICATION

In addition to being a basic human need, human communication assists us in identifying our own needs and the needs of others. The ability to communicate as an adult enables us to identify, give meaning to and understand the roots of our feelings. For example, think about Schutz's interpersonal need for affection. Infants experience the need for affection but are unable to distinguish this need from any of the other needs they feel. As a result, infants have no choice but to respond to their need for affection in exactly the same fashion that they respond to their need for food. This means that they will cry in the attempt to attract attention to themselves. Of course, the satisfaction of an infant's need for affection will depend on whether the infant's parents have learned to distinguish between the cry of hunger and the cry for affection. Unable to identify their specific needs, much less communicate them to others, infants are at the mercy of the adults in their environment.

As we gain in experience and acquire language, we learn to identify and interpret our individual needs. We learn, for example, that some of the behaviors we engage in are designed to elicit affection while others are designed to achieve social inclusion. We also learn that a need like affection cannot be satisfied by food and that a need like inclusion cannot always be satisfied by our parents' praise or approval. Yet, the ability to discriminate in either instance would have been impossible had we not learned to give meaning to our experiences, that is, to interpret our actions and associations with others. Furthermore, this ability to give meaning to experience would be impossible had we not first acquired the ability to manipulate the verbal and nonverbal symbols that make up our system of communication.

Communication also enables us to identify the needs of other people. What a person communicates and how it is done mirrors the needs that the person is experiencing. The person who likes to be the center of attention regardless of the situation may attempt to attract notice at a party by dressing in a bizarre fashion, by dancing lewdly, or by smothering everyone who passes by with unsolicited affection. Each mode of behavior is communicative. And each of these modes is characteristic of overly social people. Overly social people, you'll recall, engage in attention-getting behavior in an attempt to satisfy their interpersonal need for inclusion.

Of course, when we see people exhibiting such behavior we do not and should not automatically label them as overly social. Nor should we say to ourselves, "Aha! There is a person who has consistently met with failure in his or her attempt to satisfy the interpersonal need for inclusion." But we do tend to make inferences about them on the basis of their communication behavior. We may say to ourselves that the person's grandstanding is indicative of his or her insecurities. Then again, we may think to ourselves that the person's behavior is designed to compensate for a lack of self-esteem. In effect, when we make such inferences we identify *what we think* is the cause of the person's behavior. And more often than not, the cause that we identify is embedded in the person's needs.

COMMUNICATION AND NEED SATISFACTION

Finally, and perhaps most importantly, communication is the medium by which people assist each other in satisfying their needs. This holds true for our most basic as well as our most complex needs. For example, think about our biological needs. At one time, people did not need to bother themselves with questions about the food they ate, the water they drank, or the air they breathed. Of course, this is no longer the case. Hardly a day goes by that we don't learn of some potentially harmful additive that is being used in food processing and preservation, some toxic chemical that is being dumped indiscriminately into our streams and oceans, or some new and dangerous pollutant that is floating in the air. With each new additive, each new toxic chemical, and each new pollutant, the probability of satisfying our biological needs in a healthy manner diminishes. Consequently, citizen's groups like the Sierra Club, Nader's Raiders, and Common Cause are trying to change our present environmental situation. They have hired lobbyists, sponsored books and films, presented their case on national television, filed class action suits against major corporate polluters, and published the environmental voting records of members of Congress and the Senate. Each of these actions is aimed at insuring the satisfaction of our most elemental needs. And each action has been communicative in nature.

Communication also assists us in satisfying our safety needs. Nowhere is this better illustrated than in the symbols we use on our streets and highways. Signs that indicate we should stop, yield the right of way, or slow down for an upcoming curve in the highway have one purpose: to make our travels safer. And these signs have come about because people agreed on and established a set of symbols that communicate important information.

Since people assist each other in satisfying their respective needs, need satisfaction is a reciprocal activity. The probability of satisfying your own needs will depend on how well you communicate those needs to other people and how well you communicate with people in the effort to assist them in satisfying their needs.

Think about your current level of self-esteem. Now think about your best friend's current level of self-esteem. Do you think the two levels of self-esteem have anything in common? Of course. You probably communicate in such a way that you reinforce your best friend's behavior. In turn, your best friend probably communicates with you in a reinforcing manner. As a result, you *both* feel significant and worthwhile in each other's presence. This is what the relationship between human needs and human communication is really all about — people doing for each other. Although our focus has been on the individual, we want to impress upon you the fact that the needs you experience are experienced by all those with whom you come in contact. This includes the relative you can't stand, the friend of a friend you feel hostile toward, or the person at work who excessively flatters the boss at each and every opportunity. When you deny the needs they experience by communicating in a less than skillful manner, chances are they will respond in a like manner. As a result, the hostilities or frustrations you attribute to these people will only become worse. We simply ask: is it worth it?

Think about Christine Chubbuck. According to her coworkers, the communication skills she displayed on the air seldom carried over to her talks with people on the job. She frequently threw tantrums, constantly felt sorry for herself, and was apt to make nasty remarks about guests on a talk show she hosted. As a camerawoman put, "She dearly loved a kind word but she could put other people down without flashing an eye." Is it really any wonder, then, that Christine couldn't register with people and couldn't satisfy needs most of us take for granted. She may have desperately wanted the attention of other people, but she apparently was not willing to reciprocate.

As Christine's tragic life shows, communication does not guarantee need satisfaction. No matter how articulate some people appear to be, they will never be able to completely satisfy their needs. But this fact is more of a reflection of how little they understand the relationship between human behavior and human communication than a reflection of the flaws that are inherent in all human systems, including communication. Clearly, then, our ability to satisfy our needs is proportionate to our skill in and knowledge of the human communication transaction.

Our success in initiating and maintaining rewarding interpersonal relationships and thereby satisfying needs rests with our skills in interpreting and responding to the communication behavior of other people. We must recognize, too, all the people out there count. But in order to gain this skill we must be willing to do two things. First, we must be willing to question ourselves and look for the underlying causes of our communication behavior. Second, we must be willing to try to identify and understand the causes of other people's communication behavior. But in order to engage in either of these processes we must be willing to explore the human communication transaction.

CHAPTER SUMMARY

The case of Christine Chubbuck is an extreme one. You and the people in your life probably bear little or no psychological resemblance to her. Why, then, do we use Christine Chubbuck as an example? Put simply, we use Christine because we all need to be shocked into realizing how important we are to other people and how important other people are to us. Nowhere is this importance more evident than in the needs we experience and the ways in which we communicate to satisfy these needs. In this chapter we have demonstrated the importance of human needs to human behavior and, more importantly, the interdependency of needs and the human communication transaction. We have said that needs are motivational, vary in terms of people, situations, and importance, and, for the most part, are satisfied only through the human communication transaction. Also, we described two need systems that detail some of the most important needs we experience as well as some types of behavior that can result from these needs. Finally, we have emphasized the fact that the satisfaction of your individual needs will depend on how skillfully you communicate in the attempt to assist other people in the satisfaction of their needs.

THINK ABOUT IT

IN GENERAL

1. Select one statement or concept in the chapter with which you strongly agree. Be prepared to explain in approximately three to five minutes why this statement affects you. Be specific. Include examples, if possible, that develop your idea.
2. Select one statement or concept in the chapter with which you strongly disagree. Be prepared to explain in approximately three to five minutes why this statement affects you. Be specific. Include examples, if possible, that develop your idea.
3. Select one idea in the chapter that you would like to share with someone. It should be the kind of idea that would have special meaning to both of you because of a positive, negative, or specific type of relationship that the idea fosters. If it is not too personal, share the reason for your selection with the class.

IN EDUCATION

Many teachers feel that students no longer care about acquiring knowledge or skills but only seek grades. If this feeling is accurate, it suggests that student needs are largely deficiency needs, particularly in that high grades may mean a good or better job and economic security later. How do you feel about this belief? Is it accurate with respect to your needs? Have you ever sensed this attitude in a teacher? How did it affect you? How do you think it affected communication between you and the teacher and between the teacher and students in general?

IN THE ORGANIZATION

1. A management theorist named Douglas MacGregor suggested that there are basically two types of organizations, Theory X organizations and Theory Y organizations. Theory X organizations assume employees are lazy, disloyal, and motivated only by the almighty dollar. Theory Y organizations assume employees come to work for more than money, are ego involved with what they are doing, and take pride in their organization as well as its products. At what level of Maslow's hierarchy do Theory X organizations operate? Theory Y organizations? Perhaps you are working or have worked for a Theory X organization. How would you describe the communication behavior of the employees — as honest and open or guarded and distrustful? How would you describe employee attitudes? Contrast their behavior and attitudes with those of employees in a Theory Y organization if you've had experience with such an organization. Discuss this with your class.

2. Have you ever worked for someone who fits Schutz's description of the autocrat? How did this person communicate with employees? Did you or your fellow employees like this person, or were you and your coworkers hostile toward him or her? If you were given a choice between working for a democratic or autocratic boss, which one would you choose? If the autocratic boss paid more money than the democratic one, how would it affect your decision? Why?

IN YOUR RELATIONSHIPS

1. It's not uncommon for the needs of one party in a relationship to become discrepant with those of others in the relationship. For example, a person's growth needs may begin to emerge, while others in the relationship may still find esteem needs most important. How might this affect the parties in the relationship or the relationship itself? Would you expect changes in communication behavior? Why or why not? Are changing needs necessarily incompatible needs? Discuss this issue with others in class.

2. If you were ever involved with someone who was overly social or undersocial, what were your initial reactions to this person? Did the person's communication behavior change as you grew to know one another better? Why?

3. In discussing people who had consistently failed to meet their interpersonal needs, we implied that these people had failed to acquire necessary interpersonal communication skills. Make a list of what you consider to be necessary interpersonal communication skills. How do your current skills compare with the list? How might you acquire these skills or improve upon those you already think you possess?

SUGGESTED READINGS

Leary, T. *The Interpersonal Diagnosis of Personality*. Ronald, New York, 1957.

Before accepting Jimi Hendrix's suggestion to become "experienced," Timothy Leary was known only in academic circles. In this book, Leary describes a complex interrelationship of needs. You may want to examine Leary's analysis, and then discuss his approach as compared to those of Maslow and Schutz.

Maslow, A. H. *Toward a Psychology of Being,* 2d. ed. Van Nostrand, New York, 1968.

While we've tried to give you an introduction to Maslow's ideas in Chapter 1, it would be beneficial to read Maslow firsthand. *Toward a Psychology of Being* thoroughly explores the question of needs.

Schutz, W. *The Interpersonal Underworld*. Science and Behavior Books, Palo Alto, 1966.

If you would like to examine Schutz's FIRO model in depth, this book will prove invaluable. *The Interpersonal Underworld* begins with Schutz's postulate of interpersonal needs and then applies the postulate to a full range of human behavior.

Winch, R. F. *Mate-Selection: A Study of Complementary Needs*. Harper and Row, New York, 1958.

Winch's perspective on the relationship between human needs and human behavior is different from Maslow's and Schutz's. Winch contends that interpersonal relationships are the outgrowth of complementary needs. To make his point, he examines the needs exhibited by married couples and the degree to which the couples' needs are complementary. We think you'll find this book interesting reading as well as a useful supplement to the perspectives of Maslow and Schutz.

Wolfe, T. "The Me Decade and the Third Great Awakening." *New West Magazine,* 1, No. 10 (1976), 27.

Few writers have provided better chronicles of the sixties and the seventies than Tom Wolfe. In this article he expounds on what he believes is, in America, a quasi-religious movement that is me-oriented.

Chapter Two
Understanding
Human Communication

Supersimplifying The tendency to minimize the significance of complex communications, as well as distort their meaning.

Communication breakdown A common term people use when they have trouble making other people understand them.

Communication fidelity (a) The degree to which people interpret one another's messages as they are intended to be interpreted; (b) the degree to which the mental images of people correspond when communicating.

Kinesics The study of communicating through body movements.

Haptics The study of communicating through touch.

Vocalics The study of the use and quality of the human voice.

Proxemics The study of communicating through the use of personal space and territory.

Chronemics The study of how time communicates.

Oculesics The study of communicating through eye behavior.

Transaction This term refers to the fact that communication between people is affected by their immediate surroundings, their perceptions of each other, and their verbal as well as nonverbal messages.

No doubt you've noticed that sometimes a word is used so indiscriminately that it begins to lose both its impact and meaning. Communication is such a word. On a very conservative level, people almost exclusively use the word *communication* in reference to their transactions with other people. But on a much more liberal level, people also use the word *communication* in reference to dealings with their pets, the handling of plants that decorate their home — and even the machines in their places of work. Few words in our everyday vocabulary are open to as many interpretations or are as applicable to as many different things as the word *communication*. A computer analyst may interpret communication to mean the transference of electronic impulses from the computer's core memory to the machine that prints the computer's calculations. Yet a marriage counselor may interpret the same word to mean the transference of thoughts and feelings between husband and wife. As if that were not enough, the word *communication* can be just as easily applied to an intercontinental television transmission via satellite as it can be applied to a young couple carrying on an intimate conversation in a secluded area of a park. It is a word so rich in meaning and so broad in scope that it can be interpreted however we like and applied to almost any of the processes we have directly or indirectly experienced.

Although this broadness of use and interpretation may not seem to be a problem, let us assure you that it is. At the very least, it makes it difficult to determine the intended impact and meaning when a person uses the word *communication*. Also, the imprecise way people use this word has given rise to many misconceptions about communication. Therefore, in this chapter we would like to begin our discussion of communication by examining some of the more common misconceptions people have about it and try to set the record straight. Following this, we will concentrate on communication in terms of what it is and what it involves.

MISCONCEPTIONS

In working with business persons, students, and even other teachers we have discovered that these groups of people frequently hold some misconceptions that may undermine their communication endeavors. The most common misconceptions we have come across are that (1) we need more communication, (2) communication eliminates problems, (3) communication sometimes breaks down, (4) words have specific meanings, and (5) you cannot communicate. What do you think?

MORE COMMUNICATION

When working with organizational personnel, one of the more common complaints we've heard is that there is not enough communication in organizations. Front-line personnel complain that they seldom hear from middle managers, top executives complain that they have been isolated from those actually doing the work, and individual departments in complex organizations sometimes bicker about the nonexistence of lines of communication between departments.

More often than not, these complaints are justified. But is the problem one of not enough communication or one of quality? The truth of the matter is that most of us are confronted by too much rather than too little communication. From the moment we awaken, we are bombarded with messages from those with whom we live, those with whom we come in contact at school, people at work, and the mass media. The problem is that we are not psychologically equipped to handle all of these messages. While the eye is capable of processing somewhere in the neighborhood of 500-million bits of information per second, the brain only can compute about 500 bits of information per second. As a result, the probability of misinterpreting communication or communicating in an inappropriate manner is quite high. Alvin Toffler, the author of *Future Shock,* believes that the amount of communication in our environment has caused many of us to become supersimplifiers, that is, people who take complex communications and grossly oversimplify their significance and meaning.[1]

The point is that the quantity of communication that characterizes an environment has little to do with the quality of communication in an environment. While there can be little doubt that we need to improve the quality of communication in our lives, we do not necessarily need more communication.

COMMUNICATION ELIMINATES PROBLEMS

In "The Me Decade," Tom Wolfe relates a story about a couple who, after seeing Ingmar Bergman's *Scenes from a Marriage,* decided their matrimonial problems could be solved if they would be more candid in communicating with each other. For starters, the husband told his wife she babbled and made little sense when meeting someone for the first time. While there is nothing so terrible about that, his wife told him that he'd never been toilet trained properly and, as a result, an undesirable odor accompanied him wherever he went. From this point on the conversation became more vicious, and the couple was, at last word, in therapy.[2]

Communication is not a cure-all for the problems we experience. If we are properly skilled in communicating, it can be a highly effective medium for the resolution of problems or conflict. Unfortunately, many of us have failed to acquire sufficient skill in this regard. To assume we can eliminate problems effectively simply by being open and candid communicators, therefore, may be a mistake because communication has the potential for creating or intensifying problems, as well as the potential for eliminating problems.

COMMUNICATION BREAKDOWNS

The idea that communication can break down is widely accepted. Generally, people assume that communication has broken down when one person has failed to accurately interpret the communication behavior of another person. While this frequently happens, it does not mean communication has physically broken down. Rather, it means that we have been ineffective in communicating.

[1]Alvin Toffler, *Future Shock,* New York, Random House, 1970, p. 27.
[2]Tom Wolfe, "The Me Decade and the Third Great Awakening," *New West Magazine,* 1, No. 10 (1976), 27.

Ineffectual communication usually is symptomatic of some deeper-seated problem between the communicators. When we accept the idea that communication can break down, however, we assume that communication is the problem. As a result, we are apt to try to treat the symptom of the problem — ineffective communication — rather than directly confront the problem. Treating the symptom instead of the real problem may accomplish little in the way of making us more effective communicators.

WORDS AND MEANINGS

One of the more common mistakes that we make as communicators is to assume that the meaning we attach to a word will be the meaning everyone else attaches to the word. This is not always the case. The meanings we associate with words are a function of our individual backgrounds and experiences with other people. Because we cannot duplicate another's background or experiences with people, the meanings we have for the same words sometimes are quite different. To assume a word has only one meaning, therefore, may affect negatively our communication with people.

Consider a simple word like *ball*. In and of itself, the word means nothing. It is a series of symbols and the meaning you attach to the word reflects your past, present, and projected experiences. If you are an athlete, for example, the word *ball* probably is associated with sports like football, baseball, basketball, and soccer. If you are a debutante, however, the word *ball* probably is associated with a coming-out party and dance.

The point is a simple one: "Words don't mean — people mean." That is to say, meaning can be subjective. Consequently, you should not automatically assume that the meaning you associate with a word will be shared by those with whom you communicate. The degree to which you and others share common meanings for words will depend on the extent to which you share common backgrounds and experiences.

How many ways can you interpret some of these words?

YOU CANNOT COMMUNICATE

Have you ever made inferences about strangers while walking on a downtown sidewalk or while in a crowded restaurant or some other public place? Do you realize people make inferences about you in such places even though you have not tried intentionally to communicate to them?

We bring this up because we sometimes assume that communication occurs only when we want it to occur. Actually, communication occurs any time meaning is stimulated in the mind of another person. And like it or not, we are constantly stimulating meaning in the minds of people who take notice of us, for example, when the person across the street, unbeknown to us, watches us as we make our way up the boulevard.

Communication is not like a light bulb that can be turned on and off with the flick of a switch. We need not be even present to communicate, in fact, if a person is aware of our absence. If an instructor is aware of your repeated absences in class, for instance, you have communicated to the instructor. Then again, if you avoid the company of a group of people with whom you might be expected to affiliate, you also have communicated. In a very real sense, we *cannot not communicate.* [3] Thus, we should try to be conscious of the fact that we may be communicating to people with whom we do not intend to communicate or with people of whom we are not even aware.

Our purpose in relating the preceding misconceptions is a simple one. When people assume something is so, they communicate as if the assumption is without fault. If a person believes that quantity and quality of communication are one and the same, that communication always eliminates problems, or that communication physically breaks down, the person will use these beliefs as a guide for communication behavior. Furthermore, these beliefs and the communication behavior they produce will undermine the person's effectiveness in communicating with people in the classroom, on the job, or in the home. Hopefully, our discussion of these common misconceptions about communication will assist you in avoiding some faulty communication behavior.

COMMUNICATION BASICS

Given the preceding framework, we can now turn to some of the basic concepts about communication that have been generated in the past two decades. They include the facts that communication is symbolic; communication can

[3] James C. McCroskey and Lawrence R. Wheeless, *An Introduction to Human Communication,* Allyn and Bacon, Boston, 1977, pp. 3–9.

be intentional or unintentional; communication is multifunctional; communication is disclosive; and communication involves acts, interactions, and transactions.

SYMBOLIC COMMUNICATION: THE VERBAL DIMENSION

Realize that none of us live within "true reality." We live within the confines of our individual experiences and the meanings we attach to these experiences through our ability to communicate. Through this ability, also, we are able to share our experiences with others. When we attempt to share these experiences, we are limited in the sense that we can provide only symbols that approximate the experience. Whether we succeed in communicating will depend on whether the people with whom we communicate share the meaning we attach to those symbols. To illustrate this point, see if you have any difficulty in understanding the following passage from Anthony Burgess's book *A Clockwork Orange*.

> A dream or nightmare is really only like a film inside your *gulliver*, except that it is though you could walk into it and be a part of it. And this is what happened to me. It was a nightmare of one of the bits of film they showed me near the end of the afternoon session, all of *smecking malchicks* doing the *ultraviolent* on a young *ptitsa* who was *creeching* away in her red, red *krovvy*, her *platties* all *razrezzed* real *horrowshow*. I was in this *fillying* about, *smecking* away and being like the ringleader, dressed in the height of *nadsat* fasion. And then at the height of all this *dratsing* and *tolchocking* I felt like paralyzed and wanting to be very sick, and all the other *malchicks* had a real *gromky smeck* at me [italics added].[4]

Unless you are familiar with *A Clockwork Orange* and Burgess's nadsat (teenage) vocabulary of the future, you probably experienced some problems in making sense of the nightmare that is described. After all, it is doubtful that you have had prior experiences with symbols like *malchick, tolchocking,* or *platties*. And because you lack prior experience, you have neither referents nor meanings for these symbols and what they are intended to communicate. We can easily overcome this problem, however, by supplying you with symbols that you have experienced and have meaning for:

> A dream or nightmare is really only like a film inside your gulliver [head], except that it is though you could walk into it and be a part of it. And this is what happened to me. It was a nightmare of one of the bits of

---

[4]Anthony Burgess, *A Clockwork Orange*, W. W. Norton and Company, New York, 1963, pp. 109–110.

film they showed me near the end of the afternoon session, all of smecking malchicks [laughing boys] doing the ultraviolent on a young ptitsa [chick] who was creeching [screaming] away in her red, red krovvy [blood], her platties [clothes] all razrezzed [ripped or torn] real horrow-show [well or good]. I was in this fillying [playing or fooling] about, smecking [laughing] away and being like the ringleader, dressed in the height of nadsar [teenage] fashion. And then at the height of all this dratsing [fighting] and tolchocking [beating] I felt like paralyzed and wanting to be very sick, and all the malchicks had a real gromky smeck [loud laugh] at me.

What we are trying to demonstrate by way of this example is that sharing our experiences on a verbal dimension is not the simple process we perceive it to be. The probability of two people being able to share and understand their respective experiences is limited to the extent that they share common meanings for the verbal symbols we call words. And this brings us to the issue of communication fidelity. *Fidelity* concerns the degree to which people interpret each other's message as they were intended to be interpreted as well as the degree to which their mental images correspond. One of the aims of this book is to increase the fidelity with which people communicate. As you now realize, fidelity communication cannot be achieved unless the participants in communication have common meanings for the verbal symbols that they use.

Remember, your experiences as well as those of others are unique. In spite of their uniqueness, though, we are able to relate our experiences as well as share in the experiences of others through communicating. If we are to be successful in either sense, however, we must try to be sure that people understand the verbal symbols we use and be sure we understand the verbal symbols they use. Otherwise, we will not be able to achieve a high degree of fidelity in our communication transactions.

SYMBOLIC COMMUNICATION: THE NONVERBAL DIMENSION

Generally, when we think about communication as a symbolic activity, we tend to view it as a process in which we translate our thoughts and feelings into verbal symbols that take the form of words. But human communication is symbolic on more than one dimension. In addition to our verbal symbol system, we have a nonverbal symbol system. This nonverbal symbol system is highly complex and every bit as, if not more, communicative as the verbal symbol system with which we are more familiar. Upward of 80 percent of all our communication behavior is nonverbal in nature. Moreover we adults tend to believe what is communicated to us nonverbally when verbal and nonverbal symbols conflict. With this in mind, consider the primarily eight ways in which we communicate nonverbally: through body movements, touch, physical appearances, vocal behavior, the use of space, the use of objects, eye behavior, and the use of time.

Body Movements   While we are not in the habit of thinking about it, the way we sit in a chair in the classroom, the posture we assume when talking to a fellow employee, and the way our faces look when speaking with a friend all communicate. Studies have revealed, in fact, that there are over 700,000 ways to communicate through body movements.[5]

Basically, we use body movement or, as it is technically known, *kinesics* to communicate in four ways.[6] To begin with, sometimes we use our arms, hands, and fingers to form *nonverbal emblems* that are indicative of thoughts, feelings, and sometimes attitudes. At one time, for example, blacks used an up-raised arm and clenched fist as an emblem of black power. Currently, though, this emblem is used to communicate solidarity or commonness among people, regardless of their racial heritage.

In addition to using our appendages as nonverbal emblems, we frequently use them to illustrate visually what we say orally. These *nonverbal illustrations* are designed to augment, emphasize, and clarify what we say. A few of the many ways we use our bodies and appendages as nonverbal illustrations are: clenching our fists to emphasize a point we are making, throwing our hands over our heads to indicate we are helpless, and giving the OK sign when we are in agreement or when something is clear to us.

The third way we use body movements to communicate concerns *affective displays.* More often than not, we augment our emotional states with certain facial expressions. We smile when we are happy, frown when we are sad, raise an eyebrow when we are suspicious, or squint our eyes when we are confused. Again, we do this to communicate our emotional states and augment our verbalizations about these states.

Finally, *kinesic behavior* assists us in regulating our transactions with other people. For instance, certain kinds of kinesic behavior that we use are designed to show that we do or don't understand what another person is saying. Still other kinesic behavior assists us in regulating the flow of the communication transaction. Pausing but looking away from another person indicates that we are reflecting on what we are about to say, whereas maintaining eye contact and pausing indicates that we are finished talking and ready to listen. If we

---

[5]McCroskey and Wheeless, pp. 185–187.
[6]Mark L. Knapp, *Nonverbal Communication in Human Interaction,* New York, Holt, Rinehart, and Winston, 1972, pp. 97–107.

want to break off the transaction entirely, moreover, we may stare out a convenient window, slap our knees with the palms of our hands, or periodically look at our watch. In a way, kinesic behavior communicates the state of our communication transactions.

Touching Behavior As suggested in the first chapter, few types of communication behavior are as important to our psychological growth and well-being as touching. Technically known as *haptic behavior,* touching communicates a full range of emotions and is an important source of reinforcement. At a minimum, we use touch to communicate praise, liking, affection, and hate. We also use touch to communicate our feelings of gladness when greeting someone we haven't seen for awhile, as well as communicating our sorrow when such people must say good-by.

In our culture the degree to which people engage in touching varies. White Anglo-Saxon males, for example, are not prone to demonstrate their affection for each other through touch. Yet, Italian, Polish, and Irish-American males are quite demonstrative. Thus, the degree to which we use touching behavior to communicate depends on our backgrounds and the backgrounds of the people with whom we communicate.[7]

Physical Appearance Not long ago, an advertisement for a major men's grooming product was predicated on the notion that "the way you look says a lot about you." Indeed, the way you look does say a lot about you. While your physique, height, hair color, and skin pigmentation may not be intended to communicate, they nonetheless do. To illustrate this fact, simply think about some of the less than flattering stereotypes people have that are based on things like height, weight, and body type. Short men are very often stereotyped as little Napoleons. Fat people are frequently stereotyped as jovial, lethargic, and low in self-esteem. Then again, superthin people are stereotypically frenetic and habitual worriers. These stereotypes, however, are less bothersome than the fact that people tend to behave as if they were true. Research on person perception demonstrates that people who are short, overweight, or too thin will have less of a chance to succeed than people who are tall and athletically built — regardless of their qualifications. While such stereotypes are unfair and should be avoided, the sad truth is many of the inferences we make about people are based on something as superficial as physical appearances. In fact, research clearly indicates that the probability of two strangers communicating is predicted best by their mutual perceptions of physical attraction.[8]

[7]McCroskey and Wheeless, pp. 194–195.
[8]Knapp, pp. 63–86.

Vocal Behavior If you have ever listened closely to Orson Welles and Laurence Olivier, or Dame Edith Evans and Lauren Bacall, you know that they have something else in common besides the fact that they are fine performers. Each of them has a way of saying something about themselves when they are not speaking about themselves. *Vocalics* refers to the use and quality of the human voice. As such, vocalic behavior includes things like vocal pitch, intensity, resonation, control, and articulation. The vocalic elements of a verbal message tend to reveal information about people, such as their geographic origin. Frequently, the vocalic elements of a person's message will reveal that he or she is from a country other than the United States or from a geographic region within the United States characterized by a particular pattern of speech. And this is why we can usually determine whether a person is from England, Boston, or Brooklyn without the person volunteering this information.

Vocalic elements may also serve to amplify the intended meaning of our verbal messages. If one person says to another, "That's really good," and emphasizes "that's" and "really," it will communicate an entirely different meaning than emphasizing "good." Although the sentences are exactly alike, the former is usually translated to mean "That's really bad," while the latter is translated quite literally. In light of vocalics, the maxim that "it's not what you say but how you say it" is not altogether untrue.

The Use of Space Elevators, buses, and subways are peculiar places, but not half as peculiar as the people who occupy them. Excepting an occasional "excuse me" for instance, people in such places rarely communicate with each other. And if that were not strange enough, they appear to be in some kind of pain as a function of their close proximity. As in most cases, there is a simple explanation for the fact that people in crowded quarters are uncommunicative and appear pained. Like animals, people have spatial and territorial needs. When these needs are in jeopardy of being satisfied, people behave in certain ways to compensate for their lack of personal space or territory.

Proxemic behavior is behavior that results from our spatial and territorial needs. We use space in two ways. First, we have personal space that is like an invisible plastic bubble that accompanies us wherever we go and is capable of expanding and contracting depending on our circumstances. Second, we establish territories, that is, areas of space that are geographically fixed. Our proxemic behavior communicates in a number of ways. On elevators, buses, or subways we behave proximically as if we are alone. We remain silent and stare straight ahead — knowing full well that we feel uncomfortable. Our silence and expressionless gaze not only serve to compensate for our lack of personal space but also communicate to those around us that we do not desire company. Company would be only a further intrusion on our personal space.

Proxemic behavior is also a source of information about relationships. Something as simple as how close two people sit with one another says a great deal about the degree of their involvement. Then again, one person talking loudly and standing almost on top of another person communicates quite clearly who dominates the relationship.

Finally, our spatial, and particularly our territorial needs, are usually reflected in our living or working quarters. For example, we both knowingly and unknowingly place chairs, sofas, tables, and desks in such a way that they communicate to those who enter our homes and offices that certain parts of our homes and offices are either off limits or open to them. Like Archie Bunker, we too have our special places — albeit a chair or a room.

The Use of Objects During the latter half of the 1960s you could infer a great deal about a person's attitudes, beliefs, and values by simply looking at his or her manner of dress. If a person wore jeans, a work shirt, and a peace sign medallion, it usually meant that the person was against the war in Vietnam, against the draft, and against whoever occupied the White House. In contrast, if a person wore a Brooks Brother's suit, wing-tip shoes, and an American flag lapel pin it usually meant the person was in favor of the war in Vietnam, in favor of the draft, and in favor of whoever happened to be in the White House. Lines were that drawn.

Objectics is concerned with the degree to which physical objects like dress, body ornaments, and environmental decor communicate. Not only dress and body ornaments can be highly symbolic but also the objects we find in a person's living environment can be revealing. Something as simple as the kinds of magazines you find on a coffee table in a person's apartment may say much about that person. Magazines like *Playboy, Oui,* and *Penthouse* might be symbolic of the person's attitudes toward women. Then again, magazines like *The Atlantic Monthly, The New Yorker,* and *Harper's* might be symbolic of the fact that the person is quite literary. In any event, the point remains the same. Like dress and body ornaments, the objects in a person's living environment are communicative and disclose information about the person who resides in that environment.

Eye Behavior One of the first things many of us learn as children is that people who lie do not look straight into our eyes. There are many folk tales like this one about eye behavior. As you might guess, some are based on myth, including this one. While our eye behavior communicates many things, the degree to which we are telling the truth is not one of them. And if you don't believe us, ask a good poker player like former world champion Amarillo Slim.

In our culture, eye behavior, which is technically called *oculesics,* is expected to conform to certain norms. One of the most pervasive norms concerns attention. When we communicate with a person we assume that if he or she looks us in the eyes the person is paying attention. We should realize, though, that maintaining strict eye contact is uncomfortable for some people and, as a result, is not necessarily indicative of attentiveness.

Another norm in our culture is that sustained eye contact is an invitation to communicate. Have you ever been called on in class when you did not want to be called on? Chances are you made and briefly sustained eye contact with your teacher. Most students intuitively realize this and avoid eye contact with a teacher when they are unsure about responding to the question.

Finally, eye contact in our culture commonly is associated with physical attraction. Depending on the environment, males frequently assume that if a female is looking at him, she finds him physically attractive. Lest females take this as another indication of the macho needs of males, females frequently draw an identical conclusion when being "checked" out by a male. The truth of the matter is, though, people stare. If we notice we are the primary object in another's field of vision, it does not necessarily mean the person is enamoured with our physical appearances.

The Use of Time   Time is extremely important to interpersonal communication and our interpersonal relationships and a significant form of nonverbal communication. The study of *chronemics* — the technical term for time — suggests that in our culture we adhere to a number of norms with respect to time. For example, we adhere to the norm that one doesn't make phone calls at three o'clock in the morning unless faced with a dire emergency. Also, we adhere to time norms regarding business hours, invitations to cocktail parties, and invitations to a dinner. In the East, for instance, an invitation to a five o'clock cocktail party really means come some time after six. Almost anywhere in the United States, however, an invitation to dinner at eight o'clock means you'll be welcome at seven-thirty.

Time also is affected by our physiology. Basically, there are two types of people in our culture with two different body clocks. First, there are people we refer to as Sparrows. Sparrows live by the motto, "Early to bed and early to rise, makes a man healthy, wealthy, and wise." From a physiological standpoint, Sparrows are at their best during the first half of the day. By way of contrast, some of us are what we call Owls. Owls like to stay up late and sleep in the morning. Unlike the Sparrow, the Owl's ability to work or carry on intellectual activities is at its highest during the late afternoon or late evening. With the exception of their different body clocks, Sparrows and Owls are not really different. Yet, in our culture, the time habits of Owls often lead people to assume they are strange. Thus, the physiological effects of time also communicate nonverbally.

Time communicates in many other ways. The amount of time we must wait to see a business client communicates, the length of our pauses during a conversation communicates, and whether a person customarily is late for appointments communicates. The importance we attach to time, therefore, is not without justification.

Although we are constantly stimulating meaning by way of our nonverbal communication behavior, we have little or no control over it. This is because we do not consciously think about and plan out things like facial expressions, the pulling of an ear lobe, or a sigh. Also bear in mind that nonverbal communication varies from one culture to the next. Thus, to assume that what is appropriate nonverbal behavior in North America is appropriate in South America, Europe, Africa, or Asia would be a mistake and should be guarded against. Finally, be aware that books like *Body Language* have misrepresented the research on nonverbal communication. Nonverbal behaviors, like folding your arms across your chest, crossing your legs in one fashion or another, or sustaining eye contact, do not have one specific meaning. To act as if a nonverbal behavior always has the same meaning would be a mistake. We'll have more to say about nonverbal communication in the following parts of the book.

COMMUNICATION AND INTENT

Just as we commonly think of communication as being a verbal phenomenon, we also tend to think of communication as being a wholly intentional phenomenon. Some would go so far as to say, in fact, that communication only occurs when one person intentionally engages another person for the purpose of eliciting a specific and predetermined response. Certainly a significant portion of our communication behavior conforms to this perspective, but we seriously doubt if all of it does. Consider something as simple as dress, a nonverbal symbol that we have already discussed. You might wake up tomorrow morning, feel exceptionally good, and decide to dress in a manner that you perceive reflects how you feel. Later in the day, someone might walk up to you and say, "Hey, you really look good today." Thus, you would have communicated to that person exactly what you had intended to communicate. The day after tomorrow, however, you might also wake and feel exceptionally good but find that you are fifteen minutes late to your first class. As a result, you might dress without thinking about what you are putting on, forsake shaving or curling your hair, and rush blindly out the door. Later that day, the same person might walk up to you and say, "Are you sick? You really look bad." In other words, without intending it, your dress might communicate, that is, stimulate meaning.

This example serves to further emphasize something we said when discussing misconceptions about communication. Everything that is directly or indirectly associated with us can stimulate meaning in the mind of another person. Again, you cannot not communicate when in the presence of other people, because they will constantly assign meaning to your behavior whenever they attend to it. And they will do so in spite of the fact that your behavior is neither directed toward them nor intended to be meaningful.

COMMUNICATION AND DISCLOSURE

Since you cannot not communicate, you are constantly revealing something about yourself to the people in your immediate environment. Hence, communication is disclosive. On a nonverbal dimension, your appearance, manner of dress, and pattern of speech are just a few of the factors that disclose information about you. Appearance and dress may disclose, among other things, how fastidious you are, how much time you take in the effort to keep in shape, your taste in clothing, and maybe even your financial status. Your pattern of speech may disclose where you come from, your cultural background, or perhaps your ethnic origins. But it doesn't stop here. What you communicate verbally also discloses more about you than perhaps you want to disclose. At a minimum, your verbal communication may disclose how educated, well read, and well traveled you are. In addition, you may be also disclosing your attitudes, beliefs, and values. For instance, in a history class your comments on a political event of the past, a now defunct political party, or the circumstances surrounding a particular war may go beyond their intended impact. That is to say, your comments may communicate your present political preference as well as your present value system with respect to war, to governmental control, and to invasion of privacy. Also realize that the people around you are disclosing information about themselves through communication. Moreover, this information may cause you to make inferences about these people that are inappropriate. While people may disclose unintentionally, there is no substitute for face-to-face intentional communication. This holds for you as well as for those about whom you make inferences.

ACTIONS, INTERACTIONS, AND TRANSACTIONS

We can look at the communication event in at least three ways.[9] We can look at communication solely in terms of how our communication behavior affects

[9]Malcolm R. Parks and William W. Wilmot, "Three Research Models of Communication: Action, Interaction, and Transaction," Paper presented at the Annual Western Speech Communication Convention, Seattle, 1976.

FIGURE 2-1
COMMUNICATION DEPICTED AS ACTION AND INTERACTION

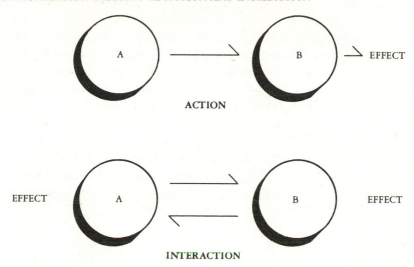

the people with whom we communicate. When we view communication from such a perspective, we are concerned exclusively with the effect of A on B. This is an *action perspective.*

A second way of viewing communication is as a form of *interaction.* The interactional model of communication is concerned with the responses of a receiver to a source's message as well as any effects the source's messages may have had on the receiver. While the interactional model is preferable to the action model, it still ignores many factors that are important to the ways in which people communicate. It does not attempt to account for the fact that there are seldom clear-cut distinctions between sources and receivers or in the perceptions of the communicators or in the environment in which communication takes place. Figure 2-1 diagrams communication as action and interaction. As you can see, these two models present communication as if communication consists of clear-cut steps. For example, the action model presents one step — A communicates to B with some effect. The interaction model presents communication in two steps — A communicates to B with some effect and B communicates to A with some effect.

Communication is much more complex than either of these two models suggests. People communicate neither in social vacuums nor in clear-cut steps where one person is assigned the role of source and the other is assigned the role of receiver. On the contrary, people communicate in noisy cafeteria lines, during emergencies such as a car accident, and other conditions of crisis and mental duress. Furthermore, under circumstances like these, one would be hard pressed to say who is the source and who is the receiver. Therefore, communication can be termed *transactional*. In effect, this means that your communication behavior as well as everyone else's, is influenced, shaped, and modified by the people and by the environment with which you come in contact. At a minimum, for example, with whom you communicate will have a noticeable impact on how you communicate and what you communicate, and these will reflect a triparte perception that you have of the person with whom you are communicating. First, your communication behavior will be influenced by how you directly view that person. Second, your communication behavior will be influenced by how you think that person views him- or herself. Finally, your communication behavior will be influenced by what you think that person thinks about what you think of him or her. R. D. Laing and his associates refer to this triparte perception as a *direct, meta,* and *meta-meta-perspective*. [10] If this terminology only further confuses you, perhaps an example will help.

Suppose two people — a young man and a young woman — go to a local pub together because one offered to buy the other a drink. Now how are they going to communicate and what are they going to communicate? Well, that depends. The young woman, who offered to buy the drink, thinks that the young man is well built, seductively dressed, and in need of companionship. This constitutes her *direct perspective* and will influence her communication behavior toward him. But the young woman also thinks that the young man is not too sure of his physical attractiveness. This constitutes her *meta-perspective* and will also influence her communication toward the young man. Last, and most confusing, the young woman thinks that the young man thinks she regards him as nothing more than sex object. This constitutes her *meta-meta-perspective* and, as in the preceding two instances, will cause her to gauge her communication behavior accordingly. Of course, all the while that the young woman is engaged in this process, so is the young man.

What we are saying by way of this example is that your perception of the relationship existing between you and another person will have a tremendous impact on your communication behavior. What we are also saying is that your judgments about how a person perceives him- or herself and how that person perceives his or her relationship with you will also affect your communication behavior.

Yet the idea that communication is transactional goes beyond this triparte perception. It also implies that how you communicate and what you communicate to another person will be influenced by how and what the person communicates to you. Even as you formulate and transmit messages to another

---

[10]R. D. Laing, H. Phillipson, & A. R. Lee, *Interpersonal Perception: A Theory and Method of Research,* Harper & Row, New York, 1966.

person, you are receiving and interpreting the nonverbal messages that the person is transmitting to you. This means that you are engaged in the process of sending and receiving information simultaneously. Because you are receiving information even as you send information, you are in a constant state of change and adaptation. That is to say, you are constantly changing and adapting your communication behavior toward a person on the basis of the communication behavior the person exhibits toward you.

Finally, how you communicate and what you communicate to another person will reflect the environment in which the transaction takes place. It stands to reason that your perceptions of what is appropriate communication behavior in certain environments will influence what you say to a person. For example, in the privacy of your home you might think nothing of berating a friend for some transgression he or she committed. But would you do the same in a library, in a quiet hotel lobby, or on a crowded bus? Probably not. In the same sense, you may use language in a gymnasium locker room that you would not use in church or at the dinner table of your boy or girl friend's parent's home. You — and most people — are sensitive to the environment in which you communicate. So, the environment, like the people you come in contact with, to a great extent, helps to determine how you communicate and what you communicate.

Up to this point, our discussion of transactional communication has focused on factors that influence your communication behavior. These same factors have the same kinds of influence on the communication behavior of the people with whom you communicate. They, too, are affected by their triparte perception of you, by the communication behavior that you exhibit, and by the environment in which they communicate with you. We can think of the transactional phenomenon of human communication as being like the components of a system. When one component in a system changes, it produces modifications in all the components of the system. The same is true of human communicators and the environment in which they communicate. Changes in people and in the environment have a direct impact on communication. Thus, the transactional model depicts communication as a system of interrelated components.

FUNCTIONS OF COMMUNICATION

In Chapter 1 we discussed the fact that one of the major functions of communication is need satisfaction. There are, however, other functions of communication. Some are directly tied to our needs and some are indirectly tied to our needs. We conclude this section with a discussion of some of these other functions that communication performs.

Affinity As pointed out in our discussion of the need for social inclusion, much of our communication behavior is targeted at developing rewarding relationships with respect to associating and interacting. McCroskey and Wheeless talk about this as communicating for the purpose of establishing affinity.[11] Affinity is based on mutual perceptions of attraction and perceived similarities, and on other perceptions of commonness.

When we meet someone whom we like, we want to avoid communication behavior that may alienate the person. As a result, we try to ingratiate ourselves to the person. For example, we communicate in an effort to find topics of common interest, to locate similarities in attitudes, beliefs, and values, and perhaps even to flatter the person a little. Once we have established a relationship, we communicate in such a way that affinity will be maintained.

Information and Understanding Communication also assists us in acquiring and understanding information that is important to us and to the people with whom we interact. When we are unsure about a comment made in class, we can ask a question, or at work we can discuss the reasons for policy changes. Also, we can consult with experts in an attempt to better understand the reasons for our or another's behavior. The more we come to know and understand, the more likely it is that we will be successful in coping with and relating to our environment and the people in it.

Decision Making Rare is the person who is completely confident in the individual decisions he or she makes. Most of us feel more comfortable with our decisions when we have consulted beforehand with competent and responsible people. Prior to the start of school we may seek advice about the classes we should take; at work we may consult with those we respect before making a decision; and in our relationships we may consult our partners before taking action that might affect the relationship. Communication not only makes consultation with others possible but also increases the confidence with which we make decisions.

Confirmation and Adaption Communication is also the means by which we determine whether a decision was correct or incorrect. For example, if we decide on a career in medicine, vote for a presidential candidate, or make a long-term relational commitment, we can assess the appropriateness of our decision on the basis of subsequent communications. If our instructors reinforce us for our work in premed, if the president conducts his or her office in a manner of which we approve, and if our relationship continues to thrive, the

[11]McCroskey and Wheeless, pp. 232–239.

beliefs underlying our decisions will be confirmed. But even if we make the wrong decision, we can adapt to the situation on the basis of what is being communicated to us.

Consistency A need as important as any of those we addressed in the preceding chapter is consistency. People like things in their lives to be consistent. They like their friends to get along with each other, want their coworkers to share their orientations toward mutual tasks, and want their children to hold onto their attitudes, beliefs, and values.

As long as our lives are characterized by consistency, there is no problem. When we experience inconsistency, however, we also experience psychological discomfort. Fortunately, this discomfort can be allayed through communication. Consider the act of buying a new car, and let us engage in wishful thinking. Prior to making a decision, we find we are equally attracted to a Porsche 911S and a Mercedes 480SL. This is a period of conflict, but inconsistency has yet to enter the picture. Finally, we make the decision and notice we feel some anxiety as a result of choosing one car over the other. Car dealers call this postbuyer's remorse, but for our purpose we will call it psychological inconsistency. The question is, How do we resolve this inconsistency and relieve the discomfort that accompanies it? Commonly, we seek out social support for our decision by communicating with significant other people. For example, we show the car to a friend or consult with a trusted mechanic. If the friend heaps praise on the car and the mechanic informs us that we made the superior choice, psychological consistency will have been restored. Indeed, it will have been restored as a function of our communication transactions with people.

Communication performs many functions, some of which are beyond the scope of this book. In addition to satisfying the needs we discussed in the first chapter, keep in mind that communication assists in developing and maintaining affinity, in acquiring and understanding information, in decision making, in confirmation and adaptation, and in maintaining psychological consistency. Also, remember that these functions are, at the very least indirectly tied to the personal and interpersonal needs we all experience.

DESCRIBING COMMUNICATION

Having covered some of the more important concepts associated with the human communication transaction, we can now turn to what is involved in these transactions.

PERSONAL AND INTERPERSONAL NEEDS

Although sometimes it seems otherwise, people do not communicate because they are in love with the sound of their own voices. As we emphasized in Chapter 1, people communicate because communication is in and of itself a basic human need and because communication is the medium by which all other human needs are satisfied.

But we humans can be an insensitive lot. And we sometimes lose sight of the fact that people communicate to us for the same reasons that we communicate to them — to satisfy needs. At one time or another in our lives, most of us have known someone who constantly called us on the phone, forever popped up in places we frequented, or always came over for uninvited visits. Initially, we were flattered by such people. Yet, sooner or later, we come to regard them as pests or nuisances, and we begin to treat them as such, in the hope that they will go away. After awhile, such people do begin to stay away. They seek us out less frequently or even quit seeking us out altogether.

Let's back up for a moment. Why do you think a person would act as if you were the only friend he or she had on earth? Unrealistic as it may seem, perhaps the person really perceived you to be his or her only friend. If you think about it, that's not so far-fetched as it sounds. For instance, let's assume that such a person has consistently failed in his or her attempts to satisfy the interpersonal need for inclusion. Let's further assume that in a moment of kindness you invited this lonely person to lunch or for a beer after class. Now, how do you think this invitation was interpreted? Probably, it was interpreted as an invitation to become friends, which might be overstepping the bounds of this single invitation. That person then might begin to seek you out incessantly. Thus, what you have come to regard as harrassment is for this person a pattern of behavior designed to satisfy the interpersonal need for social inclusion.

The point we are making here is that a person's communication behavior is the outgrowth of the personal and interpersonal needs that he or she experiences. No one purposely wants to be a pest or a nuisance — even though it may seem that way. Keep in mind, consequently, that communication involves personal and interpersonal needs. And try to be sensitive to the fact that a person's communication behavior, no matter how bothersome, is symptomatic of a deeper-seated psychological state.

ENVIRONMENTAL FACTORS

What happens once we recognize — consciously or unconsciously — that a personal or interpersonal need exists? Do we articulate the need the best we can and hope that it will be satisfied by chance? Usually we attempt to structure our communication behavior in such a way that it increases the likelihood of the need being satisfied. And we do this by surveying, identifying, and evaluating the verbal and nonverbal cues in our environment that have meaning for us. To make the point clear, consider Maslow's need for belongingness in two very different environments — say a local hangout where you spend your Friday afternoons following classes and a formal dinner party that you have been invited to attend. Social conventions at the hangout are of little importance to belongingness. Knowing this, you dress with indifference, perhaps drink with exuberance, and talk with careless abandon. Social conventions at the formal dinner party, however, are of the utmost importance to satisfy your need to belong. As a result, you plan to exhibit an entirely different pattern of behavior than that exhibited in the local hangout. That is, you plan dressing on the basis of social convention, drinking within the acceptable limits of social convention, and talking as dictated by social convention.

This example highlights two important points. First, the way in which we structure our communication behavior to satisfy a particular need depends largely on the meaning we attach to the verbal and nonverbal cues in our immediate environment. Second, different environments very often provide us with different sets of verbal and nonverbal cues. Therefore, the set of communication behaviors we exhibit also will tend to differ. Again, this points to the fact that communication is transactional.

FEEDBACK

The probability of our needs being completely satisfied ultimately depends on our skills in processing the verbal and nonverbal cues in our environment and formulating messages or communication behaviors that accurately reflect these cues. Using the preceding example, this would mean that the satisfaction of the need to belong would depend on how accurately you interpreted the verbal and nonverbal cues in the two environments and whether the communication behavior you exhibited was consistent with these cues. But how do you know if your interpretation of the verbal and nonverbal cues in your environment is accurate? Also, how do you know if the message strategy or the communication behavior that you adopt and exhibit is consistent with the informational cues in a particular environment? Quite simply, the answer is feedback.

Feedback is made up of the external communication cues that occur during and following a communication attempt. You come to know whether your interpretation of informational cues is accurate and whether your message strategy is appropriate by feedback. If you experience hunger, communicate that fact, and are subsequently fed, you have some grounds for saying that your interpretation was accurate and that your message strategy or communication behavior was appropriate. Conversely, if you were hungry, communicated that fact, and were not fed, you would have grounds for saying that your interpretation of verbal and nonverbal cues was inaccurate and your message strategy or communication behavior was inappropriate. Thus, you would probably reinterpret the verbal and nonverbal cues in your environment and formulate a different message strategy in the attempt to satisfy your need for food.

The importance of feedback to communication cannot be minimized. Feedback increases perceptual accuracy among transactants and, thereby, increases the fidelity with which they communicate. Also, feedback affects our confidence in communicating. If one person receives negative feedback from another person, it will decrease the communicator's confidence about his or her message. If feedback is positive, however, it will increase the communicator's confidence. Finally, people are more confident in their interpretations of a communicator's messages when they are able to provide the communicator with feedback.

CHAPTER SUMMARY

In Chapter 1 we stressed that communication is both a need in and of itself and the medium by which all other needs are satisfied. We also said that the satisfaction of personal and interpersonal needs depends on how skillful and knowledgeable you are with respect to the human communication transaction. In this chapter, we dealt with concepts about the human communication transaction and with facilitating the acquisition of communication skills. Initially, we discussed some common misconceptions people have about communication. Can you recall them? They are that (1) we need more communication, (2) communication eliminates problems, (3) communication sometimes breaks down, (4) words have specific meanings, and (5) you can not communicate. Then we said that (1) communication is symbolic on both verbal and nonverbal dimensions; (2) communication is both intentional and unintentional; (3) communication is disclosive; (4) communication can be viewed as action, interaction, and transaction; and (5) communication is multifunctional. Finally, we discussed some of the basic elements of the communication transaction, including personal and interpersonal needs, environmental factors, and feedback.

THINK ABOUT IT

IN GENERAL

Complete the exercises given under Think About It: In General, at the end of Chapter 1.

IN EDUCATION

1. Jim explains to Buddy that he and one of his instructors can't seem to get across to each other. Jim confides that he sought out the instructor during office hours, and although he merely wanted to discuss a point in which he held a different opinion, the encounter ended in a shouting match, and he was asked to leave the instructor's office. Buddy asks Jim what he thinks the source of the problem is, and Jim replies there just seems to be a complete breakdown in communication between him and the instructor.

What is wrong with Jim's interpretation of the source of the problem? If you were in Jim's shoes, how would you handle the problem?

2. Today there are many more exchange students on campus than ever before. These exchange students come from cultures with different nonverbal norms than those in North America. Assume that after class an exchange student asks for a minute of your time. You begin talking but notice that the student is violating your personal space by standing too close. How would you react?

IN THE ORGANIZATION

1. In many organizations communication moves from the top of the organization downward but never from below moving upward. In light of our discussion of feedback, how do you think this affects the perceptual accuracy and confidence of those on the lowest rung of the organizational ladder? How do you think this affects the organization in general?

2. The medical profession has a language of its own. Assume you are a para-professional in some aspect of medicine, and you must frequently explain illnesses, medicines, and methods of treatment to outpatients of varying degrees of intelligence. Would you use the same terminology in your communication transactions with all of your outpatients? Why or why not?

3. Most organizations run on "sparrow time." There are some organizations

that allow employees to work at a time that is consistent with their body clocks. What advantages, if any, do you see in such an approach? What disadvantages, if any, do you see in an organization strictly adhering to "sparrow time?"

IN YOUR RELATIONSHIPS

1. We have said that the way people communicate with each other will reflect the environment in which they communicate. Would you say the communication transactions you have with friends at work, at school, and in less formal environments are different? If the answer is yes, how are they different and what do they say about the nature of your relationships? If the answer is no, explain why you think they aren't.

2. We have said that communication has the potential for intensifying problems as well as the potential for resolving them. Have you ever experienced a minor problem in one of your relationships and found that communicating about it appeared to intensify the problem? If you have, why do you think the problem became more rather than less intense? Does your explanation have anything to do with the way you communicated? What communication skills must people employ if they are to avoid intensifying a problem as a function of communicating about it? Do you practice these skills? How?

SUGGESTED READINGS

Burgess, A. *A Clockwork Orange*. W. W. Norton and Company, New York, 1963.

Communication theorists are fond of the saying that "words don't mean — people mean." This saying implies that the meaning attached to a word is subjective. *A Clockwork Orange* is not only a view of the future but also a graphic illustration of how people from different cultures and from different times see different and new meanings in the words of English-speaking people.

Knapp, M. L. *Nonverbal Communication in Human Interaction*. Holt, Rinehart, and Winston, New York, 1972.

Nonverbal communication is significant, and Knapp's book synthesizes the research in and the theory of nonverbal communication. He presents it in an interesting and enlightening format.

McCroskey, J. C. and L. R. Wheeless. *An Introduction to Human Communication*. Allyn and Bacon, Boston, 1975.

Of all the basic communication texts available (that is, those dealing with the full range of the human communication transaction), this text is by far the most comprehensive. Chapter 1, which deals with misconceptions about human communication, is valuable reading for those interested in knowing both the strengths and limitations of the human communication transaction.

Montagu, A. *Touching: The Significance of the Human Skin.* Columbia University Press, New York, 1971.

Informative and written in such a way that the reader can't help but realize the beauty that is inherent in people touching, this book represents science in a most humanistic light.

Chapter Three
Understanding
Interpersonal Communication

SHOP TALK

Cultural data Information about the important norms that operate in a culture.
Sociological data Information about the groups with which a person identifies and associates.
Psychological data Information about the characteristics of a person, for example, attitudes, beliefs, values, and defense mechanisms.
Relational continuum An uninterrupted flow of events that takes place as an interpersonal relationship evolves. The relational continuum concerns the sequence of events that takes place between people following their initial meeting. This continuum ranges from simple acquaintance to intimacy.

Uncertainty reduction This is a function of interpersonal communication. It normally occurs when people first meet and communicate in the effort to learn more about each other; for example, their backgrounds and interests.
Ingratiation Communication behaviors that are designed to make people like us.
Empathy Feeling or experiencing what another person feels or experiences.
Reciprocity This term is used when people attempt to satisfy each other's needs on an equitable basis, disclose similar information to each other, and the like.

Human communication as conceptualized and described in Chapter 2 could be applied to almost any communication behaviors in which people engage. For example, it could apply to the behavior of a person who reads and processes the information printed on a highway billboard, a person watching television, two people talking on the phone, or a group of business people working on an assigned task. In short, we described human communication in its most general sense.

The question that we want to address in this chapter probably has already occurred to you: When does communication stop being just plain communication and become interpersonal? There is no obvious answer because people in the communication field have yet to agree on a completely satisfactory definition of the term *interpersonal communication.* Let us examine some of our colleagues' definitions and then our own.

INTERPERSONAL COMMUNICATION: WHAT DOES IT MEAN?

While there is little agreement on definitions of interpersonal communication, its basic elements are inherently similar to other forms of communication. Most of our colleagues would agree that interpersonal communication is verbally and nonverbally symbolic, disclosive, transactional, multifunctional,

55

and that it can be either intentional or unintentional. Further, most people would agree that interpersonal communication involves needs, is influenced by environmental factors, and requires feedback. Unfortunately for the student of interpersonal communication, unanimity abruptly stops at this point.

A SAMPLER OF DEFINITIONS

Gerald Miller and Mark Steinberg suggest that people base their predictions about communication outcomes on three levels of data: cultural data, sociological data, and psychological data.[1] They believe that during the initial stages of interaction, people tend to base their communication behavior on knowledge of the culture in which they are communicating. This means that people talk about things like sports, cities in which they've been, and even the weather. If they continue to interact, however, Miller and Steinberg suggest that the communicators will move from cultural to sociological data. This means that they will base their communication behavior on knowledge of their respective reference groups. To Miller and Steinberg, communication based on knowledge of the culture or of a person's reference groups is noninterpersonal. In order for communication to be interpersonal, people must base their communication behavior on knowledge of their respective psychologies. This means that interpersonal communication takes place only when one person's communication behavior is founded on knowledge of another person's attitudes, beliefs, values, psychological hang-ups, and the like.

In contrast to Miller and Steinberg, William Brooks and Phillip Emmert suggest that communication is interpersonal when "two to about twenty persons attempt to mutually influence one another through the use of a common symbol system, in a situation permitting equal opportunity for all persons involved in the process to influence each other."[2] Unlike Miller and Steinberg's definition, which suggests we rarely engage in interpersonal communication, Brooks and Emmert's definition is almost without bounds since some would say all intentional communications are aimed at influencing another person or persons. Moreover, while the notion of equal opportunities to influence is an intriguing one, it is unrealistic in light of the fact that in a group of seven people there are 966 lines of communication that group members could use in the attempt to influence each other.[3] The probability of

[1]Gerald R. Miller and Mark Steinberg, *Between People,* Science Research Associates, Chicago, 1975, pp. 12–29.

[2]William D. Brooks and Phillip Emmert, *Interpersonal Communication,* Wm. C. Brown Company, Dubuque, Iowa, 1976, pp. 7–8.

[3]William W. Wilmot, *Dyadic Communication: A Transactional Perspective,* Addison-Wesley Publishing Company, Reading, Mass., 1975, pp. 18–19.

equal influence, therefore, would be quite low in groups of more than three people.

The final two definitions that we will consider are those of Stewart and D'Angelo and Patton and Giffin. Since they are brief, we will discuss them collectively. John Stewart and Gary D'Angelo suggest that communication becomes interpersonal when people are comfortable in sharing their humanness.[4] The emphasis here is on sharing rather than predicting or influencing. Patton and Giffin suggest that interpersonal communication is really no different from other forms of communication with the exception that it occurs only in a face-to-face setting.[5] Rather than distinguish interpersonal communication from other forms of communication on the basis of types of data, equal opportunities to influence, or the willingness to share, Patton and Giffin suggest that interpersonal communication is distinct because of the context in which it occurs.

Despite the different meanings that people attach to the term *interpersonal communication,* there is a consistent theme running through the definitions that we have presented. Put simply, each of the preceding definitions suggests that interpersonal communication is unique. With this in mind, let's now turn to the perspective from which we will operate in the remaining chapters of this book.

A PERSONAL DEFINITION

To begin with, we believe that interpersonal communication involves predictions, attempts to influence, feeling comfortable in sharing our humanness, and that frequently it takes place in a face-to-face context. We do not believe, however, that interpersonal communication is restricted to any one behavior pattern or any one context. So where does that leave us?

As we see it, communication between people can be legitimately called interpersonal when the communication behaviors that they exhibit meet at least one of three criteria, all of which are tied to the initial and continued satisfaction of personal and interpersonal needs. First, we believe that people are engaged in interpersonal communication when their communication behaviors are targeted at satisfying needs that cannot be satisfied without the benefit of other people. These are clearly personal or interpersonal psychological needs. Second, we believe that people are engaged in interpersonal com-

[4]John Stewart and Gary D'Angelo, *Together: Communicating Interpersonally,* Addison-Wesley Publishing Company, Reading, Mass., 1975, p. 23.

[5]Bobby R. Patton and Kim Giffin, *Interpersonal Communication: Basic Text and Readings,* Harper & Row, New York, 1974, pp. 48–51.

munication when their communication behaviors contribute to the maintenance of a rewarding interpersonal relationship as defined in Chapter 1.
Finally, we are firmly committed to the idea that people are engaged in
interpersonal communication when their communication behaviors are designed to facilitate the growth of their relationship.

If you examine these criteria closely, you will find that none restricts
interpersonal communication to any particular behavior pattern or context.
On the basis of these criteria, people could be engaged in interpersonal
communication at a weekly gathering, during a long-distance phone call, or
even during an argument. After all, a weekly gathering of friends may serve to
satisfy the need for social inclusion, a long-distance phone call may contribute
to the maintenance of a long and valued friendship based on the need for
inclusion, and an argument between lovers may bring to light information
that will help the relationship to grow and to continue to satisfy their needs.

There is no certainty that the communication behaviors people exhibit will
always lead to the satisfaction of a personal or interpersonal need, contribute to
the maintenance of a rewarding interpersonal relationship, or even help the
relationship grow. But that doesn't rule out such behaviors from being called
interpersonal. In our estimation, it means simply that the people exhibiting
such behaviors have yet to familiarize themselves with the process of interpersonal communication in terms of how it unfolds and in terms of what it
involves.

THE INTERPERSONAL COMMUNICATION PROCESS

In Chapter 1 we said that the satisfaction of your needs is proportionate to your
knowledge and skill in the human communication transaction. The same is
true about the quality of your interpersonal communiction behavior. That is to
say, the probability of your interpersonal communications actually satisfying a
personal or interpersonal need, actually contributing to the maintenance of a
rewarding interpersonal relationship, or actually helping a relationship to
grow depends on your knowledge and skills with respect to the interpersonal
communication transaction. In order to realize this goal, consequently, we
need to go beyond the definition of interpersonal communication and consider
the nature of the process itself.

A SYSTEMIC PROCESS

Interpersonal communication is both orderly and sequential. Most commonly,
interpersonal communication begins on a superficial note and becomes increas-

FIGURE 3-1
THE RELATIONAL CONTINUUM

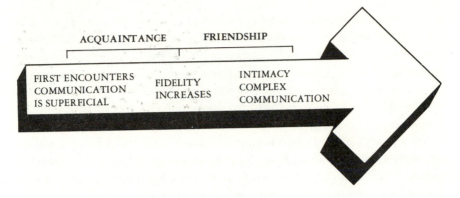

ingly complex as people assist each other in satisfying their needs, as the expectancies about the potential of their relationship escalate, and as they spend more time together.

Figure 3-1 approximates the sequence in which interpersonal communication and interpersonal relationships most commonly evolve. As suggested in this diagram, interpersonal communication concerns intially the superficial characteristics of the communicators and becomes more penetrating as the communicators move through the phases of acquaintance, friendship, and intimacy. While the relational continuum we've constructed doesn't communicate this fact, we can have a satisfactory interpersonal relationship anywhere along the continuum from acquaintance to intimacy. Going back to our discussion of Schutz's concepts in Chapter 1, we can see that a satisfactory interpersonal relationship depends on whether we and our relational partners are psychologically comfortable with the degree to which we assist each other in satisfying needs and with the level of interaction that characterizes our relationship. This is something that we negotiate and renegotiate with our relational partners throughout the life of the relationship.

What we are saying, then, is that interpersonal relationships and the interpersonal communication behavior that characterizes them will vary along a relational continuum ranging from simple acquaintance to intimacy. Further, we can have a satisfactory interpersonal relationship and enjoy rewarding interpersonal communication anywhere along this continuum. Again, it simply depends on whether we and the people with whom we are involved are comfortable with the depth of the relationship and the communication behavior that characterizes it. Given this rather general description of the process of interpersonal communication, let's now turn to a brief story depicting the meeting of two people and then analyze the story as it relates to interpersonal communication and the evolution of an interpersonal relationship.

Gramma's Attic features the two mainstays of most pubs in college towns — rock and roll music and cheap beer. To entice students away from their books on a weekday night, the management of Gramma's Attic calls every Thursday evening "Ladies Night." As you might guess, ladies night is a chauvinist ploy. Women are admitted free and provided with dime drafts so that men will be encouraged to pay admission and regular prices for beverages.

On a particular Thursday evening two people, Steve and Erica, stand on opposite sides of the dance floor. Steve is dressed simply — faded jeans, a silk-screened T-shirt, and sandals. Erica is dressed similarly — jeans, a white cotton blouse with pajama collar, and clogs. Both are relatively attractive people; both feel the need for social inclusion. As Steve scans the people on the opposite side of the dance floor his eyes meet Erica's. The stare is momentarily held and then eye contact is broken off. Steve begins to scan again, only to return to Erica. This time eye contact is made and sustained — a nonverbal message that is commonly regarded as an indication of attraction.

Steve reflects on similar experiences he has had at Gramma's Attic. He concludes that Erica is interested in him and, with this expectancy in mind, skirts the perimeter of the dance floor, intent on talking to her and satisfying his need for company.

As Steve moves toward Erica, she too reflects on like experiences while attending ladies night. On this basis, she fully expects him to approach her and attempt to initiate a conversation. Her expectancy is confirmed, and she greets Steve's "Hello" with a smile.

Steve continues by introducing himself and Erica reciprocates. A series of questions and answers follow:

> "You . . . ah, come here often, Erica?"
> "Mostly Thursday nights. How about you?"
> "Maybe once or twice a semester. It's always so crowded."
> "Are you a student at the university?"
> "No. I'm a professor."
> "Really? What department?"
> "Poli-sci."
> "You don't look like a professor."
> "Don't let my clothes fool you. I've got a closet full of her-ringbone jackets with leather elbow patches. Tonight I just felt like going Bohemian. Are you a student?"

"Sort of. I'm interning at the med center. You look surprised."

"Surprised? I frequently run into female M.D.s. I frequently hallucinate also. Yeah, I'm surprised."

"I know . . . I don't look like a doctor."

"Well, let's just chalk it up as another blow against male superiority. Can I buy you a beer?"

"I'll buy — after all, it's ladies night."

As Erica turns from Steve and moves toward the bar, his eyes carefully follow. He thinks about what has occurred and sizes up the situation to himself, "What next, a doctor! I must have appeared a real fool — no . . . I'm a professor. Good one! I hope I haven't blown it completely."

Fully aware that Steve is watching her, Erica allows a barely noticeable smile to cross her face. "One more stereotype blown out of the water." She orders the two drafts and gauges her initial feelings about Steve. "He's okay . . . not outstanding, but okay. Maybe a bit conceited." The drafts appear, twenty cents exchange hands, and she begins to dodge the mass of bodies that separate her from Steve.

"Thanks."

"Sure."

"Hey . . . I didn't mean to come off like the big time professor. You know — trying to impress the naive sweetheart of Sigma Chi."

"Sure you did. It's probably worked before."

"Well . . . I apologize. I feel foolish."

"I could have excused myself, so don't apologize. Do you like teaching?"

"Yeah . . . I like the freedom it gives me. How about you — medicine okay?"

"At first it wasn't, but it's gotten better."

"What d'ya mean?"

"Well, at first people were put off by the fact that I was a woman intern. They automatically stereotyped me as a white-coated Gloria Steinem — hell-bent on furthering the cause of sisterhood — which was true in a way, but not exactly right. Can we sit down?"

Steve places his open palm on the small of Erica's back and gently guides her to an open booth where they sit down. She doesn't seem to mind him touching her, and Steve interprets this to mean that she is at ease with him.

"You were saying that people didn't have you pinned down exactly . . . "

"Well, they were right about me being somewhat of a feminist. Medicine always has been a locked door for women, regardless of how bright they were. But that wasn't the primary thing. I wanted to be a doctor. And that's what they couldn't seem to get through their thick heads. So at first I was miserable . . . "

"How have things changed?"

"I'm good. And after a while, they began to realize that I was."

"That was enough to change their thinking?"

"I don't know if it changed their thinking, but it made them respect me."

"You're okay, Doc, you know that?"

Erica returns Steve's compliment with a smile and affectionate stare. They continue to talk and share their thoughts freely. At the evening's end, they make tentative plans to see each other and then go their respective ways.

Simplistic and accelerated as the preceding story is, it says a lot about the way an interpersonal relationship begins to develop and about the interpersonal communication behaviors that promote its development. Among other things, it suggests that first encounters are influenced by predictions based on communication variables that are predominately nonverbal, that decisions to initiate communication frequently are based on prior experiences, and the initial comments made during a first encounter are targeted at pin-pointing commonalities between communicators.

NONVERBAL COMMUNICATION

When people seek out relative strangers in the attempt to satisfy a personal or interpersonal need, they have little data to go on beyond the meaning they attach to the environment and the behaviors of the people with whom they come in contact. Usually, this means that they will gauge their own communication behavior and make predictions about communication outcomes on the basis of general information, most of which is nonverbal.

One source of such general information is the environment itself. Most of us have learned that there are communication behaviors that are appropriate in certain kinds of environments. We have learned, for instance, that there is a communication behavior pattern that is appropriate in places where people go to socialize — like Gramma's Attic. We base our communication behaviors on this knowledge and use it to make predictions about the outcome of our communication behaviors. Further, we use this knowledge to assign meaning to the communication behaviors of other people. Steve and Erica's familiarity with Gramma's Attic probably led them to predict that they could satisfy the need for inclusion there. In turn, this knowledge probably assisted them in deciding on their own communication behaviors and in assigning meaning to the communication behaviors of others.

A second general source of information that people use when they seek out others is physical appearance. You will remember from Chapter 2 that people infer a great deal about others on the basis of appearance. In this example, Steve and Erica probably developed expectancies about each other based on their physical appearance. Since they were described as relatively attractive, we would think that they used this information also to develop a set of expectancies about their mutal desirability. Their casual dress also might have prompted them to assume mistakenly that the other was a student. Of course, these expectancies further served to guide their communication behavior.

Finally, Steve and Erica probably developed a set of expectancies about their interest in each other on the basis of their eye behavior. Most of us are well aware that sustained eye contact may communicate attraction. But more than that, it is also commonly interpreted as an invitation to communicate. So it was with Steve and Erica.

What we are saying here, then, is that people rely heavily on nonverbal cues when they are in the process of seeking someone out. Most notably, they rely on the nonverbal cues contained in the environment: physical appearances, body language, and eye contact. These nonverbal cues assist people in deciding on appropriate communication behaviors, in making predictions about the outcomes of their behaviors, and in assigning meaning to the behaviors exhibited by others.

THE DECISION TO INITIATE

Whether or not we actually decide to communicate with someone depends largely on how confident we are in our interpretation of the nonverbal cues that we have observed. In turn, our confidence depends on how accurately we have interpreted such cues in the past. For example, if we have found that people attend certain environments for particular reasons, that an attractive person finds us attractive, and that sustained eye contact is an invitation to communicate, we should be completely confident in our interpretations of nonverbal cues in similar kinds of environments with similar types of people. On the other hand, if we have found that our interpretations have frequently been inaccurate, or if we have had only minimum contact with an environment and with people like those whom we now confront, we are not as likely to try to initiate communication with a stranger.

Finally, previous experiences in a specific environment or in one that is similar will affect the way in which we attempt to initiate communication. The social conventions that operate in a particular environment will dictate the way in which people attempt to initiate communication. If a decision has been made to communicate, people will use their previous experiences and knowledge of social conventions as a basis for determining what to say initially. In our example, Steve and Erica began to talk to each other by greeting each other and exchanging names.

TWENTY QUESTIONS: UNCERTAINTY REDUCTION AND INGRATIATION

Following an exchange of names, our hero and heroine talked about their occupations and provided each other with clues about their interests. Although we didn't see the conversation through, we implied that more of this kind of information was exchanged as the evening progressed.

When people meet for the first time a great deal of question asking takes place. These questions serve the communicators in at least two ways. First, as communicators gain knowledge about each other by asking questions, they will begin to reduce the uncertainty they felt prior to, and immediately following, the initiation of the communication transaction.[6] Second, they may be able to ingratiate themselves by finding common interests.[7] For example, if Steve discovered that Erica liked skiing and he was knowledgeable about the sport, he could use this topic to ingratiate himself, that is, to gain her acceptance.

NEED COMPATIBILITY

Up to this point, we have concentrated on the factors that influence people prior to the communication attempt and on some of the interpersonal communication behaviors people exhibit once they actually begin to communicate. Now the question is what happens following a first encounter between people like Steve and Erica? Although they appeared to satisfy each other's needs in

---

[6]Charles R. Berger and Richard J. Calabrese, "Some Explorations in Initial Interaction and Beyond: Toward a Developmental Theory of Interpersonal Communication," *Human Communication Research,* 1 (1976), 99–112.

[7]Murray Davis, *Intimate Relations,* The Free Press, New York, 1973, p. 4.

this single encounter, does it mean necessarily that they will continue to do so in future encounters?

The tentative plans that Steve and Erica made to see one another again are not uncommon during the beginning phase of what may become an interpersonal relationship. But there is no guarantee such commitments will be honored. Sometimes they are used as convenient devices to excuse oneself from a communication transaction. After all, it's much easier to turn down an invitation for a second meeting over the phone than face-to-face.

Whether or not this will actually happen, however, depends on how two people such as Steve and Erica feel about the relationship after they physically separate. Once they return to their residences, they probably made *intrapersonal,* or mental, evaluations of their first encounter. Such intrapersonal evaluations commonly center on the issue of need compatibility. According to Schutz, "compatibility is a property of a relationship between two or more persons, between an individual and a task situation, that leads to mutual satisfaction of interpersonal needs and harmonious coexistence."[8] In the case of Steve and Erica, whose meeting grew out of their respective need for social inclusion, the probability of their meeting again would depend on two factors. First, it would depend on whether they mutually perceived their inclusion needs to be compatible in their initial encounter. Second, it would depend on whether they projected need compatibility in future encounters. And this brings us to the issue of expectancies.

EXPECTANCIES

If Steve and Erica believe that they can assist each other in satisfying their mutual needs, they will develop a positive or favorable set of expectancies about the potential of their relationship. In turn, these favorable expectancies will influence the communication behaviors they exhibit when they meet again. Because they perceive each other positively and believe in the potential of their relationship, they will communicate in a manner that is likely to confirm their mutual perception and belief. In a sense, their communication behaviors will serve to accent the positive factors that they see in each other.

On the other hand, if they develop a negative set of expectancies following their first encounter, chances are they would not honor their commitment to meet again. Even if they did, their communication behaviors probably would confirm the negative set of expectancies each had developed. In this case, their communication behaviors would highlight the negative factors that they see in each other.

[8]William Schutz, *The Interpersonal Underworld,* Science and Behavior Books, Palo Alto, 1958, p. 105.

TIME AND CONFIRMATION

The process of evaluating need compatibility will continue throughout the life of an interpersonal relationship. Likewise, expectancies will operate throughout the life of a relationship and may change as it develops further. It is crucial to realize that need compatibility and expectancies will be judged and formed recurrently on the basis of our communication behavior and that of the people with whom we are involved. Thus, while Steve and Erica may have come away from their first encounter with the belief that their needs were compatible and with a positive set of expectancies, there is no guarantee this will be the case in subsequent encounters. It would depend on whether their communication behaviors perpetuate the belief of need compatibility and the positive set of expectancies that they had developed. Similarly, there is no guarantee that their relationship will become increasingly complex as they spend more time with each other. Again, it would depend on need compatibility and their expectancies about the potential of their now established relationship. While they may have compatible needs and hold onto positive expectancies as long as they center the relationship on the need for social inclusion, they may find that the opposite is true when needs like affection or behavior control enter the picture.

COMMUNICATION

The ways in which our interpersonal communication behavior changes as a relationship passes through the stages of acquaintance, friendship, and intimacy is detailed in the final part of this book. But there are some very general matters concerning communication that we should discuss at this point. As we've already said, judgments about need compatibility and the formation of expectancies will be based on the communication behaviors people exhibit. Thus, the probability of having a successful encounter with someone, much less a relationship, is, in the final analysis, determined by interpersonal communication skills.

Also, the fidelity with which people communicate will vary depending on how superficial or complex a relationship is. While we disagree with Miller and Steinberg's contention about what constitutes "true" interpersonal communication, we believe that the fidelity with which people communicate will increase as they exchange more and more information about themselves. However, this does not mean necessarily that the quality of their communication also will increase because intimate information about another person can be used for destructive as well as constructive ends.

Finally, we emphasize the fact that the movement of interpersonal communication from the superficial to the complex will be influenced by the environment in which most of the communication occurs and by the roles of the communicators. In our story, for example, we described two people becoming socially involved with each other. The potential for intimacy and intimate communication in such a relationship is quite high.

But what if our story had dealt with a first encounter between a teacher and student following class, a top-flight executive and a union organizer, a forest ranger and a family camping, or a recreation leader and a group of thirteen-year-olds? Would you say the potential for intimacy and intimate communication is as high in these cases as in the case of Steve and Erica? Probably not. Realize, then, that our interpersonal relationships and the communication behavior that characterizes them are influenced by our environments and by the roles we must assume in these environments.

CONCLUDING REMARKS

We have said that interpersonal communication is a systemic process. By this, we mean that interpersonal communication begins superficially and becomes increasingly complex depending on (1) the needs that people assist each other in satisfying, (2) their expectancies about the potential of their relationship, and (3) time. Also, we said that people can have and enjoy rewarding interpersonal relationships anywhere along a continuum ranging from acquaintance to intimacy depending on whether the participants are comfortable with the depth of their relationship and the communication behaviors that characterize it.

In our story, we depicted two people engaged in what commonly is known as the acquaintance process. We also described the communication behaviors people exhibit prior to and following an initial encounter. While we didn't carry this relationship through the phases of friendship and intimacy, keep in mind the fact that judgments about need compatibility and expectancies are as important to friends and intimates as they are to acquaintances. Above all, remember that judgments about need compatibility and the formation of expectancies are based on the way you and those with whom you are involved communicate.

INTERPERSONAL COMPETENCIES

Let's conclude this chapter by examining some of the commitments people must make and the skills they must acquire if they are to become interpersonally competent. Achieving such competence is not an easy task because, at the very least, it involves a reexamination of the assumptions on which interpersonal communication behavior currently is based, and, at the very most, it may demand abandoning some customary interpersonal communication behaviors. While it would be impossible to isolate all of the commitments or areas of competency that effective interpersonal communication demands, we think the following are representative.

TIME

Many songs have been written around the theme of time, and we recall bits of two songs that make points worth mentioning. The first song begins with the premise, "What a friend we have in time." The second song ends with the premise, "Time, oh good, good time — where did you go?"

It seems to us that the first premise is particularly true for the very young. To them, time is perceived as a friend because there seems to be an inexhaustible supply of it. But as we grow older, the second premise seems more appropriate, for we learn that time is anything but inexhaustible. Perhaps this is why we have incorporated phrases like save time, bank time, spend time, and waste time into our day-to-day patterns of communicating.

Since interpersonal communication develops in an orderly and sequential fashion from superficial and nonintimate levels to more complex and intimate ones, doesn't it seem that the continuum of time is important? Think about those relationships that you regard as the most rewarding and meaningful ones. How long have they been in existence? For the most part, they probably have existed for a significant span of time. The point is that enduring and rewarding interpersonal relationships do not come about overnight. They take time to develop.

Let's consider also the meaning behind one person's commitment of time to another. Time is perhaps the only thing we have to give to another person that is an unknowable quantity. For example, consider the commitment two people make when they agree to marry. Such a commitment implies sharing worldly goods, bodies, joys, and sorrows. But are these kinds of sharing the more important facets of the commitment? Or is the most important facet of the commitment the fact that they agree to share their futures?

Time is extremely important both to interpersonal communication, as when we take time to really listen, and to the growth of our interpersonal relationships. We need to be mindful of the significance of our commitments of time, as well as those of the people with whom we are involved.

COMMITMENT TO SELF AND OTHER

Just as interpersonal communication demands a commitment of time, it demands that we reexamine our initial orientation when we communicate with another human being. For example, have you ever thought about the use of the pronoun "I"? In the context of interpersonal communication its significance cannot be minimized. Most of us assume an "I" orientation when we begin communicating with another human being, that is, we have the attitude that it will serve to satisfy our wants and desires and not necessarily the needs of the person we communicate with. Think about it.

> Person A: "Why did you talk with him? (I want to know why . . .)
> Person B: "I needed to find out about the assignment . . ."
> Person A: "Did you mention the party?" (I want to know if . . .)
> Person B: "I really thought it wasn't my responsibility."
> Person A: "Why?" (I want to know why . . .)
> Person B: "Well, I didn't organize the party."
> Person A: "So . . ." (I don't feel that is a very good reason . . .)
> Person B: "What do you mean, so? If I had organized the party then I would feel responsible for the guest list but since I didn't, I don't."

Although communication behavior is, to an excessive degree, "I" behavior — I want this; I need her; I cannot do without him; I think it would be bad for me — it is significantly affected by other people, for as R. D. Laing so accurately points out, "The presence of these others have a profound reactive effect."[9] The way in which you believe that others perceive you will influence the way in which you behave.

While you need not strip yourself of your individuality in the effort to make your interpersonal communication transactions more rewarding and effective, you must be sensitive to the needs and feelings of the people with whom you interpersonally communicate. To reemphasize the point, you must realize that the probability of your individual needs being satisfied as a function of interpersonal communication is increased when the transaction also serves to

[9]R. D. Laing, H. Phillipson, and A. A. Lee, *Interpersonal Perception: A Theory and Method of Research*, Harper and Row, New York, 1966, p. 4.

satisfy the needs of the people with whom you communicate. What we are saying here, then, is that interpersonal communication involves two commitments in order to be rewarding and effective. It involves a commitment to self, but at the same time it involves a commitment to other people that reflects your sensitivity to what they are experiencing and what they feel.

EMPATHY

Too often people go about their business as if the world they happen to see is the world that everyone else happens to see. As a consequence, they become intolerant of ways of behaving and thinking that are contrary to theirs. But the world one person sees is not necessarily the world that another person sees. And when we fail to recognize this, we not only deny the idea of transaction but also increase the likelihood of meeting with failure in our attempts to establish interpersonal communication. When we fail to recognize that the other person perceives the world differently, we are likely to misinterpret the informational cues fed back to us. As a result we also are likely to develop inappropriate communication strategies. How do we overcome the tendency to assume that another person sees things as we see them, feels things as we feel them, or formulates thoughts and opinions as we do? We attempt to learn how they see the world and attempt to interpret informational cues as they would interpret them. In other words, we try to empathize, that is, to visualize and relate to, other people's perception of the environment.

DISCLOSURE AND TRUST

Have you ever noticed how some people hide their own weaknesses but invite others to talk about theirs? Perhaps it's simply a function of ego defenses coming to the forefront. Then again, perhaps it's a function of our belief that if we reveal some weakness to another person, he or she will exploit the weakness. Regardless of the reasons, the tendency to invite disclosure without reciprocating detracts from the effectiveness of interpersonal communication. Think about such a relationship. How long do you think the relationship can continue before some suspicions are raised? Probably not very long at all because the failure of one person to reciprocate very often leads to the other having feelings of distrust. Moreover, it almost always causes the person who initially disclosed information to become more cautious and guarded about their internal states.

Empathy means trying to see the world as other people see it.

Although rewarding interpersonal relationships cannot be built on a foundation of distrust and suspicion, it does not mean that we must disclose ourselves entirely. Rather, we must be willing to share ourselves with others as the situation demands.

RECIPROCITY

Above all, interpersonal communication involves reciprocity. When we disclose ourselves to others, we expect them to reciprocate. And when we try to see the world as they do, we expect them to return the favor.

The idea of reciprocity, though, is best demonstrated perhaps by the fact that when we engage in communication behaviors designed to assist other people in satisfying their needs, they are likely to engage in behaviors that help us to satisfy our needs. Think about it. When was the last time you engaged in communication behavior that assisted a person in satisfying a need — say a need like belongingness or social inclusion? How did you feel and how did this person react?

Normally, when we help someone to satisfy a need, we can't help but think well of ourselves. Is it possible, then, that by assisting a person in satisfying a need like social inclusion, that person assists us in satisfying a need like self-esteem? Of course it is, but it goes beyond this. By engaging in behaviors that facilitate satisfaction of a particular need, we increase the probability that this very person will assist us in satisfying exactly the same need. This kind of interdependency, binding humans to each other, makes the notion of reciprocity an essential part of the interpersonal communication transaction. Bear in mind that when we deny the needs of others through what we say and do, we diminish the quality of our own lives.

CHAPTER SUMMARY

This chapter has provided an overview of some of the more important elements associated with interpersonal communication. We have demonstrated that interpersonal communication is not restricted to specific communication behaviors in specific contexts. We have described interpersonal communication as a process that begins on a superficial note and may become increasingly complex as a function of needs, expectancies, and time. Finally, we have stressed the fact that interpersonal communication is a reciprocal activity that requires a number of commitments by us and by the people with whom we come in contact.

THINK ABOUT IT

IN GENERAL

Complete the exercises given under Think About It: In General at the end of Chapter 1.

IN EDUCATION

1. Assume the role of teacher. During your office hours a student enters your office and expresses a desire to talk about a problem he or she is having. You know little about the student other than that he or she doesn't talk much in class but does well on assignments. The student begins to disclose sensitive psychological data. While you realize self-disclosure normally is reciprocal, you are bothered by the information with which you've been provided and the position in which you've been placed. How are you going to communicate

with the student? Can you see any danger in a teacher and student disclosing psychological or intimate information to each other? If so, what are they and why do you consider them dangerous? Do you see anything positive coming out of the situation that we've asked you to assume? Why or why not?

IN THE ORGANIZATION

1. We have said that the fidelity with which people communicate goes up as they acquire more information about each other. Yet, in many organizations managers are discouraged from eating lunch with subordinates or socializing with them in less formal environments. What effect on communication is such a company policy likely to have? Think about the effects as they relate to your future or present occupation, and consider some of the communication strategies you might employ to thwart such a policy.

2. Job interviews are a very special form of first encounters. Usually, the interviewer knows something about the job candidate prior to the interview, but the job candidate knows little about the interviewer. Assume that you have been granted an interview for a job that meets your career needs. How might you apply the information presented on a first encounter to enhance the probability of landing the job?

IN YOUR RELATIONSHIPS

1. Have you ever wanted to know someone very much but when given the chance, blown the encounter completely? If you have, analyze the encounter in terms of the communication behavior you and the other person exhibited. Given the opportunity to meet this person again, how would you change your communication behavior?

SUGGESTED READINGS

We will be the first to admit that we don't have all the answers about interpersonal communication. The information presented in this chapter is biased in the sense that it reflects our academic training, backgrounds, and current attitudes and beliefs regarding the process of interpersonal communication. The following books discuss interpersonal communication from perspectives that range from slightly to highly discrepant with our own. You may profit by examining them in contrast with this book.

Brooks, W. D. and P. Emmert. *Interpersonal Communication*. Wm. C. Brown Company, Dubuque, Iowa, 1976.

Miller, G. R. and M. Steinberg. *Between People*. Science Research Associates, Chicago, 1975.

Patton, B. R. and K. Giffin. *Interpersonal Communication: Basic Text and Readings*. Harper & Row, New York, 1974.

Stewart, J. and G. D'Angelo. *Together: Communicating Interpersonally*. Addison-Wesley Publishing Company, Reading, Mass., 1975.

Wilmot, W. W. *Dyadic Communication: A Transactional Perspective*. Addison-Wesley Publishing Company, Reading, Mass., 1975.

Part Two
Interpersonal Communication
and Identity

Have you ever wondered why friends behave a certain way in one situation and differently in another? Have you ever considered carefully the factors that influence your initial reactions to people when meeting them for the first time? Have you ever thought about the fact that each of us develops a set of expectancies about our behavior and the behavior of those with whom we come in contact? Part 2, which focuses on the nature and influence of our individual identity systems, addresses these kinds of questions. Each of us develops a unique identity system that influences, among other things, our attitudes toward ourselves and others, our interpersonal communication skills, and our abilities to satisfy our individual needs as well as the needs of those with whom we communicate. Once understood, these unique identity systems can be altered so that we can become more effective communicators.

Part 2 is divided into five chapters. Chapter 4 broadly discusses the development of the human identity system in terms of the major factors that shape it. Chapter 5 breaks down the identity system into its interdependent components and considers the impact of these components on our interpersonal communication behavior. Chapter 6 concerns the nature of human perception, and Chapter 7 extends this information to the formation and influence of human expectancies. Finally, Chapter 8 discusses some of the ways we deal with these expectancies when our own or another's communication behavior violates them.

Chapter Four
Identity Formation:
The Making of a Person

Identity A general term concerning how people view themselves.

Positive Characterized by desirable aspects of existence.

Negative Characterized by undesirable aspects of existence.

Prenatal environment One's environment prior to birth.

Surrogate mother Any individual, or even an object, that substitutes for the role of one's real mother.

Peer group Two or more significant individuals who are perceived as being of the same status or level.

Significant others Individuals from whom we desire approval.

Life space One's experiences at any given point in time and the people who play a part in them.

Consistency A term used to describe psychological balance or harmony.

Internal consistency A state of harmony or the lack of conflict among things like attitudes, beliefs, and values.

External consistency A state of harmony between our perceptions of our environment and the things actually taking place in our environment; for example, perceiving that someone likes us and then having that person tell us he or she likes us.

Internal-external consistency A state of harmony or lack of conflict between things like our attitudes and our perceptions of what is taking place in the environment; for example, an attitude that war is bad, while the nation is at peace.

Inconsistency A state of disharmony or conflict.

Cognitions Thoughts, feelings, attitudes, beliefs, values, and so on.

As Dr. Frederick LeBoyer points out in his best-selling *Birth Without Violence*, life is both exciting and frightening at the moment of birth. Following nine months inside a confined but secure and pleasurable prison, we are forced into a new existence. The walls of the prison begin to tremble and quake, forcing us down a dark tunnel of seemingly infinite length. Then it happens — lights and sounds come into the range of our senses and we become aware that we have escaped the tremors which have rocked and thrown us about like a small boat on a violent sea.

> . . . everything explodes.
> The whole world bursts open.
> No more tunnel, no prison, no monster.
> The child is born.
> And the barrier . . . ? Disappeared, thrown away.
> Nothing! — except the void, with all its horror.
> Freedom! — and it is intolerable.
> Where am I . . ."
> Everything was pressing in on me, crushing me, but at least I had a form.

My mother, my hated prison — where are you?
Alone, I am nothingness, dizziness.
Take me back! Contain me again. Destroy me!
But let me exist . . . [1]

Perhaps it is only fitting that the prospect of a new existence both frightens and excites us. Life holds few guarantees or certainties, for example, about what we will ultimately be like or what we ultimately will accomplish, or about the lives we will inevitably touch. The only certainty is that we will be a human form with a unique identity.

In Chapter 1 we said that people must examine their own communication behavior in order to acquire communication skills that indicate their sensitivity toward the needs of other people. This chapter, which is concerned with the question of identity formation, is designed to facilitate just such a process of introspection. Realize:

No one else has seen the same world as you have.
No one else sees the world as you do.
No one else will ever see the world exactly as you do.
No one else has experienced life as you have.
No one else has an identity just like yours.

We are all individuals in all senses of the word and unique in our perceptions of ourselves and of the world around us. Let us explore the factors that give rise to a sense of identity and relate them to the process of interpersonal communication.

IDENTITY FORMATION IN THE DEVELOPMENTAL YEARS

How we see ourselves plays a major role in the decisions we make about interpersonal communication. At a minimum, how we see ourselves influences with whom we communicate, when we communicate, where we communicate, what we communicate about, and how we communicate. While we all have the need for rewarding interpersonal relationships, we tend to be somewhat selective in the development of such relationships.

Generally, we want to know something about the nature of the other person so we can make intelligent decisions regarding the potential depth of the relationship. At the same time, the other person seeks knowledge about us. So how do we exchange this information? By interpreting another's communica-

[1]LeBoyer, Frederick, *Birth Without Violence*, Alfred A. Knopf, New York, 1975, p. 27.

tion cues, we reach a decision or create an image regarding that person's identity. On the basis of the mental image that we have of the other person, we make numerous decisions influencing the type of potential relationship and the path of communication activity to be taken with that individual. Therefore, it is to our benefit to have some idea of how we got to be who we are, how we can change who we are, and how other people interpret who we are.[2]

SOME ASSUMPTIONS ABOUT HUMANS

To begin this discussion of our identity and its formation, let us review some ideas we have regarding the nature of members of the genus Homo sapiens. First, all humans have an orientation to avoid that which they perceive as painful and to seek that which they perceive as pleasurable. At times, this may involve seeking the least painful of two or more painful alternatives or the most pleasurable of two or more pleasurable alternatives. All living organisms seek to maximize positives and minimize negatives. Since each individual has a different path of experience that provides the base from which specific positive and negative evaluations are made, each tends to develop different concepts of what is painful and pleasurable, uncomfortable and comfortable, and positive and negative.

Our second assumption, discussed in Chapter 1, is that humans have an inherent need system that has varying levels of satisfaction. It would seem reasonable, then, to assume further that movement toward a need satisfaction level would be positive and a lack of movement or a movement away from a need satisfaction level would be negative. The degree of positive or negative reaction would be dependent, of course, on the individual and the state of his or her need system.

The third assumption, derived from Maslow's safety need, is that humans need consistency. We feel that consistency is viewed as a positive state and inconsistency as a negative state. However, the nature of consistency is individually derived and what is consistent for one may be inconsistent for another. Logic is not applicable. If the events we experience do not occur in some consistent or orderly manner, we humans would be in a perpetual state of uncertainty and never be able to satisfy our need for safety, security, and orderliness.[3] This is most obvious in the case of external consistency. If we turn the steering wheel of a car to the left, we fully expect the car to turn to the left.

---

[2]Many authors have addressed the issue of how identity is formed, what it is, and how it affects behavior. We are particularly indebted to Chad Gordon and Kenneth Gergen for their outstanding work in collecting so many different points of view in one publication, *The Self in Social Interaction,* John Wiley and Sons, New York, 1968, 1.

[3]L. Festinger, *Theory of Cognitive Dissonance,* Stanford Univ. Press, Stanford, 1957.

If it does not, the car would be in an inconsistent state, and we would be in a negative state. We would want to take some action to minimize this condition or alter it in such a way that it becomes positive. In this case, the solution may be simply to avoid driving a car or being in the vicinity of cars being driven. In the interpersonal sense, external consistency may relate to the idea that most of us prefer being perceived in the same way by people in our environment. In a specific situation, when others do not perceive us as having the same identity, we typically take some action, either physical or psychological. When our friend John emits a communication behavior that we interpret as meaning "I think you're a good person," and our friend Susan emits communication behavior that we interpret as "I think you're a turkey," we have different options open to us in the effort to resolve this inconsistency. Perhaps the most common reaction would be to stop referring to Susan as a friend — a process that tends to limit our life space.

It is important also that we maintain consistency internally, as in our attitudes. It would be inconsistent to have a negative attitude toward the Watergate situation and a positive attitude toward American politics in that time frame. In the same sense, it is difficult to maintain a positive attitude toward friends and a negative attitude toward the behaviors that they engage in. The effort toward consistency in how we perceive ourselves and how we would like to perceive ourselves is also an internal state. In this case, the difference in mental images would have major effects on our general orientation toward communication behavior in various situations.

To further add to the complexity of our existence, people also attempt to attain similar internal and external states. We prefer people to perceive us somewhat as we perceive ourselves. In the example above of John and Susan's inconsistent comments, we would tend to like John if we have a high perception of ourselves and dislike Susan; but if we think we really are a "turkey" and are not bothered by that judgment, we would probably like Susan more than John. Our expectancies of another person's behavior and how we go about resolving violations of those expectancies will be covered in Chapters 7 and 8. For now, it is sufficient to indicate that humans generally treat inconsistencies as negatives, and operate psychologically to avoid their occurrence, and attempt to resolve those that do develop.

Let it suffice to say at this point that the effort toward consistency interacts with our notions of positive and negative and that our experiences result in psychological states that bring great pressure on our identity system. Since our needs satisfaction levels, their importance indexes, and the methods (communication behavior) used to fulfill those needs are a function of our world experience, the importance of the identity system to our comfortable existence is obvious.

In summary, then, we think that most people view consistency and need satisfaction as positive aspects of existence. The need for an identity and for confirmation of that identity assume high positive priorities for most of us. We also point out that no two identities are the same. Let's now examine the reasons why identities differ, and the role that communication plays in forming those identities.

INHERITED TRAITS

Some characteristics like body build, body size, eye color, hair color, skin tone, and sex are inherited, that is, received genetically from our parents, and consequently we have no control in their initial formation. Although our technology has advanced so that we can alter these features (with high-heeled shoes, reducing salon treatments, breast enlargement or reduction operations, contact lenses, hair tints and dyes, pigment change, and even sex operations), alteration of the nonphysical self is more difficult. It is difficult because these psychological aspects of our identity are learned shortly after conception and operate primarily at the subconscious level.

When we become aware of a physical aspect of ourselves and learn what it means (that a person weighs an excessive amount by American standards, for instance), we can compare this meaning to what we as a human want it to mean and take corrective measures. But what do we do when we have an obnoxious trait and find that our peer group recognizes it? It takes concentrated effort to gain awareness and then to alter this item in our identity and to eliminate the communication cues that others were interpreting to mean that we were indeed an obnoxious person.

Generally speaking, we all start life with basically the same body structure. We each have the same number of limbs, eyes, nerves, and vital organs. Our respiratory systems, digestive systems, nervous systems, and sensory systems operate in basically the same way. However, a large number of individual differences exist within this set of characteristics. We do not have identical capacities to sense the world about us. Furthermore, even though we have similar brain structures, we have different mental images. Thus, the interpretation of what we sense differs for each individual.

Summarizing, there are certain facets of our physical structure that we inherit from our parents and that are a part of our personal identity. As we learn what these items are, we learn how to evaluate them and how others evaluate them. We proceed, then, to either accept or change our perceptions and the perceptions of others regarding these aspects.

THE LEARNING PROCESS

The development of individual identity is a life-long process. However, the influence of the early years of life provides such a strong base that its impact is evident throughout the life of the individual. This is reflected in the age-old maxim, As the twig is bent so grows the tree. The environment shapes your sense of identity from the point of birth through adulthood.

During the first five years of our lives, before we develop a refined thinking process, our ideas of self-identity are formed to a large extent by what other people tell us. As Ratliffe and Herman point out: "You tend to be what you think you are. You tend to think you are what you say to yourself you are. You tend to say to yourself what you are by listening to people around you tell you what you ought to be, think, feel, say and do."[4] The communications of important people in your life space are either positive or negative. Miller and Steinberg note that humans are constantly trying to achieve control of their environment, trying to reach points of consistent pleasure.[5] It is the result of such efforts that formulate our ideas of identity. The role of communication in forming identity is to allow one knowledge of the existence of an environment, to allow one to exert influence upon that environment, and to allow one awareness of the success, nonsuccess, or failure of those attempts. Again, Miller and Steinberg note that "the development of self-identity is not primarily a function of communication, but rather a consequence of the outcomes of a person's communicative efforts to achieve environmental control."[6] The concept of environmental control may be seen as an effort to achieve need satisfaction levels, maintain states of consistency, or avoid painful states of existence. Let us examine in some detail the shaping procedures that formulate identity.

The Environment of the Infant Following conception, the first sensory mechanism to become active is the tactile system. The fetus becomes aware of changes in its surrounding environment through a sense of touch and pressure. It can discriminate between pain and pleasure as a result of this sensory organ and, thus, may shift position to avoid uncomfortable postures and to seek pleasurable ones. After the child is delivered and forced to utter its first oral activity, it is exposed to what will become the focus of its life space — oral communication. The child is unaware of this yet, but through constant repetition begins to discover that when in a state of pain, oral activity quite often brings about relief. The child learns the pleasures and pains of the body.

[4]S. A. Ratliffe and D. M. Herman, *Adventures in the Looking Glass,* National Textbook Co., Skokie, Illinois, 1974, p. 11.
[5]G. R. Miller and M. Steinberg, *Between People,* Science Research Associates, Chicago, 1975.
[6]Miller and Steinberg, p. 80.

In most cases hugging and caressing are viewed as producers of pleasurable states; lack of milk, wet diapers, roughness, and harshness are viewed as producers of painful states. To further enhance the differences, the child begins to notice that painful states are replaced by pleasurable states if certain behaviors are exhibited. If this were not so, if the parents were not responsive to the baby's cry of distress or did not handle the baby with intimate contacts, then the child would tend to be frustrated even to the extent of switching the concepts of what is painful and pleasurable to what is painful and more painful. The results of such a perspective would have major impact on the child's identity system and ultimately upon the interpersonal communication behavior utilized by that individual.

Normally raised children recognize pleasure in intimacies and warmth from the parents in the form of touch and sounds such as cooing and ahhing. Soft, warm voices are desired while harsh, rough, and cold voices are undesired. The innate need for belongingness and love, discussed in Chapter 1, is operative at birth. The child begins to classify those communications from the environment that reflect gains toward that need as pleasurable and communications that indicate movement away from that need as painful. These classification activities become more evident as the child matures in his or her ability to discriminate between incoming stimuli and to infer sources of these stimuli.

Recognizing that warm voices are associated with parental approval and thus pleasure, and cold voices are associated with parental disapproval or pain, the child responds to the first instances of purposeful shaping by external oral activities. Feeding time no longer consists of just pleasure associated with the procurement of milk. It also is associated with the movement toward the need of belongingness and love, and it now includes negative aspects if certain behaviors occur, such as, knocking the food off the table. The parents begin using the conditioning principles of reward and punishment (in some cases unwittingly) to produce the desired behavior in their child. The child begins to recognize that pleasurable states are acquired only if certain behaviors are utilized and that these states are withheld or replaced by painful states if other behaviors are utilized. Toilet training is a good example. First the parents seat the child on the commode at about the appropriate time in order to familiarize him or her with the proper procedures and the general situation. The child, of course, will not understand immediately and the parents will initiate efforts to teach the child that the proper place to perform excretory functions is in the bathroom. Teaching will be positively or negatively reinforced with warm voices and a lack of negatives or cold voices, spanking, and a lack of positives.

Such a small part of the environment as warm or cold voices can drastically influence an identity item like lovability, the quality of attracting affection from others. Can you see the difference in a child's self-perspective on this one item if raised in an environment of warm voices (which are communications from the environment that one is loved) versus being raised in an environment of cold voices (which are communications from the environment that one is not loved)?

During the first several months of life, the infant does not see things in the environment as good and bad, but as exclusively good or bad. In addition, the child's perspective does not remain constant across various situations. Judgments about objects and people in the environment are predicated on the immediate situation and whether the child is in a positive or negative state. Sullivan discusses the example of the hungry baby who cries.[7] The mother interprets this communication as indicating the baby is in need of milk and supplies a nipple. If the nipple produces milk, then the baby is satisfied, in a positive state, and categorizes the nipple as "good." However, if no milk is produced, then the nipple is categorized as "bad." As the infant matures, he or she transfers the prior evaluation of the nipple to the nipple producer — the mother. If the mother produces a positive state, then she is a "good" mother; if not, then she is a "bad" mother. This process of generalizing positive and negative traits and associating them conceptually with related objects and persons occurs with maturation. It is during this period, after the infant begins to discriminate self from other parts of the environment, that personal identity items are formulated that will provide the basis for relating to other individuals in later life.

Once the child has developed skills at verbalizing, the opportunity of the parent to shape the child's identity increases a thousandfold. Even the process of acquiring language is a shaping procedure. Typically, the child begins to make sounds that resemble words in the parents' vocabulary, such as "Mama" and "Dada." When this occurs, the parents get excited and shower the child with hugs, caresses, and vocal reinforcement. Using positive reinforcement to get the learning stages of language acquisition started is almost always used. But when the child has acquired a small vocabulary and begins to string words together into phrases and sentences — watch out! — negative reinforcers appear.

"No! You're saying it wrong again!"
"If you say 'ain't' one more time . . ."

Through efforts to maximize positives and minimize negatives, the child develops a language structure and an appropriate vocabulary.

The mother-child relationship in the past had the most influence on the child's development of personal identity. The typical mother of 1930 spent her

[7]H. S. Sullivan, *The Interpersonal Theory of Psychiatry*, W. W. Norton and Company, New York, 1953.

entire day with or in the presence of the child. Since World War II, when mothers worked in defense factories, this has not been the case. From the 1950s the resultant pressure for the mother to assist in increasing the family's financial state and to gain personal autonomy has split further the mother-child relationship. In all probability, this trend will continue, if not escalate. Thus, the general concept of the role of the mother has undergone major changes. No longer will the mother be home with the child almost constantly from birth to kindergarten age. Being in the age of the working mother, the child is finding that the significant people in his or her early life include not only the mother and father but also a surrogate mother in a babysitter, nursery school teacher, or play school leader. The effects of such a division are unknown, yet we can look at the last generation of humans (whose surrogate mothers were at the least the television set) and distinguish differences in tendencies and behavior from previous generations. The natural reaction of the older generations is one of fear of the subtle changes, yet we cannot determine on the basis of present evidence if such alterations as increased intelligence, more worldly perspectives, higher tendencies toward sociability, and higher instances of mental frustration are really for the benefit or detriment of the preservation of the human race. We can certainly observe changes not only in values but also in the intensity with which such values are held. Regardless, changes in identity formulated during the child's first five years will occur and emerge as the child of today develops into an adult.

Sociocultural Economic Impact Parents also provide the child with identity items that are a function of the sociocultural economic environment in which the family unit exists. The social environment includes the relationship between parents and between each parent and the child. The communication that occurs verbally and nonverbally provides the foundation for the child to integrate behavior patterns and notions into a sense of self. If one parent communicates to the other in an aggressive, domineering manner and receives positive reinforcement for such behavior, the child may generalize that such communication behavior is appropriate for him or her. If the parent's social life is of a particular nature and the child observes the apparent positive reinforcement received by the parents for such a social life, the child may tend to adopt a similar social life. The following poem illustrates the impact on a child of the early period and of the environment to which the child is exposed.

If a child lives with criticism
He learns to condemn
If a child lives with hostility
He learns to fight

If a child lives with ridicule
He learns to be shy
If a child lives with shame
He learns to feel guilty
If a child lives with tolerance
He learns to be patient
If a child lives with encouragement
He learns confidence
If a child lives with praise
He learns to appreciate
If a child lives with fairness
He learns justice
If a child lives with security
He learns to have faith
If a child lives with approval
He learns to like himself
If a child lives with acceptance and friendship
He learns to find love in the world[8]

As the child learns what produces positive and negative states in the world, these behavior patterns and concepts are integrated into the personal identity. The child also learns how to handle negative states and begins to substitute alternative cognitions and behavior for the anxiety and frustration brought about by such negative states.

Between the ages of three and five the child begins to differentiate boys from girls. Sex differences are recognized. These physicial differences also carry social and psychological differences that are reinforced by mom and dad, and these become critically important core items of the identity. Stereotypically, boys are expected to be brave, adventuresome, exploring, aggressive, and dominant over the opposite sex. Stereotypically, girls are expected to be sweet, timid, content, subtle, and submissive toward the opposite sex. Men wear one type of clothing and play with masculine toys, while girls wear a different type of clothing and play with feminine toys. These toys most typically represent the general orientation of masculinity and femininity that the parents desire the child to portray upon maturation and may include general orientations toward occupational roles. Boys play with fire trucks, guns, and race cars and being boss, while girls play with mock ovens, baby dolls, clothes, and maid services.

At present, a number of women have managed to overcome their sex role conditioning. Sex roles, which always existed, have undergone major changes

[8]Dorothy Law Nolte, "Children Learn What They Live," in *Looking Out/Looking In*, Ron Adler and Neil Towne, Holt, Rinehart and Winston, San Francisco, 1975, p. 43.

in the past two decades. Women's liberation is active in the late 1970s. In all likelihood the sex roles portrayed by the men and women of the year 2001 will be distinctly different from those of today. Children will have adjusted to different positive states relative to communication behavior personifying sex. In other words, basic core elements of the identity system will undergo changes in the next few generations because of alterations in the parental and cultural environments that will provide positive reinforcement for different core elements of the identity than past generations experienced during their formative stages.

Sex roles are only one of many different aspects of personal identity that are formulated by the social and cultural environment provided by the parents. Our manners are also conditioned by the parents' reflections of sociocultural customs. "Please," "Thank you," "Yes, Ma'm," "No Sir," and "I'm sorry" are taught to the child through the utilization of positive and negative reinforcement. Observe, however, that manners are not universally the same. In some parts of Africa a child is taught to shake hands with both hands while in our American culture, a one-hand-extended handshake is dictated.

The cultural notion of time is another aspect of personal identity. This aspect of time becomes associated with keeping a grudge in a case study mentioned by E. T. Hall.[9] A military government group occupying the atoll of Truk in the South Pacific was approached by a native exclaiming that a murder had taken place and that the murderer was in the village. Rushing to the scene, they could find no evidence of disruption nor the supposed murderer. Finally, they discovered that the murder had happened seventeen years earlier. Time does not heal wounds for the Trukese. Hall related another story about an Indian chief who, when promised an outstanding racehorse for some future date, walked away in dismay. Yet, when later offered a swaybacked old nag to be delivered immediately, he was exuberant.[10] The future had little reality for this group of Indians. The only time that mattered was the present.

What are your identity items associated with time? Are you an "on time" person? How much time do you allow to others at different stages between psychological acquaintance and psychological intimacy? When you're listening to another person, do you give him or her full benefit of that time, or do you split it with other thoughts rambling through your head? How do you allocate your time in an average day? Honest responses are somewhat shocking, aren't they?

It is through the learning process that such basic components of identity as ethical values and religious values are developed. Were it not for the shaping

[9]E. T. Hall, *The Silent Language*, Fawcett Publications, Greenwich, Conn., 1959, p. 26.
[10]Hall, p. 23.

by our parents, would we think of ourselves as ethical? Would we be religious? In all probability, we would not. We would be scraping to meet elementary needs in a human-eat-human world. The continued existence of society and culture is dependent upon instilling in the personal identities of youth basic values by which continuation of the human race has a high potential for success. This conditioning can be authoritarian in nature, for example, consider Hitler's youth program. Mao Tse-tung and his book produced the Red Guard, which was an effort to insure the perpetuation of that society by indoctrinating and shaping the core value system items in the identities of its youth. Our culture is not much different in this regard. The value or religious system that you have been shaped to acknowledge was in all probability presented in your youth as a positive state by your immediate environment — parents, relatives, and so on — with negative reinforcement for nonconformity provided with ease. Do not react to this with abhorrence. If youth had no foundation for an ethical and religious system, they would have no guidelines with which to reach a state where reason could be applied and such decisions independently made. In other words, you probably would not live to reach the point of emotional and intellectual maturity that would allow you to make such decisions on your own. In later years, we may increase or decrease the degree to which these values are operative in our identity as the positive or negative rewards for such involvement vary in our environment.

Peer Group Environment   Our identity system is further shaped by our peer groups. Given that our need for belongingness and love is extremely active and rarely totally satisfied, the unwitting shapers have a powerful weapon to use at their will. With positive and negative states being determined by the degree of achievement of basic needs (in a psychological sense), the giving or withholding of affection or comradeship becomes directly associated with the production of those states. Thus, we may well adapt personal identity items of our peers in an attempt to reach a positive state. As James said, "A man has as many different social selves as there are distinct groups of persons about whose opinion he cares."[11]

Consider those individuals who leave home to attend college. The inclusion need becomes extremely active. Concern is felt for whether they will feel as if they belong and if they will have friends and dates. The dormitory life on a college campus contains numerous strong pressures to conform to a new norm that can create changes in individual idealities and behavior. Most males undergo strong pressures for sexual success indexes.

Of course the female has respective pressure to be a successful dater. A

[11]W. James, "The Self," in *The Self and Social Interaction,* ed. C. Gordon and K. J. Gergen, John Wiley and Sons, New York, 1968, I, 42.

class of students was asked to define promiscuity in the college environment. After hemming and hawing for thirty minutes, the only response was that people who sleep with five different persons six nights a week are definitely promiscuous.

In a similar sense, the individual who moves to a new job is also subjected to pressure from fellow employees to conform to a new norm. This may lead to a change in the individual identity system. A person who was raised under low economic conditions may feel the pressure to alter various attitudes and values as a result of accepting a position where the fellow employees were raised under high economic conditions. A college student who works a night shift may well undergo pressure in the form of ridicule by other employees. If the work environment also becomes a major social environment, individuals under severe peer pressure may alter not only their perspective toward higher education but also their own desires and abilities to succeed in educational attempts. Of course, for peer pressure to be effective, it must be a dominant influence at that particular time period.

Significant Others Within any environment, we are influenced by the individuals who are significant to us. Significance may be in the form of authority, admiration, or desire. In a sense, we anticipate what the significant other's expectancies of ourselves are or what they would require of one in order to like them, and in many instances we adapt or at least try to adapt ourselves to conform to those expectancies.

In the vocational environment, the significant other may be the supervisor who controls promotions and pay increases. To some extent people will attempt to personify themselves to that individual as the type of person the supervisor would admire. Should sufficient positives be offered, that personification may be internalized as an active part of the identity system.

Within the educational system, the significant others could be a teacher, a parent, an administrator, or a fellow student. Regardless of position, the more esteem we have for the other, the more authority the other has over our positives, or the more desire we have for a relationship with the other, the more we may be affected by the other individual.

Educational Environment The education system and the reaction of significant people in it form a neat package of positive and negative reinforcements that affects the components of our identity. If you get A's on your report card and your parents and peer group give you positive reinforcement, you develop the idea that you are the type of individual who gets A's, and you will adopt all the nonspecifics associated with getting A's, that is, intelligence, capability, composure, and competence. On the other hand, should you receive D's and

F's, your perspective of who you are will be drastically altered. Teachers also may have an effect upon the identity system. Individuals who receive positives from one teacher may adopt a lifestyle and identity designed to perpetuate the positives. The identity formation process is so complex that even nonchalant behavior on one person's part can have an influential impact on another person.

One young man's life was totally changed during the high school years. Prior to this time he had existed in the ghetto and was developing an identity comparable to the "hood" of the 1950s. On entering high school, he excelled at football, basketball, and other sports. Whereas once he had to frighten others to fulfill his identity and satisfy his need for belongingness, he now found such behavior was no longer necessary. His attitudes were changed further by a simple incident. Back in those days, high schools required male students to wear belts. Being the rebel he thought he was, naturally to wear a belt was to give in to authority — and he wouldn't do that. The principal, who had a reputation for being tough, caught him in the hall and brusquely ordered him into the office. There, to the amazement of the youngster, the principal offered him his belt to get through the day. This very simple, unplanned occurrence in the education environment had drastic impact on his identity. Athletic prowess altered his interpersonal behavior toward peers while a show of concern for him as an individual altered his perspective toward authority.

In addition to grades and student-teacher relations, the identity system is also affected by what one learns in a formal sense. Taken as a whole, then, the educational environment has a tremendous effect on the identity system.

CHAPTER SUMMARY

Remember that each time we refer to the environment influencing your sense of identity we are talking about your interpretation of communication cues from sources external to yourself. It is only through analyzing communication cues that you even know an external world exists. It is only through communication that your significant others affect you and you affect others.

Our identity is not a singular concept. It is a complex interrelationship of three primary components: personal identity, social identity, and ideal identity. Each represents a different perspective of ourselves in our life space. The following chapter continues to describe how one's identity is formed but considers each of these components, their interaction, and the resultant effect upon interpersonal communication.

In this chapter we described the process by which our identity begins to take shape. It is important to understand this process because your identity and the identities of others have a tremendous effect on the process of interpersonal communication. With this in mind, we said that individual identities are shaped by: (1) prenatal and postnatal environments, (2) the socioeconomic circumstances of the family unit, (3) peer groups, (4) the system of education, (5) and those people we regard as significant forces in our lives. Remember that environmental communication is the medium by which our identities take shape and that our individual identities have an immeasurable impact on interpersonal communication behavior.

THINK ABOUT IT

IN GENERAL

Complete the exercises given under Think About It: In General, at the end of Chapter 1.

IN EDUCATION

1. Discuss in class how your identity has been influenced by the educational system. Try to focus on specific facets of education, for example, subject matter, teaching methods, sizes of schools, and the socioeconomic status of students — which do you think had a major impact on your identity and your current skills as a communicator?
2. How has your identity changed as a result of your schooling? Consider how your identity changed as you moved through the various levels of education. Also, think about changes in your communication behavior that accompanied changes in your identity.
3. List the five most significant teachers in your life. Why were they significant? How did they affect your identity and the ways in which you interpersonally communicate? For example, have you used their communication behaviors as models? If so, explain why.

IN THE ORGANIZATION

1. Many organizations like their executives to assume a corporate rather than individual identity. In effect, this means personnel should behave in a manner

that is consistent with the image the organization wants to portray. How would you react to such a policy if you were employed by one of these organizations? Do you think an executive's corporate identity carries over into his or her social relationships? If so, what effect might this have on the person's interpersonal communication behavior and interpersonal relationships?

2. Generally, the people we work with have a real influence on our identities. This influence can be either positive or negative, depending on how they communicate with us. In turn, we have the same kind of influence on our coworkers. Assume you are working with someone who exhibits communication behavior like that exhibited by Christine Chubbuck. Knowing that healthy identities make for a healthy organization, how would you communicate with this person in the attempt to influence positively his or her identity?

IN YOUR RELATIONSHIPS

1. Sarah Kiesler, a well-known social psychologist, found in her research that identities that are comprised of both male and female characteristics are more healthy than identities that are strictly masculine or feminine. Generally, this means males who are not afraid to show emotions associated with females (for example, crying when happy) and females who are not afraid to show emotions associated with males (for example, assertiveness and aggressiveness) are best equipped psychologically to cope with and relate to people. Many parents now guard against their children assuming communication roles that are strictly masculine or strictly feminine. What's your reaction to Ms. Kiesler's conclusion and this practice of parents? If you are currently a parent or someday plan to be one, will you now avoid creating situations that require your children to assume strictly masculine or feminine communication roles? Why or why not?

2. How has your sex affected the ways in which you communicate with people? Are you a sexist communicator? How do you know? Are nonsexist communicators more skillful than sexist communicators? If they are, what might you do to become a more skilled communicator in situations where both sexes are represented?

SUGGESTED READINGS

Gordon, C. and K. Gerger. *The Self in Social Interaction.* John Wiley and Sons, New York, I. 1968.

This scholarly book is perhaps the outstanding current compilation of ideas about the identity system, its development and consequences. The advanced student will find it challenging and meaty. It is heavy with theory and not recommended for entertainment reading.

Note: See Chapter 5 for additional readings associated with the identity system.

Chapter Five
Exploring the Identity System

Personal identity Who you believe you are.

Social identity Who you believe other people think you are.

Ideal identity Who you believe you would like to be and to be seen as.

Identity system The composite of personal, social, and ideal identity in interaction with each other.

Behavioral set A collection of identity items that become operative as the situation and context changes. These identity items affect communication behavior used in that situation.

Core identity Those identity items that group together as the overriding principles of life. Included are such items as beliefs, values, ethics, and morals.

Identity item A cognition or thought.

Weighted item An identity item that assumes varying levels of importance as the situation and context changes.

Behavioral options Alternative ways of behaving that have various consequences.

This chapter is concerned with breaking down the identity system into its components and showing how each has developed from environmental communications and how each influences the interpersonal communication transaction. We are concerned that you gain not only a theoretical insight into the identity system but also a practical awareness of the relationship between your identity and your interpersonal communication behavior. This should provide an insight into the behavior of others and provide alternative explanations for their interpersonal communication behavior.

One's total concept of self is composed of at least three primary components that are complexly intertwined and often difficult to discriminate in everyday life. Each of these components affects the others in a continuing dynamic fashion. For the purposes of discussion we offer the following definitions:

1. Personal identity: The perspective each of us has of ourselves.
2. Social identity: The perspective each of us has of other's view of ourselves.
3. Ideal identity: The perspective each of us would like ourselves and others to have of us.

The term *perspective* appears in each of the above definitions to further establish the idea that each of us is an individual. Each of us believes that we have found reality, that we have found truth. We react, interpret, and behave as if we are correct in our view of the world. Often, we additionally assume that everyone else has the same reality or truth that we have. This, of course, is a major error that often has dire interpersonal consequences.

In test situations, students often redefine these terms. We hope you do not make the error of defining *social identity* as "what others think of me." This is incorrect because you do not know what others think of you. You only assume or guess what mental images they have of you based on the communication cues you have received and interpreted from them. You may have interpreted those cues wrongly. You may have missed the important cues. These people may have sent out the wrong cues to represent their mental image. Millions of things could have caused a low fidelity communication link. You will behave toward others based on your assumptions and perspectives. Therefore, all anyone has is a perspective of truth, and each of us has a different one.

PERSONAL IDENTITY

Personal identity is basically who you believe you are. It consists of the conscious and unconscious perceptions we have of ourselves. These perceptions are based on environmentally learned criteria. These include evaluations of physical features (such as height, weight, body build, hair color, skin color, length of fingers, and complexion) that are made in such a manner as to represent attributes like beauty or handsomeness and femininity or masculinity. They include evaluations of physical and mental abilities as well as cognitive states such as values, beliefs, attitudes, and opinions. As you can readily see, personal identity is basically anything about ourselves that can be situationally identified and evaluated.

As you read this book, all of your personal identity items are not operative. Your ability to play tennis, for example, is not of serious concern to the present situation. However, were we discussing the relative merits of various athletic events, this item might become relevant to the interaction and enter the conscious portion of your mind.

Personal identity items, individually and in groups, affect our interpersonal communication behavior. An item may be operative either at the conscious or unconscious level. Prior to becoming operative through context or environment, the item is classified as dormant. At any one time millions of items are dormant, awaiting situations where they will be called on to assist in making behavioral or cognitive decisions.

Some personal identity items are deeply rooted, of extreme importance, and very difficult to alter. This does not mean that these concepts are unchangeable; rather it means that of all the facets of your personal identity, these few group together as the overriding principles of your life. As such they are

I AM_____ ?   I AM_____ ?   I AM!! _____

Discovering who you are is a process.

FIGURE 5-1
PERSONAL IDENTITY CORE

VALUES
ETHICS
CULTURE
ATTITUDES

relatively solidified. We call this collection of items the *core* of the personal identity. Figure 5-1 exemplifies the core of the personal identity as the core of an apple. It typically includes such dominant items as religious beliefs and values, cultural beliefs and values, ethical beliefs and values, and some ingrained attitudes.

The personal identity core is surrounded by all other aspects of our personal identity. The farther removed from the core an item is located, the easier it is to alter and the less important it is in terms of influencing your interpersonal communication behavior. Figure 5-2 exemplifies the manner in which each of the personal identity items is intertwined with each other item and with the core. Because of our need for consistency, we strive to maintain some degree of balance in terms of individual assessments of the various items composing our personal identity. That is, we recognize our limitations and we compensate for them by making general rather than specific internal evaluations of ourselves. For example, we seldom evaluate ourselves as both a good and bad tennis player. Instead, we generalize that we are an average tennis player with a good forehand and a not-so-good backhand. Because of our striving for a positive identification, there is the tendency to ignore the negative aspects of our personal identity. This is not to say that we are incapable of admitting deficiencies, but rather that we rarely make conclusive statements about our more noticeable shortcomings. Rare indeed are the individuals who can admit to themselves that they are bad chess players without qualifying the comment through an internal or external rationalization process. Typical examples of this type of behavior are "I'm just learning," "You can't expect miracles overnight," "What do you expect me to do against a player with twenty years

FIGURE 5-2
OVERALL PERSONAL IDENTITY

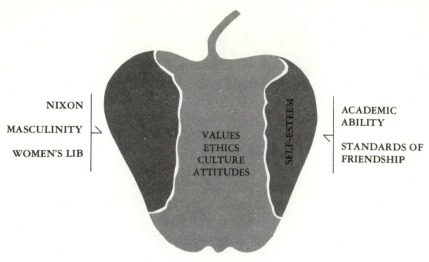

of experience?" or "It's a silly game anyhow." It is exactly this tendency toward positive self-identification that leads to confusion between our ideal identity and our personal identity. We discuss the negative aspects of this confusion later in this chapter.

Since who we believe we are plays such an important role in determining the communication behavior we tend to utilize in an interpersonal situation, it may be of some benefit to take a moment and assess our personal identity. Remember that many items are dormant and many other items are operative at the subconscious level. Introspection is a word that has been abused but still is apropos. It means to look into yourself, to discover those aspects of your identity that affect your behavior daily, but have been relegated to the unconscious level as a function of repetition after forming habitual behavior patterns. Make a list of five adjectives to start (for example, aggressive, intelligent, nervous, sociable, and competent). Now rate yourself on a scale of 1–10 on each adjective. Don't be bashful and try not to cover up. Be as honest as you can in this process of self-awareness.

In all probability you have not consciously thought much about many of the items listed above. The fact that you have responded indicates that these items are or could be part of your personal identity if an appropriate situation developed. If we were to take this one step further and ask you to rate yourself on a list of nonsense syllables, in all likelihood you would do so. We can and will evaluate ourselves on the basis of concepts which have no actual meaning. Our effort to establish a personal identity is so strong that where no meaning exists we will assign a meaning based upon our experience with vaguely similar concepts from the past.

Once we have general or specific ideas about our personal identity, we try to communicate that facet of ourselves to others. Up to this point we have been considering those communications from the environment that form our personal identity. For a moment let's consider those communications we make to our environment about our identity. It is important to emphasize that we are continuously doing so and that much of this communication is not consciously sent out. Based on our experiences (which help form our personal identity), we formulate behavior patterns designed to represent ourselves to other people in a responsible manner. Assume that a young woman believes that she is attractive and intelligent; she will attempt to communicate these personal identity items to others by her selection of verbal and nonverbal behavior. Typically she will surround herself with artifacts associated with these items. She would tend to draw upon her experiences in observing people who she thought were attractive and/or intelligent and, in a sense, mimic their behavior and adopt artifacts associated with attributes in the observed individuals as additional communication cues. A certain style of clothing or a certain posture or walk might be adopted and used as communication cues representing her personal identity items.

Consider those individuals who think of themselves as intelligent. If all the intelligent people that they know talk extremely fast, what do you think the odds are that they will adopt that behavior as a communication cue?

Who we think we are and our experiences with other people of similar qualities provide the background for the communication behavior we utilize as communication to ourselves and to others. Why do people have a motivation for changing hair color, hair style, and dress style as current fashions shift? It would appear that most people have a fairly strong personal identity item associated with contemporary attractiveness. Thus, by adopting the current styles, individuals not only communicate to themselves that they are indeed contemporarily attractive, but also communicate this to others from whom positive reinforcement is expected.

As we continue our discussion of identity and interpersonal communication, the concept of consistency will appear often. When we are discussing the effort to be consistent, keep in mind that consistency is an individual concept. What is consistent in your mind is not necessarily consistent in your employer's mind or your mother or father's mind.

Most of us have done things in our lives we now regret, things that, as we look back on them, seem totally inconsistent with who we think we are and how we ought to behave. Yet, if we can go back and remember our thoughts just before the behavior, it probably seemed quite logical and not at all inconsistent with our personal identity. How often have we heard or said to ourselves, "Well, it just seemed the right thing to do at the time." Reviewing the videotape of a motorcycle race, one rider was heard to say, "Well, I can't believe I took such idiotic chances. It just seemed like I had to drive over my head to win. I am not a reckless person and if I ever do that again black flag me the hell out of there!" A girl friend once said, "It's just not like me to spend that much money, but all those sales were just too good to resist."

It may be beneficial for you to stop a moment and recall at least three types of behavior in which you were involved that seemed quite logical at the time, but in retrospect you recognize that other people might have reacted with a comment like, "But that's just not like you" or "That's not the person I know." If you have access to the people who might have reacted this way, ask them what they thought you had in mind when you behaved as you did. Discuss the reactions in terms of their interpretations of the situation and the communication cues. You might want to share these experiences with your classmates and get their reactions also.

What kinds of behavior have others performed in your life group that seemed inconsistent from your viewpoint? List three examples and attempt to estimate the reasoning process that the other individuals went through before they behaved so peculiarly. If you have access to the people involved, ask them to pin down their reasoning for such behavior and compare it with your estimates. Discuss the reactions in terms of your expectations of their behavior.

Due to our need for consistency within and between the elements composing personal identity, decision making in regard to behavior (and communication) includes an instantaneous skimming of the personal identity items to determine which are relevant in this situation and their respective importance level. These items then are more important than others at that time and thus are weighted when making decisions. The various behavior options open to us are then compared to these weighted items for that situation, and the behavior that will produce consistency and best satisfy our basic needs on the basis of past experience will be determined.

This is an appropriate time to return to the adjective list you made earlier when looking at your personal identity. Assign values to each of the items according to their personal importance to you based on the following scale:

Most important	5
Very important	4
Important	3
Not very important	2
Least important	1

You should now have some notion of your weighted personal identity items (though remember that this is certainly not an exhaustive list). Consider an instance when you must make a communication behavior decision between an item weighted at 5 and an item weighted at 3. Will 5 always win? No, we don't believe so, because the situation may affect our weighting values. In completing the weights, you were reacting to the situation you were in at the time. As the situation changes, so does the weighting system. Consider, for example, discussing premarital sex with your parents; then consider the communication behavior you adopted in discussing premarital sex with your friends (both male and female). The communication cues used to represent your feelings on this issue were probably different. The context or situation changed. New identity items became active and either caused shifts in importance levels or through a unique combination overwhelmed a highly weighted isolated item such as one's attitude toward premarital sex. Examples of what appears to be a shift in identity are numerous. However, we believe that the identity does not radically shift or change, but rather that different views of one's identity are presented as the context or situation shifts and changes.

For example, you may consider yourself to be a good athlete. When you are in a situation that involves other athletic students, your communication cues may be strong, overt declarations of your athletic prowess. If we alter the situation to include students who care little about athletics, your communication cues may assume a more subtle quality without the boastful technique used earlier. Consider your communication cues representing your feelings about religion. The communication cues selected vary in situations involving other individuals whose views are quite different. Assuming that you have as an item in your personal identity the idea of politeness, one can discern the various cues utilized in being polite in a shopping crowd, being polite on a first date, and being polite after ten years of marriage.

We believe that our tendency is to behave in such a way as to promote maximum positive consistency among situationally weighted elements of our personal identity. Fortunately, the totally complex nature of the personal identity becomes somewhat simplified with the development of behavioral sets or habits. This process is similar to the development of perceptual sets, which are discussed later.

These behavioral sets are related to role playing. *Role playing* is basically a set of communication cues that we utilize in conjunction with a situational view of identity. The collection of items in our personal identity that comprises the behavioral set or role for a particular situation is, in essence, a window we present to allow others access to our identity in a certain situation or context.

When you sit down for a discussion about your future with your best friend, you find yourself most comfortable utilizing the communication behavior that resulted in the development of your relationship. Those cues personify the role of best friend. Yet, when you are discussing the same topic with your professor, you have a different behavioral set toward what communication behaviors will be acceptable in your role as student. In the same sense, when you sit down with your employer to discuss your future, a different set of communication cues will be utilized to represent your identity in the context of employee. Most of us prefer to have others view us positively and consistently. Therefore, a role, which may be defined as selected behavior representing a specific and contextual view of your identity, includes to some extent other people's expectations of our identity.

The tendency to be consistent is also operative between behavioral sets. In our earlier years, the need for consistency was not strong. We could easily switch from being a doctor to being a clothes designer to being a rodeo clown. But as we mature, the pressure to settle on less of a variety of behavior sets increases. The need to decide on an occupation, the increased pressures we feel as we attempt to personify various behavioral sets, and the increased expertise demanded of certain roles exemplifying those aspects of our identity require us to make major decisions as to who we are and how we want other people to view us. Young adults, beginning at approximately age sixteen, quite often experience what has been called an *identity crisis.* You may know others who are in that state, or, possibly, you may be in the midst of your own identity crisis. Typically, peers and other respected individuals in our lives encourage us to "find our real selves." What they are attempting to communicate is that in today's society members are expected to avoid major shifts in the identities portrayed through roles.

You have probably experienced such roles as child, student, roommate, woman, man, sibling, or friend during which you engaged in different communication behavior. "Find your real self" means becoming aware of the core element of your personal identity and allowing that core to become operative in each of the behavioral sets or roles with which you become involved. Different roles in different situations are not disturbing from the consistency viewpoint as long as core elements are operative, but different roles in the *same* situation produce frustration and anger not only within ourselves but in those around us about whom we care most.

To adopt the role of child when interacting with your parents and to switch to the role of employee when you go to work is quite appropriate. But if when you go to work, you assume the role of child on some days, the role of citizen on other days, and the role of student on still other days, you won't keep your job long. The same principle applies in our interpersonal relationships. While on a date you are expected to assume the date role. If you switch from date to spouse and then to child, odds are you will not get many more dates. In fact, people will begin to wonder about you.

How many roles did you utilize today? Take a moment and list at least three. Indicate the most outstanding changes in your behavior, and the behavior that remained constant. What does this behavior represent to you? How do you think it was interpreted by others?

SOCIAL IDENTITY

Our perception of how others perceive our identity is termed *social identity*. What we think others think of us has major ramifications for our selection of communication behavior. There is the strain for positive consistency between significant other's perceptions of us (or at least our perception of their feelings) and also the strain for consistency between personal identity, social identity, and our idealized identity.

Take the time to make a new list of qualities. Without checking back on your previous list, place a circle around the number you think your best friend would give you and place a square around the number you think your worst enemy would indicate about you. Observe the differences in your social identities. What different communication behavior did you engage in during interactions with these two individuals that could cause such apparently different interpretations of your identity? What communication behavior does each of these individuals utilize in your presence that causes you to believe that they think of you this way?

An example of the strain for consistency between social identities may be as follows: you may feel that John and Linda believe that you are a good person, that you have good attitudes, or that you are beautiful, vivacious, and great fun. On the other hand, you may feel Paul and Ann think that you are stupid, that you are obnoxious, incompetent, and without social manners. This creates an inconsistency and we are likely to engage in some activity to resolve this state. Possibly we may interact with Paul and Ann and attempt to alter their perspective in John and Linda's direction, or we may derogate Paul and Ann and treat their opinion as worthless, or worse, treat them as worthless. A

How we think others see us is not always correct.

number of alternatives are available to resolve that inconsistency and will be covered in more detail in Chapter 6.

Another inconsistency state is possible if once our social identity is established with each person, behavior on their part becomes inconsistent with our social identity and will produce in turn action on our part. For example, a change would be if John and Linda suddenly treat you as if you were a bad person of a dull, boring nature or if Paul and Ann were suddenly to treat you as if you were intelligent, worldly, and socially desirable. Because of our urgency to obtain and maintain positive social identity, we may tend to ignore or misperceive the negative aspects communicated by John and Linda and the positive aspects communicated by Paul and Ann. Remember, *we are not affected by what other people really think of our personal identity. The only thing of importance to our state of identity and consistency is what we think they think.*

How other people really think of us does not affect our communication behavior. Our communications are based on what we believe that they think of us. What we believe others think of us is so important that we devote the entire next chapter to addressing the concept of perception. Material in that chapter should be applied as you create a sense of social identity.

IDEAL IDENTITY

The need for positive consistency in individuals implies that each individual has a notion of what is positive and what is negative in his or her life space. While we feel that the need for consistency is innate and a human is born with the ability to discriminate between pain and pleasure, the method of fulfilling the consistency need, of extrapolating pain to punish or pleasure to reward, and of inferring positives or negatives in one's environment is learned. We do not know that a hug and a kiss is comforting and a slap or spanking uncomfortable until we learn it from experience. We do not know that cowardice is negative and bravery positive until we learn this. The goals themselves (levels of need fulfillment required for satisfaction) are a result of base-level items in our personal identity interacting with the environment to which we are exposed.

The degree of love or feelings of belongingness we require to fulfill our innate need for these qualities is determined by the amount we receive relative to various situations and points of time in our development. This interacts with other items of our personal identity. It is affected by our learning the quantities and qualities of various communication cues related to those needs in different situations. On this basis, you make decisions about how much love or belongingness support from the environment you should receive.

The goals we set for fulfillment of our needs, in a situational sense, may be considered a unit forming what will be termed an *ideal identity*. The ideal identity results from an individual's response to the question, "What sort of person should a person like me be?" Thus, as we go about our everyday activities, we are striving to reach a point of consistency between our present personal identity and our idealized identity.

If we believe that on a scale of 1–10 we are about a 5 on sensuality, yet we believe that a person like us should ideally be an 8, then we will engage in activity to reach the level of 8. As we involve ourselves in various self-oriented communications designed to raise our value on this personal identity item, occasionally the ideal becomes lowered and occasionally we approach that ideal.

To give you a feel for the idea of ideal identity, go back to the list of adjectives you used earlier and rate yourself as you would ultimately like to be. You should now have some notion of your ideal identity on a limited scale of items. To really advance your knowledge of yourself, compare the answers you gave for personal identity with the responses you just gave for ideal identity.

If your scores are comparable, most likely you are satisfied with your life space (unless you were lying to yourself) and are exerting efforts to remain in such a consistent state, though probably not for long. Soon you may experience the raising of your ideal identity to higher levels on selected items. If you discovered large differences between your personal identity score and your ideal identity score, you are more likely to be in a state of stress in attempting to reach the ideal state of balance.

Different scores, which indicate widely disparate notions of personal identity and ideal identity, must be considered very carefully. Occasionally the ideal identity is so far out of reach that the striving for consistency causes severe mental and physical anguish. We are not saying that one should not have high goals, but instead that one should have built-in steps to climb to reach distant goals. The psychological comfort obtained by reaching subgoals will enhance the opportunity to "catch the brass ring." With subgoals to achieve, the inconsistency that inevitably results from minor setbacks will not be disastrous.

Another aspect of idealized identity is that it never loses its impact on our lives. As soon as we reach a goal that we thought would fulfill the ideal identity item, we become engrossed in behavior to maintain that level or we insert higher or different goals to replace achieved ones. Although we may consider ourselves comfortable with a number of friends, we tend not to stop making new ones. The violinist may never be satisfied completely with the total performance; the top athlete must work continuously to remain the top athlete. Problems are created especially in interpersonal relationships when one party begins to take the other for granted and ceases efforts to maintain the satisfaction level of identity items such as love and belongingness. Communications to the other individual regarding worth, value, lovability, or desirability begin to decrease. As this happens, the other person begins to question his or her need satisfaction achievement, and the identity system begins to handle this violation of his or her expectations. Quite often the result is to seek out another partner who will provide communication cues that one has indeed achieved an ideal state. It would seem, then, that one should consider the impact of communications regarding the other's achievement of what is considered ideal, for the other may go elsewhere in striving to reach or maintain an ideal state. One must also recognize that an alternative is available to those individuals who feel they have reached their goal of idealized identity items — a different goal. They may also seek confirmation that the goal has been reached from a variety of other sources. Thus, a potentially dangerous situation exists in regard to reinforcing communication behavior. If, however, the foundation of the relationship is built on solid, high fidelity communication exchange, the potential for a wandering or disenchanted partner or spouse is drastically reduced.

In order for meaningful relationships to develop and continue, then, it is critical that we recognize in ourselves and in others the continual seeking and need for communication cues from the environment that support the struggle for ideal identity achievement.

The idealized identity is developed in much the same manner as our present self. Perhaps the factor that is primarily influential in developing dream selves is the media. In the unreal world of television and film, movie stars, sports heroes, and politicians are presented as personifications of femininity and masculinity need satisfaction in the role of the everyday person. As a result, ideal identities seem so far out of reach of the average person that major shifts have occurred, particularly in the sexual orientation of today's society. Thumb through a few magazines or spend a couple of hours watching television and you'll be amazed at the number of advertisements using what could be loosely termed a sexual appeal. Consider for a moment the number of products in the local drug store for both men and women with the purpose of exuding communication cues designed to enhance perceptions of sexual desirability. Excessive concern with reaching goals based upon these incorrect reflections of the real world may result in neurotic behavior so deviant from society's norm of expectation that removal from society may occur.

The interaction between personal, social, and ideal identity produces the determining factors in deciding most of our interpersonal communication behavior.

FIGURE 5-3
OUR IDENTITIES INTERACT WITH THE IDENTITIES OF OTHERS

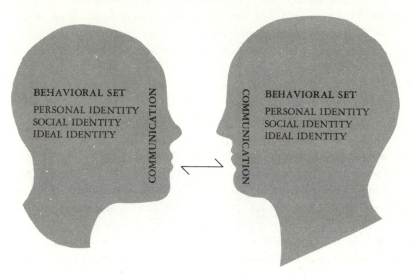

IDENTITY INTERACTION

As we meet new people, our identity system plays a major role in the types of communication we give to the other individual. In turn, that individual's identity system will affect the communication cues given to you. Each individual has a behavioral set for the situational context of the transaction. Figure 5-3 shows two individuals about to meet. Each one has a personal, social, and ideal identity, and a behavioral set for the situation. Thus, they will attempt to reveal a particular view of their identity system to each other.

Depending upon the state of the identity system (which includes need achievement indexes and situational references) of each individual, the communication cues emitted will reflect the personal identity or the ideal identity in an effort to create a social identity consistency. It should be evident that none of these subsets of identity are independent. They are interdependent and reflect communications received in the past interacting with communications received from the present.

Some individuals may withhold conscious communication cues until enough information is gathered about the other individual to make a decision regarding the potential success of a relationship. These individuals are, of course, communicating nonintentionally through the nonverbal mode of communication and by the mere fact that they are withholding information about themselves. The other individual will make judgments about these people's identity and proceed with the transaction on that basis. However, when judgments about identity are based only upon nonverbal communication cues, the potential for error becomes extremely high. Thus, relationships that may have developed into strong, satisfactory friendships sometimes do not mature simply because of a lack of sufficient information about the other.

Individuals may initiate interactions by giving communication cues representing their ideal identity (a state they have not yet reached). It is not unusual on first dates for people to "put their best foot forward." Occasionally, that "foot" is an artificial one. As the relationship progresses, revelation of the white lie has a high potential for destroying whatever gains had been achieved.

This points out the necessity of not only knowing your identity system but also feeling satisfaction with that system. If you confuse your personal and ideal identities, the communication cues you utilize may give another person a totally incorrect perspective of you. When this error is discovered, the other typically feels cheated or lied to. Occasionally, dissatisfaction with one's personal identity in conjunction with a strong need for inclusion and affection will lead to purposeful and planned misrepresentation. Ultimately, this will result in inferior relationships. As will be discussed in Chapter 8, manipulation of yourself or of others leads to relationships founded on falseness. As such they are in themselves false.

Perhaps the identity transaction that has the highest potential is one in which both parties start off by revealing relatively unimportant personal identity items. This allows both parties to build their repective social identities slowly and allows an ease of correction for misinterpretations. This base (which for a student consists of information such as name, major, classification, courses, and so forth) provides a foundation on which both parties may make decisions regarding the identity situation and the potential for a relationship.

Self-esteem is a vital identity item that plays a major role in determining our communication behavior. Self-esteem is the extent to which one approves of one's own identity system. Self-esteem is, in part, a function of the degree of positive consistency between our present personal identity, our social identity, and our ideal identity. The closer we approach our goals (need satisfaction) the more we approve of ourselves. The higher our perception of our ability to achieve those goals, the higher our self-approval. In addition, self-esteem also is a function of the consistency between how we see ourselves and how we believe others see us. This varies according to the situation and the behavioral set utilized for that situation. Thus, we have as many indexes of self-esteem as we can conjure situations. Most research, however, is based on a general or overall index of self-esteem. This involves obtaining a synthesis of situationally pertinent items from individuals relative to their self-perceived value.

Some individuals, however, become absorbed in only one group of identity items, where low self-esteem is operative, and allow that small facet of the total identity to become continually active and influential in all contexts. In most cases that person fails to recognize the positive aspects remaining in the totality of the identity complex and thus becomes deficient in communicating aspects of the identity system other than the negative one being concentrated upon. This, of course, tends to perpetuate the overgeneralization of low self-esteem as the inconsistency between personal, social, and ideal identity broadens.

CHAPTER SUMMARY

We examined the identity system and its development in some detail because it is the identity system that primarily influences communication in our interpersonal relationships.

Identity is formed by communication from our environment. The identity system consists of three components: personal identity (how you see yourself), social identity (how you believe others see you), and ideal identity (how you would like to see yourself and be seen by others). Personal identity consists of a core and surrounding elements. Behavioral sets consist of those elements of our identity which are situationally bound.

Based on our identity system and the situational context, we communicate to other humans in attempts to develop mutually satisfactory relationships as a function of the interaction between the identity system and the need system.

THINK ABOUT IT

IN GENERAL

Complete the exercises given under Think About It: In General, at the end of Chapter 1.

IN EDUCATION

There is little question that teachers and the assignments that they require can potentially affect changes in the core identities of students. Often, this means that students may change the values that they acquired from their parents and home environment. What changes, if any, have occurred in your core identity as a function of attending college? Have these changes affected the ways you interpersonally communicate with people on the job or at home? If so, in what ways? Have any of these changes negatively affected relationships that were healthy prior to your attending college? If so, what does this say about your sensitivity or insensitivity to the core identity of others? Also, what communication skills are demanded of you if these relationships are to return to a healthy state?

IN THE ORGANIZATION

Most of us learn at an early age that bribery is unethical. Further, most of us incorporate this conclusion into our value system. Assume that you are an executive with a multinational corporation such as Lockheed Aircraft. Your superior discusses an overseas sales trip you are about to take and informs you that you are to transfer a large sum of money to a foreign official who will have a major influence on the type of aircraft that his country purchases for its nationalized airline. In other words, your superior asks you to be an intermediary in a bribe. This is not only inconsistent with your value system, but also places you in an awkward position as a communicator. How are you going to explain to your superior that you cannot comply with the request, but at the same time not risk your job? Consider the alternatives, including a change in your core identity to rationalize complying with the request.

IN YOUR RELATIONSHIPS

We said in Chapter 3 that the fidelity with which people communicate tends to increase as they learn more about each other. On the basis of this conclusion, one might argue that people need to reveal their personal, social, and ideal identities completely to each other. Take a position on this view and discuss it with other class members.

SUGGESTED READINGS

Argyle, M. *The Psychology of Interpersonal Behavior.* Penguin Books, London, 1967.

This book surveys the field of pyschological study of behavior between people. The focus is upon social motivation, techniques, and skill; self-image and self-esteem; eye contact; groups and culture; and social behavior and mental disorders. The chapter dealing with self-image and self-esteem is of particular note.

Fromm, E. *Man for Himself.* Holt, Rinehart and Winston, New York, 1947.

This book deals with problems of ethics, of norms and values leading to the realization of man's self and of his potentialities. Different types of ethics are discussed in terms of applications and problems. The role of human nature in the development of the self is also discussed.

Goffman, E. *The Presentation of Self in Everyday Life.* Doubleday & Company, Garden City, New York, 1959.

This book is intended to serve as a handbook showing one sociological perspective from which social life can be studied. This is done by considering the way in which individuals in ordinary work situations present themselves to others, the way they guide and control the impression others form of them, and the kinds of things they may and may not do while sustaining their performances.

Gordon, C. and K. J. Gergen. *The Self in Social Interaction.* John Wiley & Sons, New York, I, 1968.

This book sets forth basic issues and themes of major scholars who have addressed the issue of self. As mentioned previously, this work is of major proportions and certainly worthy reading for anyone who wishes to delve deeper into the concept of self than presented here.

Laing, R. D. *Self and Others.* Penguin Books, London, 1969.

This book is an attempt to weave experience and behavior into a consistent theory as they are in real life. This is done by discussions of the modes of interpersonal experience and the forms of interpersonal action.

May, R. *Man's Search for Himself.* W. W. Norton & Company, New York, 1953.

In this book the author discusses insights of psychology on the hidden levels of the self. It also discusses related ideas in the fields of literature, philosophy, and ethics. The aim of the book is to show how man can find a center of strength within himself.

Sullivan, H. S. *The Interpersonal Theory of Psychiatry.* W. W. Norton & Company, New York, 1953.

This book was prepared from the unpublished lectures of Dr. Sullivan. The core of Sullivan's work is the psychiatry of interpersonal relations or the study of communication between people. The lectures in this book discuss the development of the self-system during various developmental stages and interpersonal relations.

Swensen, C. H., Jr. *Introduction to Interpersonal Relations.* Scott, Foresman and Company, Glenview, Illinois, 1973.

This book centers on the theories that have been proposed about the nature of relationships. These theories are psychological and sociological in perspective. Discussion of communications and the double blind, nonverbal communication, social exchange, attitudes, need, and role theories are included.

Chapter Six
Identity and Perception

SHOP TALK

Closure This term refers to our tendency to fill in information which has been left out of a communication stimulus; for example, completing a drawing of something with which we are familiar.

Perception The meaning we give to our experiences.

Selective perception The tendency to tune into that part of our environment which is most relevant to our past experiences or our immediate psychological state.

Selective exposure The tendency to expose ourselves to communications that are consistent with our identity and to avoid information that is inconsistent.

Selective attention The tendency to attend to communications that are important to our identity and be inattentive to communications that are perceived to be minimally important.

Selective recall The tendency to recall experiences that have had a major impact on our identity and to forget those of little consequence.

Perceptual organization The tendency to pattern new experiences with the environment on the basis of past experiences with the environment.

Autistic thinking The tendency to perceive what you want to perceive.

Closemindedness The tendency to perceive things in black and white terms exclusively.

Openmindedness The tendency to perceive things broadly rather than in only black and white.

Assimilation The tendency to accept points of view that are perceived to be closer to one's own than they actually are.

Contrast The tendency to reject points of view that are perceived to be farther from one's own than they actually are.

Ethnocentrism The tendency to view and judge others on the basis of our own standards.

Stereotyping Perceiving an individual as a member of a category of people rather than as an individual.

The halo effect The tendency to selectively perceive or evaluate all the communication behavior of another person as positive.

Perceptual attribution Attaching certain positive or negative qualities and motives to people on the basis of their communication behavior.

Noise Any stimulus which interferes with communication and perception.

Have you ever read a book on the advice of a friend and found it wasn't the exciting tale your friend suggested it was? Have you ever seen a film in the company of a date and found that the two of you disagreed about the message that the film was attempting to convey? Why do you think people who normally are quite rational argue and scream at each other about the respective merits of two political candidates?

This chapter will focus on the aspect of communication that involves the reception and interpretation of communication cues from the environment and the people within it. As we progress through various facets of the interpersonal perception process, the factors that contribute to the potential for communica-

113

tion error will be discussed. The ultimate goal of this chapter is to assist you in becoming aware of why you perceive the world the way you do in terms of interpersonal communication behavior.

Communication traditionally has been divided into the two elements of sending and receiving. We indicated earlier that these processes occur simultaneously during interpersonal communication transactions. The receiving or perception element of the transaction is so critical to developing meaningful relationships, it will receive separate treatment.

We build our concept of reality through perception, which gives us information about the environment. Earlier we discussed the development of the identity system as a function of our environment. Since our environment is perceived during the development process, we could say that our identity would not exist without the ability to perceive. At the same time, one must recognize that as we mature our perception of the environment is greatly affected by our identity system. Thus a circularity develops whereby identity and perception become interdependent.

Perception is an active process in which we receive stimuli, recognize and interpret them, and perhaps act in response. However, much of the perceptual act occurs at an unconscious level. We are not consciously aware of most stimuli that bombard our sensory mechanisms during a normal day. Nor are we consciously aware of the majority of our interpretations that eventually lead to communication behavior. This chapter is designed to foster an awareness of our dependence on perception and thus the importance of its accuracy.

Let's note again that each of us has a different view of reality, that each of us has a different identity, that each of us has a different need system, and that each of us has had different experiences that result in different memories. Because of these differences, truth in absolute terms does not occur in interpersonal communication behavior. You communicate on the basis of that which you perceive to be true regardless of its authenticity. Since it would obviously be to our benefit to base our communications on actual truth rather than assumed truth, the importance of being aware of those psychological processes that affect our perception of truth cannot be minimized.

Before proceeding with this chapter, it would be beneficial to examine your interpersonal perceptions. Make a list of at least five qualities that your best friend seems to possess and that the person you like least seems to lack. Attempt to identify why you feel that they have or do not have those qualities by writing a short paragraph that describes the communication cues that they utilize and why you believe those cues represent those qualities. Examine each of your perceptions under each of the following processes to ascertain the potential you have to make erroneous perceptions.

PERCEPTUAL REGULARITIES

Although we each perceive the environment through different sets of senses, the process of perception has a number of regularities.

CLOSURE

Closure is a tendency to perceive a complete mental image where there is incomplete data. We tend to perceive a pattern and jump to an interpretation without fully examining the pattern or without receiving sufficient information about the pattern. What do you see in Figure 6-1? A triangle? Look again. Would not a more precise interpretation be three lines, none of which are connected: one is horizontal and the other two are vertically inclined? Is it ridiculous to be that specific? Probably in this case, but what if one were perceiving love or freedom instead of a triangle?

Read the message in Figure 6-2 quickly. What is wrong with this message? Look again. People who read fast develop a perceptual pattern of skim reading. They only look for "meaning" words, while slower readers see each word. Compare the reaction to these messages of your parents or other adults with that of a young child just learning to read. The young child is learning and developing a perceptual pattern of closure. The adult is already locked into a way of perceiving the environment.

Read the following sentences:

> The _____ jumped over the moon.
> The cow jumped over the _____.
> The _____ jumped over the _____.

How good were you at closure? The ability to complete patterns is increasingly essential in the modern world. But it does have drawbacks. For instance, the

FIGURE 6-1
EXAMPLE OF PERCEPTUAL CLOSURE

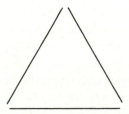

From Raymond S. Ross, *Speech Communication: Fundamentals and Practice,* 3rd edition, © 1974, pp. 22, 24, 25, 27. Reprinted by permission of Prentice-Hall, Inc., Englewood Cliffs, New Jersey.

FIGURE 6-2
OTHER EXAMPLES OF PERCEPTUAL CLOSURE

last sentence above was originally, "The dog jumped over the fence." In one sense, we led you away from that inference. In another sense you jumped to a conclusion with insufficient information. Do you just "halfway" listen to others and then use your closure ability to construct a mental image of what they were trying to say? Obviously the potential for communication error is extraordinarily high, as is the potential for a person to be frustrated when one doesn't understand the communicator.

SELECTIVE PERCEPTION

While this will be discussed in more detail later, selective perception is a perceptual regularity that leads to fidelity in our mental images. Selective perception is the tendency to perceive things on the basis of our experiences and present psychological state. Basically, the term *selective perception* is founded on the fact that people can focus on only a limited portion of their environment at any specific moment. That limited portion is the result of their past experiences and present psychological state.

Since people can neither duplicate the experiences nor psychological state of others exactly, we frequently perceive different things when observing the same phenomenon. As a case in point, consider two people who observe the same traffic accident. The first person, who just finished a game of tennis and is still alert, has been driving for twenty years. The second person, who feels sluggish as a result of eating too much at lunch, favors buses to privately owned automobiles. Given these two descriptions, what do you think the chances are that the two people saw the same thing when the two cars collided? Would you say that they are not good?

The point is that no two people selectively perceive the world in the same way. And the more we can recognize this fact, the more understanding we can be of different opinions and reactions to events. This does not mean that we have to change our mental image, but that through such understanding, arguments founded on different perceptions are more easily discernible and possibly resolved.

PERCEPTUAL ORGANIZATION

As the brain receives information representing a facet of the environment, it attempts to create a mental image. In such efforts, one of the first steps is to organize the material in a meaningful way. Thus, we are dependent upon our past experiences with that material or similar material in an effort to bring order to the massive amount of information we are receiving. Such efforts produce a natural bias on our part that is consistent with our past experience. We tend to organize in a manner consistent with the available information, given our experience with that information previously. Let's look at some examples where only your personal background plays a role in your perception. Concentrate on Figure 6-3 and Figure 6-4 before reading further.

Figure 6-3 is most often seen as either a vase or twins looking at one another. Either perception is correct depending upon whether you placed the black area in the foreground or in the background. Figure 6-4, however, has only one "correct" interpretation — the word "sly." This word is difficult to interpret because the amount of contrast between the word and the background is very limited. Our attempts to make sense of our environment may produce tension, frustration, and anxiety when they are not successful. Did you give up on Figure 6-4? Our efforts to handle those communication cues in our interpersonal transactions that we cannot easily organize in some way also often result in frustration and so forth, but avoidance can be extremely detrimental to the relationship.

FIGURE 6-3

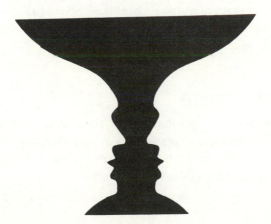

Do you see a vase or twins?

From Raymond S. Ross, *Speech Communication: Fundamentals and Practice,* 3rd edition, © 1974, pp. 22, 24, 25, 27. Reprinted by permission of Prentice-Hall, Inc., Englewood Cliffs, New Jersey.

FIGURE 6-4

Can you see the word?

Since our past experience introduces an organizational bias in our perception of the environment, each of us organizes our environmental perceptions differently. Furthermore, because of differences in past experience, some individuals are better prepared to organize their perceptions in specific environmental situations. This gives them more representative mental images of that environment, whether it is a person or an object. One way to increase our abilities to organize in a meaningful manner is to continually solicit evidence as to our correctness or incorrectness and use that information as a basis for future perceptions.

Having discussed aspects of the perception process that most humans utilize, we suggest that you review each of those aspects in light of the impact they may have had in your perception of the environment and, more specifically, the people in that environment.

PERCEPTUAL ORIENTATIONS

Given that each of us has a separate and distinct perceptual system, we nonetheless utilize similar orientations in interpreting our environment. In some cases, we are concerned with general orientations to the world around us, in others with short-cut methods of inference.

AUTISTIC THINKING

Our tendency to perceive what we want to perceive is termed *autistic thinking*. It involves the interpretation of our environment in such a way that reasonable interpretations become confused with desired interpretations. We once knew two students who had been going steady for three years. Cheri had gone to college in hopes of meeting someone who would care for her. Near the end of the three-year period, John was having second thoughts about the relationship and began to subtly give her cues as to his feelings. He began to work late at the library, to forget dates, to be too busy studying to spend that evening with her. Cheri reacted to this shift in the situation by perceiving that John loved her so much he was going to extra efforts (including forsaking her company) to prepare himself to support her in the manner in which she was accustomed. Ultimately, this led to a disastrous conclusion.

The confusion of a reasonable interpretation and a desired interpretation often results in such different perceptions of the state of a relationship that when the actual feelings are finally forced into the open, the result is total dissolution of the relationship. This same problem in terms of perception of events or others in the environment can cause communication error and stress in any kind of relationship from professor-student to wife-husband, to employer-employee. A suggestion we make continually throughout the text is to often stand back from a situation and ask yourself, "Is this really a reasonable interpretation of what happened? Am I just reading into it what I want to read into it?"

OPENMINDEDNESS VERSUS CLOSEMINDEDNESS

This orientation toward external events is often described as a personality variable. It is, however, directly related to perceptual orientations. Individuals who are closeminded or dogmatic are authoritarian, self-opinionated, and see the world through a very small peephole. Typically, they have an extremely high regard for specific authority figures, whose communications they perceive as meaningful and truthful, and a disregard for less significant individuals, whose communications they perceive as questionable and false. Closeminded people generally live within a restricted value and belief system and tend to perceive things in terms of black or white rather than black, white, and possibly grey. In other words, they have a distinct perceptual set that distinguishes only opposites. In such people's opinions your communication (and possibly you) is either right or wrong with no possibility of a middle ground. The degree of closemindedness is dependent to some extent on the degree of commitment or involvement such people have with that aspect of the environment. They are intolerant of change or differences of opinion. The particular perceptual set that they have can rarely be altered by reasonable argument. Alteration can occur, but most likely only by a highly valued authority figure.

Given the above description of perceptual tendencies, most of us can immediately recognize either a boss, teacher, or student who fits the category of perceptual orientation called closeminded. What is your reaction to that person? In all likelihood, it is negative. Consider further, then, those instances in your life space where, perhaps only on a single topic, you are closeminded. How do you think those people observing you react to that perceptual orientation in you?

ASSIMILATION-CONTRAST

Perhaps the open-closeminded orientation could be further demonstrated by looking at the principles of assimilation and contrast. Basically, when we have a particular perceptual set, cues from the environment that resemble or are similar to our own are assimilated. Assimilation may occur by broadening the perceptual set or by perceiving those cues as being more similar than they actually are. When those cues are at a point of dissimilarity or in opposition to our perceptual set, we tend to push them farther away or contrast them with our own. Sherif, Sherif, and Nebergall present this idea in light of the attitude change theory and the notion of ego involvement.[1] They suggest that on any particular issue we have a latitude of acceptance and a latitude of rejection that is affected by the degree of ego involvement we have on that issue. In between exists a latitude of noncommitment. For the purpose of illustration, Figure 6-5 exemplifies a closeminded individual's perspective and an openminded individual's perspective. Remember, a closeminded individual generally views all things this way, while the highly ego-involved individual would have this perspective only in relation to the issue in which high ego involvement is maintained. Regarding communication cues from the environment about premarital sex, the closeminded individual will perceive the vast majority as automatically false or discrepant with what is "right." The openminded individual, however, while maintaining basically the same personal position on premarital sex, would totally reject only the extremist point of view. Unfortunately, in addition to rejecting the majority of communication, the closeminded individual also rejects the majority of people. Once an association is established between the cue and the person, he or she is treated by the closeminded person in the same manner. The openminded person, because few cues are totally rejected, maintains an openminded perspective on the majority of people also. We suggest that openminded people have infinitely more individuals in their life space and thus have a higher potential to develop more social relationships than closeminded individuals.

[1]C. W. Sherif, M. Sherif, and R. E. Nebergall, *Attitude and Attitude Change*, W. B. Saunders Co., Philadelphia, 1965.

FIGURE 6-5

ATTITUDES TOWARD PREMARITAL SEX

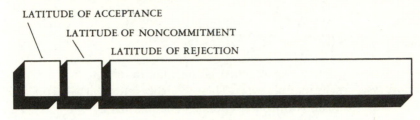

LATITUDE OF ACCEPTANCE

LATITUDE OF NONCOMMITMENT

LATITUDE OF REJECTION

A CLOSEMINDED PERSPECTIVE

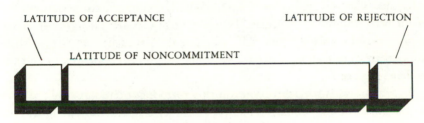

LATITUDE OF ACCEPTANCE   LATITUDE OF REJECTION

LATITUDE OF NONCOMMITMENT

AN OPENMINDED PERSPECTIVE

ETHNOCENTRISM

Another orientation that can affect our perception of individuals in the environment is that of ethnocentrism, which has been defined as "an unconscious tendency to view and judge other people by our own customs and standards. We place ourselves, our ethnic or social group at the center of the universe and rate all others by how close they come to our center."[2] An ethnocentric presentation may occur in relation to your country, religion, race, geographic location, lifestyle, occupation, or any number of concepts that may conceivably project a sense of "rightness" or "goodness." Is it practicable to perceive that another group of individuals (whether a minority or majority, of our religion or another) is wrong or bad or less in some way than we are simply because they have a different "something?"' Do we have any absolutes today? Do we allow ourselves to perceive a range of relative values?

The ethnocentric perspective has major implications for our perception of others and their communication behavior. This, of course, ultimately narrows the mere number of people who are eligible to exist in our life space. In today's mobile, integrated society, can we afford to be ethnocentrically exclusive? Is

[2]R. L. Applebaum et al., *Fundamental Concepts in Human Communication*, Canfield Press, San Francisco, 1973, p. 89.

the stereotype of the rich snob any different from that of other ethnocentric individuals? Speaking of stereotypes, let us examine this mind set.

STEREOTYPES

An individual who stereotypes others is engaging in inferences about the identity system of a group of people. These inferences are often based upon folk tales, rumors, and other ill-conceived sources of information. Stereotypes are instant mental images that are not based on purposeful communication cues from an individual. They are mental images that become active for any individual who falls into a classification. We become automatic and robotlike in our perception of individuals. Typical stereotypes are: all fraternity and sorority members are rich and self-centered; all A students are bright; all F students are dumb; all hippies have no values; all professors are robots; and all students are pests.

As you can easily see, stereotypes quickly introduce prejudice either in favor of or against the individual. When you consider that the individual was not judged on his unique identity system, but rather was prejudged on the basis of hearsay and tales, perhaps you will also consider that prejudice emerging from that stereotype is equally erroneous. Unfortunately, once a prejudice is operative, all communication cues are perceived in light of that prejudice.

THE HALO EFFECT

Consider for a moment a person that you like and a person that you dislike. Run through your mind a series of mental images of their communication behavior patterns.

If you can open your mind, the odds are that they occasionally behave almost exactly the same. Yet, when the person we like behaves one way, we say, "Hey, that's cool," and when the one we dislike does the same thing, we say, "Wow, what a dummy!" This is partially the result of what is termed *the halo effect*. Once we have established a person as positive or negative, we tend to evaluate all their communication cues from that single perspective. In fact, we'll go beyond merely reacting to the communication cues that are easily recognized and begin to search out that which may possibly be interpreted as either positive or negative.

Consider the impact of the halo effect upon our life space. When meeting someone new, we make inferences about the person's indentity system based upon primarily nonverbal cues. We then automatically begin to evaluate the person as positive or negative. If we give the person a positive evaluation, we proceed to mingle with the person, to learn more about the person, and to begin to share purposeful disclosures of our identity system. Perhaps a few weeks later we decide this individual is not the kind of person with whom we want to become good friends, and we begin to search elsewhere. But what happens to the person we evaluated as negative? Do we give the individual a two- or three-week trial period? In most cases, the answer is "no." We immediately begin to rule the person out of our life space by focusing on cues that we can interpret negatively. We will avoid communicating with the individual when possible. In fact, we may even seek reinforcement from others for our opinion and thus begin to prejudice them against this person.

Consider the situation where you're walking between classes, you encounter a relative stranger, and you say, "Hello," with a big smile. The other person responds with a raised eyebrow that you interpret as "Get lost!" Thus you immediately begin to infer negative aspects about the person's identity system. But what if, just prior to your meeting that person, he or she had flunked a test, wrecked the family's car, or lost a best friend. Under those circumstances, he or she didn't want to say hello to anybody. Yet you would take it as a personal effront and walk away muttering. "What an obnoxious person. I'm glad we didn't speak — looked kind of freaky anyhow." Is that the kind of perceptual behavior that will lead to a life space filled with people?

We strongly suggest that all of us should make conscious efforts to withhold immediate judgments. We should wait until adequate information about others has been received before making decisions that will rule them out of our life space.

The preceding section has discussed perceptual orientations in light of individual manners of viewing the environment. It should be noted that extremes of each orientation are rare. Most of us move along a continuum from low to high application of each orientation in terms of general outlook and specific situations. We suggest this material would be more meaningful to you if you went back over each orientation and identified at least one concept for each orientation to which you would say, "Yes, I have that orientation toward _____ concept," or "No, I don't have that orientation toward _____ concept."

PERCEPTUAL ATTRIBUTION

Generally, we do not have to walk around a building to recognize its existence, and we assume that it has four sides. We make the assumption based on our past experience with visually seeing the front of a building. We are able to conceptualize at least three dimensions even if we see only one or two dimensions. We know on the basis of past experience that people have a backside and have depth to their body even if we only see a picture of them. We attribute to them the third physical dimension without having to physically see it for ourselves.

We have a tendency, however, to go beyond merely assuming the existence of a physical object or body. We also assume a psychological dimension to exist for any individual we sense. That assumption is based on inferences that we make from the communication cues we have attended to and interpreted regarding the other person.

INFERENCE

An image is constructed of the other individual's identity system. The reasoning is of an inferential nature. By this we mean that one may look at a particular set of cues associated with an individual, such as clothing, attractiveness, or footwear, and infer the kind of person he or she is. We all know others do this but rarely do we recognize that each of us is doing the same thing. Why does one dress up for the first date with another? Because we know the other is going to get some idea of the kind of person we are by the clothes we wear.

The multitude of cues that we utilize for such perceptions is innumerous. Every category of nonverbal cues discussed in Chapter 2 comes into play. One might call humans the great synthesizers. Rarely does one particular cue determine our perception of another's identity, but rather a synthesis of all cues leads to a general impression. (This is not so for stereotypists, ethnocentrics, and closeminded individuals.) As we get to know the other person better (receive more communication cues), we may alter our initial perception.

CAUSALITY

A crucial inference that we make in constructing the perceptual package is that of why other people behave as they do. We tend to perceive others' behavior (cues) from a cause-effect perspective. If we watch someone stumble while walking (effect), we may assume the cause to be the catching of a toe in a crack (cause). In a like manner, we perceive a cause (love) to every effect (kiss) in the interpersonal situation. This colors and has an impact on our perception of the other individual. We also assume that the cause we assign to an effect is correct. Perhaps this will be clearer if you think of your perception of cause as being an answer to the question, "Why did the other person behave that way?" The answer to that question affects the overall perception of that individual and is based upon your perceptual system and communication cues that immediately preceded it. The potential for error is very high. A person may be late for a date or an appointment. You may infer from this communication cue of time that the cause of such lateness was the individual's lack of concern for you as a person. Numerous causes could have been perceived from this cue, but based on the state of your perceptual system, you will typically perceive one cause and then proceed to behave toward the other on the assumption that you were correct.

Causality inference, as with all aspects of perception, is different for each individual, because each of us has a different perceptual system and attends to different cues from the environment. Thus, two individuals observing the same behavior may infer different causes for the same behavior. Yet, if they were to communicate to each other about the third party, each would believe initially that the other inferred the same cause. If the differences in perception are not brought to light, the fidelity of their communication will be low and possibly create friction in the relationship. Furthermore, both could have made incorrect inferences and be doing a disservice to the third party, and potentially they may be lowering the standing of their relationship to that individual.

Two female students reported their reactions to the communication cues of another female student. One student indicated she felt uncomfortable with the third girl because of her lack of eye contact. She kept looking around "as if she was looking for someone more important to talk to." The second girl reported that she liked the third girl, but had been bothered by a "twitching in her eyes." An interview with the third girl revealed that she felt very uncomfortable maintaining direct eye contact because "it always bothered me when others looked right into my eyes. I felt like they were trying to invade my private thoughts."

This example illustrates three different "causes" for the same behavior. Each girl assumed her particular inference was known and accepted by the others. On the basis of what turned out to be incorrect causal inference, the two girls perceived the third differently. Neither girl was motivated to go beyond her initial reaction. This is a common communication error. We tend to forget that for each time we have incorrectly inferred the motives of another, someone has incorrectly inferred our motives.

We suggest you examine your use of communication cues that lead to inferences about other people. Review your responses to the exercises in Chapter 5. Are the cues you use quality cues? Do they lead to high fidelity communication? These questions will not be easy to answer because most cues and inferences occur at the subconscious level. You will have to be introspective to locate cause-effect connections that you have come to use automatically. Most of us do use some poor quality cues. This will give you the opportunity to examine old "forgotten" cues in light of the following question: "Is this the kind of communication cue a person like me should use to evaluate other human beings?"

INFLUENCES ON PERCEPTION

The mental image created as a result of external stimuli is influenced by a number of factors. Each factor is interdependent with each other factor. In other words, rarely does a single factor solely influence our perception. Thus the system by which mental images are constructed is complex. The perceptual system is composed of at least the following factors: (1) past experience, (2) environmental indexes, (3) total identity system, (4) situational identity, and (5) need state.

PAST EXPERIENCE

This factor includes more than simply a memory of facts, figures, and solid objects. It is a subset of the identity system, but of such importance that separate treatment is deserved. Included in our past experience are such concepts as events, language, previous interpretations of select stimuli, and the outcome of such interpretations and subsequent behavior. If someone says "red" or "love" or "hi," our past experience with those symbols allows a general interpretation. In addition, past experience allows us to interpret the range of nonverbal stimuli including the raised eyebrow, furrowed forehead, dress, car, and so forth. The generalized picture we create is influenced by the environment in which the communication cues are generated.

THE ENVIRONMENTAL INDEX

This factor includes an analysis of the physical environment within which the transaction is taking place and the immediately preceding verbal and nonverbal stimuli. Thus we may derive different mental images for the phrase "I love you" while sitting in an auto looking at the moon on the local Lover's Leap than we do while performing on stage or meeting people at a family reunion.

The previous interpretations may also assist in determining which of several meanings to give to an ambiguous word like "red" (a color or a communist) or a sign like a raised fist (an emphasis or a fight) or an eyebrow elevation (he's interested or he thinks I'm wrong).

THE ROLE OF IDENTITY

In Chapter 4 we discussed how our identity was formed, what it consists of, and how it affects our communication behavior. In Chapter 5 we discussed the individual components of our identity and their potential effects on interpersonal communication. Because of the interdependent nature of many complexities in our psychological processes, emphasis should again be placed on the impact of our identity in efforts to construct mental images of our environment.

Interpretations of verbal or nonverbal cues are affected by the three factors of identity and their relationship to each other. If we have a high personal opinion of ourself and believe others do also, our tendency is to interpret cues from the environment as being positive (up to a point). You may have had the experience of knowing someone who could not recognize obvious insults. In fact such a person may walk away with the feeling, "Gee, isn't it great that my friends and I are so close that we can insult each other and both know it's just in fun." The orientation toward self and how one expects others to perceive that self can color the interpretation of communication cues.

The total identity system includes our attitudes, beliefs, values, and general orientations toward ourselves and our general environment. The specific situation that we find ourselves in, however, brings specific aspects of our total identity to bear on the act of perception.

SITUATIONAL IDENTITY

We have already established how a behavioral set may influence the communication cues that we utilize to represent our identity. That same behavioral set also influences the manner in which we interpret cues from others. It brings into focus specific aspects of our identity system and past experience. Thus, the communication, "I love you," may be interpreted as a slap in the face if one is trying to present an image associated with a corporate president or a student in the classroom at the time. At the least an embarrassing emotion would be attached. If we are trying to appear worldly and an old friend rushes up, slaps us on the back, and loudly proclaims, "What's going on rookie?" We would probably not interpret that as a gesture of friendship.

Thus, as we find that a situational identity is operative, we tend to perceive the environment in light of that situational identity.

NEED STATE

This factor has overriding implications for the possibility of misinterpreting environmental cues — seeing cues that are not there or missing cues that are present. When a need has not been satisfied in a long period of time or when the need achievement level has not been reinforced in some time, the individual begins to seek out information that would tend to lead to need satisfaction. Shipwrecked sailors with no food begin to hallucinate situations in which they are surrounded by food. A person lost in the desert will soon hallucinate "water, water everywhere." The same principle operates when psychological needs are starving. When for some time one has not satisfied a belongingness and love need or a need for inclusion or affection, a slight glance from another may be interpreted as a gesture of friendship or the desire for friendship. One may tend to focus only on those cues that may represent friendliness and thus overlook cues that may be intended to say, "Slow down, you're trying too hard to be my friend." Individuals may begin behaving in an over- or underpersonal manner and also begin to perceive the environment in light of those orientations. In other words, their view of reality becomes altered, thus influencing their concept of truth that forms the basis for behavioral decisions. These factors influence the perception of the environment from the point of neural impulse to the creation of a mental image.

Review the sections called Think About It in Chapters 1, 4, and 5 in light of their impact on your perception of the environment and specifically the people in that environment. Write a short paragraph for each of the five influencing agents that relates that material to your personal perceptual experiences.

Now that we have examined the psychological aspect of perception that involves our interpretation of communication cues from the environment, let us further explore the manner in which those cues are processed by the perceptual system.

THE PHYSIOLOGICAL ASPECT OF PERCEPTION

Our ideas of the world and of our identity are the result of a complex mental activity generally termed thinking. Our thinking efforts, however, are based on information that we have interpreted from stimuli provided by the five senses. Human beings have intelligence. This allows us to conceptualize raw sensory data as representing reality. The fact remains, however, that these cognitive abilities would be valueless without base level data provided by the sensory system. Thus, we should consider the act of perception as a two-phase process consisting of sensation and interpretation.

The basic characteristics of everyone's sensory system are almost identical, but no two individuals have exactly the same system. Unfortunately, in interpersonal transactions we often overlook the possibility that another's sensory system may be different from our own. We tend to assume that everyone else hears exactly what we do, sees exactly what we see, smells, touches, and tastes exactly as we do. A moment's reflection should reveal that this is not the case. Technological advancements have allowed many to achieve similar seeing and hearing abilities through eyeglasses and hearing aids, but psychological variables so influence what we sense that to submit the above assumption is folly. Since the physiological and psychological aspects of perception are so interrelated, some reference to the latter will occur in the following sections.

STIMULI

We all exist in an ocean of stimuli — sights, sounds, smells, tastes, and touches. Each of these is transmitted from the environment to our sensory system over a channel. Sight is transmitted by light waves, sound by sound waves, touch by pressure, and smell and taste by chemical means. The various senses may be operating simultaneously in receiving stimuli. One may hear the words "I love you" and see the smile on another's face, while also smelling the other's aftershave lotion or perfume, touching his or her body, and sensing the aftertaste of a kiss. With so many stimuli being absorbed at the same time, it is not unusual that our view of the other may be somewhat generalized. When one further considers that stimuli are constantly being absorbed into the sensory system, the complexity of our thinking and attribution efforts becomes evident.

Stimuli are thought of as that which may activate a sensory system. Given this definition, many stimuli that affect the sensory systems of other creatures are not available to humans because of inherent limitations in our sensory system. We can hear only a certain range of sound waves, see a certain range of light waves, feel a certain range of pressure. We must recognize also that we do

FIGURE 6-6

INSTRUCTOR

STUDENT   STUDENT

not have access to all the stimuli in our environment. In Figure 6-6, the instructor stands at the front of the classroom. The student "seeing" from the far left will not receive the same stimuli as the person "seeing" from the far right. Thus, each individual may perceive the nonverbal communication emitted by the instructor differently.

BODILY PERCEPTUAL PROBLEMS

Stimuli that interact with a sense organ are transormed from a light or sound wave into an energy unit. This energy unit is moved through the nerve system to the brain. During the journey, the energy unit may be altered or blocked by psychological activity. This psychological activity is primarily subconscious.

A second potential problem occurs if the energy impulse reaches the brain. Many nonimportant stimuli in the form of energy impulses reach the brain. In order to cope with such stimuli representing the fact that you have your shoes on (pressure), a portion of the brain makes a decision regarding the value of incoming impulses. It decides whether to awaken the remainder of the brain to act upon those impulses or simply to allow them to dissipate. These decisions are psychologically controlled. Thus, a family living next to railroad tracks soon adapts to the noise of passing trains in the night, yet are able to instantly awaken at the sound of a baby's whimper.

Unfortunately, this ability is not always used to its maximum effectiveness. The concept of noise is most often thought of as anything that interferes with the quality of perception. It may include the barking dog next door, the radio commentator, frustrations, pressures, hangovers, or emotion. The level of noise that you allow to interfere is in part related to the amount of effort you put forth to concentrate or pay attention to specific communications.

As the impulses arrive, the brain begins to make decisions as to what they represent. It begins to interpret the environment based upon three levels of sensation. These levels of sensation may be differentiated by the ability of the brain to construct that part of the environment that created the initial stimuli.

The first level is that of detection. Here we are simply aware that something has happened. We do not know what has just occurred, but we develop a feeling that something has happened. After talking with a close friend, you may get a feeling "that something was wrong." Or you may enter a room and feel that something has changed, but you just can't quite put your finger on it.

The second level is that of recognition. This normally results from "looking for" certain types of impulses; thus other impulses become retarded. For example, have you ever looked for a friend in a crowd? As you scan the faces you are primed to recognize a particular face. It jumps out at you. The halo effect is another example. This was discussed in more detail earlier. If we are in a depressed mood, we become very alert to cues or stimuli from the environment that may reflect negatively upon us. We will also overlook those cues that may be positive.

There are good and bad points regarding this level of sensation. It allows the athlete to react quickly; it allows us to focus on a particular stimulus in a mass of stimuli. Yet, at the same time it often results in our responding too quickly, without enough information. Reacting in such a manner would not seem to be beneficial for developing interpersonal relationships. If, for example, you heard that a stranger was an obnoxious type of person, you may prime yourself to recognize those obnoxious qualities without waiting for sufficient information to make such an important evaluation of another human being. Look at Figure 6-7. It is a picture of a young, vivacious, pretty lady in a hat with a feather on top. Look at her again. This is not a picture of a young lady, but actually a picture of an old witch. The odds are high that you will have difficulty seeing the old witch because you have primed yourself to see a young lady. Think about this in terms of your interpersonal relations. If you are primed by your friends to see another as a snob, can you really enter into a transaction and recognize that person's good qualities?

FIGURE 6-7

Do you see a young or an old woman?

From Raymond S. Ross, *Speech Communication: Fundamentals and Practice,* 3rd edition, © 1974, pp. 22, 24, 25, 27. Reprinted by permission of Prentice-Hall, Inc., Englewood Cliffs, New Jersey.

The third level of sensation is that of identification. This level is concerned with the fidelity of the communication between the environment and the mental image you create. It requires much more information that is analyzed not as a function of priming, but rather as a function of the clarity of the impulse and your perceptual system. Thus, identification goes beyond recognition in terms of the effort expended to construct the mental image. This is the minimum level for fidelity perception. It involves all of the preceding discussion of psychological perceptual tendencies.

MEMORY

Memory certainly plays a major role in perception. In fact, it is the foundation for human existence. On our ability to recall the past hinges the very concepts of experience, language, symbols, consistency, and identity. While considerable research has been conducted on our memory system, controversy still exists as to its operation. Two primary lines of thought are prevalent. First, that memory consists of two phases — short term and long term. Proponents of this view feel that all interpreted impulses go to a short-term memory area. If the particular image (that is, address, phone number, experience, and so forth) is not of enough importance or is not rehearsed, then it simply dissipates. Assuming it is of high importance or is rehearsed, then the mental image proceeds to an area designated as long-term memory. How are you at remembering names? Are names important enough in your life space to go to long-term memory?

The other perspective on memory indicates that everything goes to long-term memory permanently, but that we have different abilities to recall particular items. Thus, everything we have experienced is in our memory and whether we can consciously construct a mental image (remember that name) depends on our ability to locate the storage area.

Another perspective on memory suggests that our memory may be divided into at least three memory systems, each with a number of subsystems. The three systems most often considered are an experience system, a concept system, and a linguistic system. This perspective emerged from research on amnesia where it was found that various types of amnesia produced difficulties in remembering independently those three areas. The suggestion is that we have different storage areas for each category that perhaps operate differently.

The preceding material on the physiological aspects of perception do not have a direct application to your interpersonal communication. However, awareness of the utter complexity of this process should lead each of us to consider the high potential for error — the potential to actively behave on the basis of low fidelity communication. The consequences of such behavior are obvious in light of the high divorce rate, the strife between parents and children, and the innumerous uncomfortable situations we face each day.

We strongly suggest that unless we human beings begin to question our individual methods of perception, the pressures of the twenty-first century may lead us to a very unhumanlike condition. For example, during the next week, make an effort to be consciously aware of your perceptions of at least five other people. Select at least one particular attribute that you infer about each person and double check its accuracy. This may be accomplished by specific observation of that person, in conjunction with communicating with them about that particular quality. Keep a record of the extent to which your perception of that person increased or decreased regarding that attribute. Ask yourself why your perceptions changed in light of the material in this chapter. Consider the amount of double checking that you wish to do in the future.

CHAPTER SUMMARY

We have presented an insight into both physiological and psychological aspects of perception. The orientation of this material has been to expose those aspects that are primarily subconscious and thus unquestioned. Interpersonal perception is a lot like riding a motorcycle in city traffic — when you stop being alert, you're in trouble.

Perceptual regularities (closure, selective perception, and organization) are discussed in light of the potential to miss important environmental cues and to organize those cues that are received in a biased manner.

The orientations we have toward the external world induce further potential to create mental images that are not representative of the environment. With most of us using one or more of the orientations in some aspect of our life space, the potential to interpret selected cues in an erroneous manner becomes increasingly high. Autistic thinking leads us to perceive what we want to perceive. Closemindedness narrows our perception of acceptable communications and ultimately acceptable people. Ethnocentrism leads to judgments of others based on how similar they seem to be to us. Stereotyping leads to prejudgments on the basis of generalized rather than specific information. The halo effect produces a tendency to generalize perceptions of communication based upon our attraction toward others.

All the above occurs as a result of our ability to attribute identity qualities or motives to others based on their communication. Too often these attributions or inferences are based on too little information.

The primary influences on the inferences that we make of others and the mental images we construct of our environment are five interdependent aspects: past experience, environmental index, total identity, situational identity, and our need state.

Any or all of the psychological aspects of perception can influence the reception and retention of stimuli. The sensation of stimuli may be affected by psychological evaluations, thus blocking and/or distorting the mental image.

THINK ABOUT IT

IN GENERAL

Complete the exercises given under Think About It: In General at the end of Chapter 1.

IN EDUCATION

The principle of selective attention suggests that we are much more attentive to communications that support the way we see ourselves and the world. In education, for example, students appear to be more attentive to information that they perceive has direct application to their career goals than to information that they perceive to be only marginally relevant to these goals. How is this going to affect perceptual accuracy and communication in those courses perceived as only marginally relevant? Are students likely to learn as much or engage in communication as frequently as they do in courses with direct application to their majors? What are the ramifications of selective attention in education?

IN THE ORGANIZATION

1. Assume the role of a federal arbitrator who must mediate contract negotiations between a large corporation and a major union. Unless a contract is negotiated and ratified within forty-eight hours, the union members will strike. There are three perceptual sets operating in this situation: (1) management's, (2) the union's, and (3) your own. These perceptual sets can't help but affect the interpersonal communication behavior of all parties involved. How might perceptual attribution affect communications in this situation and how might you handle it?

2. A West Coast insurance company salesman with a high rate of success is asked to conduct a sales meeting with the company's midwestern personnel. Communication techniques are discussed and the participants leave the meeting intent on employing these techniques with potential policy buyers. Six months later, company statistics suggest that while sales on the West Coast continue to climb, sales in the Midwest have dropped. Why do you think this might have happened? Has your explanation anything to do with perception and its affects on interpersonal communication?

IN YOUR RELATIONSHIPS

We have talked about perceptual attribution from both an inferential and causative perspective. Think back to a time you inappropriately attributed psychological qualities to a relational partner, and also assigned an erroneous psychological motive to the person's behavior. How did this affect your interpersonal communication behavior and the state of your relationship? What dangers do you see in the process of perceptual attribution? How might you thwart them? What communication skills (for example, empathy, reciprocity) must you sharpen to thwart negative, perceptual attribution?

SUGGESTED READINGS

Bartley, S. H. *Perception in Everyday Life.* Harper and Row, New York, 1972.

This is an interesting approach to perception from the nonverbal communication point of view. While not directly oriented toward person perception, it does relate the various sensory mechanisms to aspects of everyday existence.

Borden, G. *An Introduction to Human-Communication Theory.* Wm. C. Brown Publishers, Dubuque, Iowa, 1971.

This is an excellent introductory book to general communication theory. Chapters 3 and 4 focus on the perception process and should prove insightful to the beginning student.

Borden, G., R. Gregg and T. Grove. *Speech Behavior and Human Interaction.* Prentice-Hall, Englewood Cliffs, N.J., 1969.

Chapter 1 of this basic text will provide a more detailed expansion of the relationship between the physiological and psychological processes of perception. While not directly oriented toward interpersonal perception, it does an excellent job of describing the process of perception.

Fabun, D. *Communications: The Transfer of Meaning.* Glencoe Press, Beverly Hills, California, 1965.

This is an excellent supplement to the beginning course in interpersonal communication. Written in a manner in which students can immediately relate to, it focuses on the reception and transmission of meaning.

Laing, R., H. Phillipson and A. Lee. *Interpersonal Perception.* Tavistock Publications, London, 1966.

This book combines theory and method in developing and exploring a new perspective of interpersonal perception. As such, it is most appropriate for the advanced reader.

Ruch, F. L. and P. G. Zimbardo. *Psychology and Life,* 8th ed. Scott, Foresman and Co., Glenview, Ill., 1971.

Part 4 of this text is concerned with stimulation and information processing. It provides material that will supplement an understanding of the perception process.

Taguiri, R. and L. Petrullo. *Person Perception and Interpersonal Behavior.* Stanford University Press, Stanford, Calif., 1958.

A collection of primarily original works, this book provides a theoretical scientific approach to the phenomena of person perception. Rigorously written, the book is a must for advanced scholars. It is not recommended for beginning students.

Chapter Seven
Expectancy Formation: What We See Is What We Get

SHOP TALK

Manipulation Treating, using, exploiting, and/or controlling the self and others as things rather than as individual human beings.

Sociocultural unit A group of people who have directly or indirectly developed a broad, collective set of expectancies regarding the behavior of individuals associated with that unit.

Expectancies Those mental images that one anticipates to be true or those events one anticipates happening.

Violation of expectancies The negation of an expectancy by its absence or alteration. (a) Actual The occurrence of a valid negation; (b) Interpreted The incorrect perception of a negation, which is treated as an actual violation of expectancies.

Whether or not it's wise, most of us feel secure in the belief that the world we see tomorrow will be pretty much the same as the world we see today. We also tend to feel secure in the belief that friends, relatives, and coworkers will appear no different next week than they appear this week. Put simply, we expect our physical and psychological reality to remain relatively constant and consistent. For example:

1. We expect to behave in a manner consistent with our identity.
2. We expect others to behave in a manner consistent with our beliefs about their identity.
3. We expect others to behave toward us in a manner consistent with the identity that we have attempted to communicate to them.
4. We expect others to behave in a manner consistent with the norms of our sociocultural units.

This chaper is concerned with questions about how your identity system interacts with your environment in producing expectancies concerning yourself and the people around you. We are specifically concerned with questions about how we operate to fulfill our expectancies and how we handle situations in which our expectancies have been violated. This is important not only because communication cue exchange plays a major role but also because it will give you an insight into your communication behavior and the communication behavior of your friends under common, everyday stress-producing situations.

INDIVIDUAL EXPECTANCY FORMATION

As has been maintained throughout this text, consistency plays a major role in affecting our communication behavior. The demand for consistency is derived from Maslow's need for safety. This need indicates that humans require order and predictability to exist. If we were not able to predict that the car would turn left when we turned the steering wheel to the left, our safety need would go unsatisfied. In the same sense, were we not able to expect the car to perform consistently, our predictions would be tenuous, and we probably would not attempt transportation by that means. It is through the striving for order and predictability that individuals develop expectancies not only of the world about them but also of themselves. Each moment of existence then is filled with numerous expectancies. Many of these expectancies are related to the physical environment (for example, the roof will not fall; feet will remain downward; the earth will not open) and are never consciously perceived in the normal course of existence. In a like manner, many of our constant expectancies relate to our communication behavior and that of others and are equally unconscious. The development of these expectancies and the nature of expectancy violation are major determinants of everyday interpersonal transactions. One's expectancies of self and others are a function of five interrelated areas: the sociocultural unit, past experiences, the identity system, the state of one's relationships, and the situational context of one's communication transactions.

THE INFLUENCE OF SOCIOCULTURAL UNITS

A sociocultural unit is a group of people who have directly or indirectly developed a broad, collective set of expectancies concerning the behavior of humans belonging to this unit. Thus, we could look at the sociocultural unit of the United States or the sociocultural unit of Texas or the sociocultural unit of the local neighborhood or the sociocultural unit at work. Typically, the collective set of expectancies of any one sociocultural unit includes a majority of the expectancies of a larger sociocultural unit (which encompasses the smaller unit). Individual members of the work unit recognize the expectancies of the city unit as well as the expectancies of the state and national units.

We are familiar with major differences between national units. The Japanese behave (dress, act, and so forth) different from the Russians or Africans or Americans. The differences in behavior between work units such as blue collar workers and white collar workers is equally obvious. The differences between social units (groups of friends) is not always so obvious. Yet in each case, one can discern that the members of a unit have expectancies of other members' behavior.

During our developmental years, we learn the expectancies of the larger sociocultural units. We also learn to expect like behavior from other members of those units and to expect different behavior from other units. As we mature

Sociocultural expectancies include the laws by which we are governed.

and move in and out of many smaller units, we also learn a variety of new and sometimes quite different expectancies.

The expectancies at each level of sociocultural units are developed for the purpose of maintaining a comfortable existence for itself and its members. Units require of their members (1) knowledge of the norm of behavior in that unit and (2) conformity to that norm of behavior. Norms of behavior represent the collective set of expectancies of a sociocultural unit. Each unit's norms are formulated through a variety of means. Some norms are developed on a majority rule basis, while others are instigated by power position rule. Still others are operative simply out of habit. The scope of a unit is constantly in flux because some people die and others are born, and some people move from one unit to another. Youngsters have little say in the unit's expectancies and adopt parental behavior that is eventually accepted as the way things are. People moving into a new sociocultural unit must become aware of and conform to the new set of expectancies in order to communicate to unit members that they are a part of that unit.

The power position rule method of establishing expectancies occurs most often in units that do not align themselves with a democratic system. Organizations or units like the military, large corporations and educational organizations tend to utilize this method of establishing expectancies. Occasionally, a sociocultural unit of friends will develop where one or two leaders will determine the behavior expected of members of that collective group. When the power position rule method has been utilized, deviation from the rules of behavior is serious and the violators are confronted with sometimes drastic means of correction. The object of correction ranges from insuring that you do not ever violate an expectancy again to leader reassurance that power is still held.

The United States government is an example of the majority rule basis for development of societal expectancies. It is also found in various spectrums of social life. Under a democratic governmental policy, the effort to maintain democratic processes in all facets of society is evident. Local organizations and social clubs typically establish a set of rules on the basis of majority consent to those rules. Within social units such as a group of friends, rules are generally unspoken. They emerge from a group consensus that was formed without ever referring to expectancies or rules of behavior. They are mutually agreed upon through the ebb and flow of communication transactions involving everything but the expectancy itself.

In examining norms of behavior, perhaps the most evident is our system of written expectancies. The books of religion, of course, provide sets of expectancies that the majority of humans acknowledge and use as guidelines of behavior for themselves and others. In the socioculture of the United States and in subsets of this culture, various expectancies are written in the form of laws. Further expectancies of a social nature are written in the many books covering the social graces, etiquette, and special occasion rules such as weddings and parties. These written expectancies are primarily associated with the larger sociocultural units. Smaller units adopt many of the expectancies of larger units. Each smaller unit will, however, have small deviations from the larger unit because of the greater opportunity for continued communication.

The vast majority of expectancies are not written. They are passed along from generation to generation, from old members to new members, by verbal and nonverbal communication. The general category of everyday manners are rarely written. How individuals socially interact with others of different sex, status, power, age, and propriety are learned by observation and verbal instruction from members of the unit. The appropriate way to shake hands, the appropriate amount of eye contact, and the appropriate body space limitations are just a few of the behavior patterns we learn from our sociocultural unit. We literally learn what our unit expects of us and then we, in turn, expect that from others in our unit. Thus unit expectancies and individual expectancies are maintained over long periods of time. The set of expectancies that we learn from our sociocultural unit, however, are only a subset of the total expectancies we maintain.

As we mentioned previously, at any given moment we are in more than one sociocultural unit. With each level of unit assuming some of the larger unit's expectancies, one should remember that as we go through a typical day we move from unit to unit at the same level. One may start the day communicating within the family unit, go to work and communicate within the work unit (or possibly within several work units), move on to school and communicate within class units and/or friend units, go for a snack after school and communicate with a friend unit, and finally return home to communicate within the family unit again. Each of us may have a different typical day, but all of us will move from one unit to another during the course of a day. As movement occurs, our expectancies of our behavior and the behavior of others will change as the unit changes. In summary, we expect of ourselves and others that which our relevant sociocultural unit expects of us.

THE INFLUENCE OF THE PAST, PRESENT, AND FUTURE

The expectancies we learned from our sociocultural units are only a part of our past experience. In one sense, all expectancies are founded on past experience. When confronted with new situations, we refer to similar experiences in our past to develop new expectancies. Our past influences not only our sociocultural unit but also our identity system, need state, and our communcation behavior, and it provides the basis for decision making in attempting to maximize positives and minimize negatives. It is through our past experiences that we relate ourselves to our environment. If, in the past, we experienced promptness when we make a date for eight o'clock, we expect the other person will be dressed appropriately and be ready to go at eight o'clock.

If we have had unpleasant experiences with persons of the opposite sex, we expect to have more unpleasant experiences. If we have had genuine and warm relationships with people in our life space, then we expect genuine, warm relationships with new acquaintances.

Our past experiences are tempered, however, by our present situation. The context in which we find ourselves affects the expectancies that we have of ourselves and others. We expect ourselves and others to behave in certain ways when interacting in the local pub, and we shift our expectations when attending a formal dance. The present affects us in the sense that if we are with our friends in the dorm room, we can expect one type of behavior. If we're with our friends in church, we can expect an entirely different type of behavior. Our expectancies change based on our present situation. The context in which we find ourselves, in a sense, assists us in deciding what we can expect in terms of another's behavior. We develop expectancies of just about everyone's behavior, even a stranger's. When walking across campus, you do not expect a stranger to jump up and mug you in broad daylight. But at night your expectancies are not quite so firm, especially if you're a female.

Before entering a particular social context, you anticipate what it is going to be like and thus develop expectancies. Think back to when you walked into this class. We would suspect that you had expectancies that the instructor would present stilted lectures and that you were going to spend the entire semester writing down everything said, memorizing it, and spitting it back on a test, probably multiple choice. We hope that's been violated. Or remember how you felt as you decided which job to take. The decision you made was influenced by your expectancies regarding various factors associated with that job. As you went to work the first day, remember how you expected it to be?

Our projections of the future certainly affect our expectancies of the present. If, for example, we project that the world will end in 1990, our expectancies of ourselves and others in the present would be different from those we would have if we did not have this projection. Consider the expectancies you had of your behavior and that of your partner when you projected getting engaged and married, and compare those with the expectancies you had prior to your first date.

So even for situations that we haven't been in yet, we look at similar ones of the past and develop expectancies on that basis. Consider a professor who teaches in an informal style and compare him with a professor employing a strict lecture format. Assume you're going to talk to each professor. Different expectancies will be developed about their behavior, even though you've never talked with a professor before. You're going to anticipate how they're going to behave or what it's going to be like. Football players do this the night before the ball game. As they fall off to sleep, they're hiking the ball, they're catching the ball, they're throwing the ball, they're kicking it, they're blocking somebody (and are they ever doing it well!) They really have these expectancies. As it turns out, this is a very good thing, because it does improve one's ability to play. Actors and acrtesses do the same. In fact, we all do this without consciously realizing it in the majority of instances.

THE IMPACT OF IDENTITY

It seems rather evident that humans treat the violation of positive expectancies as painful or negative. Our human orientation remains one of maximizing our positives and minimizing negatives. (Stop for a moment and consider the state of the world if everyone maximized their positives by minimizing other's negatives.) The dominant orientation of the American culture at this time is to WIN. Winning with the concepts of personal identity, ideal identity, and social identity consumes the greater amount of our time interacting with others.

While each individual carries with him or her expectancies based, in part, on the sociocultural unit and past, present, and anticipated future experiences, one's identity system is the major influence on expectancies. These expectancies form such an integral part of our psychological world that the vast majority remain buried in our subconscious only to become evident when violation occurs. In addition, many violations are realized and resolved without our consciously being aware of such happenings.

We feel that each person's view of the world is bound by his or her individual identity structure. Expectancies are heavily influenced by who you think you are, how you believe other people see you, how you would like to see yourself, and how you would like others to see you.

As discussed earlier, humans expect and operate on the expectancy of consistency, particularly in the areas of personal identity and social identity. If you believe you have a good memory, then you expect to remember things. If you beleive you are a good athlete or a good dancer, then you expect to perform well in athletic events or on dancing programs. You also expect others to recognize those more important aspects of your personal identity. Others should also recognize your outstanding memory, athletic ability, work skill, or dancing prowess. If you believe a particular person loves you, then you expect loving behavior from that person. If you believe a friend thinks of you as intel'ectually capable, then you expect your friend to behave that way. One must recognize, however, that all of these expectancies are to some extent influenced by the behavioral set that is operative at that moment. Our discussion of unit differentiation and the impact of the present situation and context is particularly meaningful because they determine in part the behavioral set that we select at any given moment. Since the behavioral set is a selected group of identity items that are reflected in our communication behavior, which shifts from moment to moment as the situation and context shift, the expectancies of self and others are also in a constant state of flux.

Although Chapter 5 was not cast in the framework of expectancies, you may want to review it because of its concern with the identity system.

A part of the context that has a major bearing on our behavioral set and in turn on our expectancies is the type of relationship we believe we have with others who are present.

THE INFLUENCE OF RELATIONSHIPS

Prior to meeting people for the first time, our expectancies are broad and general. We apply the expectancies learned from the sociocultural unit and our past-present experience. The moment we come in face-to-face contact, however, our expectancies become less general and more specific. We analyze the communication cues emitted by others, form some notion of their identity, and begin to expect certain behavior from them. Strangers, of course, are doing the same thing to us. Details of this process were discussed in Chapter 6 and will be further explained in Part 3. It is through the communication cue exchange that each develops specific expectancies of the other. As more verbal and nonverbal communications are exchanged, the expectancies one has of another become refined and detailed. Decisions are made, based upon your analysis of the other's communication and the person's confirmation or denial of your expectancies, regarding how far along the relationship continuum you would like to progress. Such a continuum is shown in Figure 7-1.

Under rare circumstances, a relationship may start further along the continuum, but most relationships start at a level of 1. The relationship concept may be viewed from at least three perspectives: (1) where person A places the relationship, (2) where person B places the relationship, or (3) where the joint feelings of each individual place the relationship. In the same manner that a chain is only as strong as its weakest link, a relationship as a unit or joint feeling can progress only as far as the lowest stage indicated by one of the two members. If person A would place the relationship at a 6 level and person B would place it at a 4 level, the relationship could be viewed from the point of view of person A, 6, or the point of view of person B, 4. But when viewing the relationship from a joint perspective, we can say only that as a joint, meaningful relationship, it has progressed only to the lowest level, 4.

The expectancies that each has of the other are based on the respective points of view. Person A would be expecting communication behavior from the other at the level of 6 while person B would only be expecting level 4 communication behavior. As the distance between persons A and B increased, the tension and frustration resulting from violation of expectancies also would increase. Most of you probably have observed a relationship in which one individual thought it was at a 9 and the other thought it was at a 2. Major expectancies of each other were violated. This often results in termination of the relationship. The key to avoiding this situation lies in reciprocal disclosure early in the relationship, which allows expectancies to have a more valid base than the usual assumptions each makes of the other. Relationship types present another problem. Within work or educational situations, individuals occasionally

FIGURE 7-1

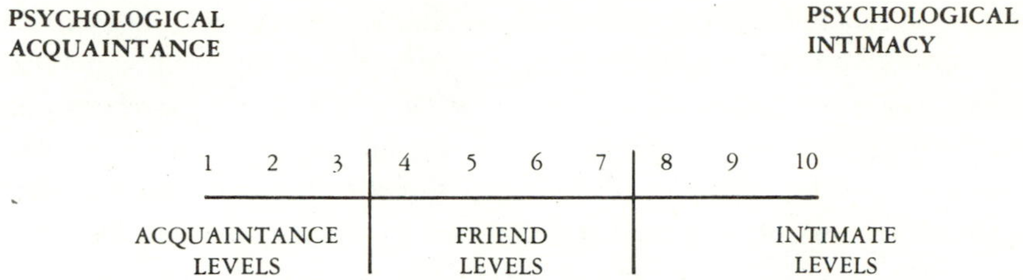

PSYCHOLOGICAL   PSYCHOLOGICAL
ACQUAINTANCE   INTIMACY

```
      1    2    3 │ 4    5    6    7 │ 8    9    10
   ─────────────────────────────────────────────────
    ACQUAINTANCE  │     FRIEND      │    INTIMATE
      LEVELS      │     LEVELS      │     LEVELS
```

Relationships generally begin with psychological acquaintance.

confuse employer-employee or teacher-student relationships with friendship relationships. When the parties involved view the relationship type differently, they of course have differing expectancies. When these are violated, any type of relationship may be doomed. Confusion of this nature is most often caused by misinterpreting each other's communication cues. The resolution of this situation without termination or trauma lies in communication about the nature of the relationship in an emphatic manner.

As relationships progress from level to level, the expectancies increase in quantity and importance. As will be discussed later, mutual trust is critical to a relationship. It would seem, then, that the continued confirmation of expectancies is directly related to that concept.

Expectancies that individuals have of another can only be known by the other party through the exchange of information. Quite often we assume that the other has the same expectancies we have. Yet, if we stop for a moment and consider the factors that form expectancies, it should be obvious that this is an illogical, erroneous assumption. While each of us makes inferences about others through verbal and nonverbal communications, the more information we have, the more likely our assumptions are valid. The amount and quality of communication that is exchanged must increase for the expectancies to be valid and in turn for the relationship to legitimately progress.

Unfortunately, many individuals persist in taking short cuts to solid relationships. Overlooking violations of your expectancies of yourself and others is, in essence, manipulation. A relationship built on manipulation ultimately will fail. A relationship that persists in spite of continued violation of expectancies is unrealistic.

THE INFLUENCE OF INTERPERSONAL NEED STATES

The state of our interpersonal needs, such as belongingness and love, inclusion, control, and affection, is a major factor in the expectancies that we have of ourselves and others. If a particular need is not satisfied, then it is active. We expect ourselves to fulfill that need. Depending on the state of the relationship we have with other people, we expect them to know our need and to assist us in fulfilling it. If, for example, we are in need of affection, we engage in communication behaviors designed and expected to satisfy that need. Of those individuals in our life space, we may select the individual whom we expect will most fulfill our need at that particular time. We then expect that person to do so. If the person does not, our expectancy is violated, and we will be in an inconsistent state and may resolve that state by terminating or reducing the relationship level.

To a major degree, relationship level is influenced by the extent to which both parties recognize and conform to the expectancies of the other, relative to such major factors as identity and needs.

In summary, we focused on the development of individual expectancies as a function of the sociocultural unit; past, present, and anticipated future experiences; the identity system, the relationship level, and the interpersonal need states. Once developed and active, our expectancies become predominantly subconsciously active in affecting our communication behavior to ourselves and others. An expectancy rarely becomes conscious unless it is thought to have been violated. When this occurs, it has drastic implications for the communication behavior utilized in interpersonal relationships.

EXPECTANCY VIOLATION

Before proceeding, take a moment to recollect several instances that you have experienced when people in your life space behaved differently than you expected them to. Try to visualize how you reacted to that behavior and the impact of your reaction on the relationship.

There seems to be two ways in which expectancies may be violated. Both assert that the violation is valid and intentional. Both are maintained in the eyes of the beholder. Both types of violations will result in efforts on your part to resolve the inconsistency inherent in a violated expectancy. First, let us draw examples from the perspective of violated expectancies within the sociocultural unit. Remember, violations occur from the point of view of the expectancy holder. In the following case, the expectancy holder is the sociocultural unit itself.

SOCIOCULTURAL UNIT VIOLATIONS

First, an actual violation may take place. If the sociocultural expectancy is that individuals will not drive in excess of fifty-five miles per hour, but you are caught driving at sixty-five miles per hour, then an actual violation has occurred. In a social sense, if the unit expectancy is that men do not hit women, but a man strikes his date, then an actual violation has taken place. The sociocultural unit will react and resolve that violation.

Since we are viewing this from the eyes of the sociocultural unit, however, a second means of violation is possible. An interpreted or perceived violation is considered and treated as an actual violation even though it may not have occurred in real terms. Consider in the previous case that you were really driving only fifty-five miles per hour. Yet the police officer's radar was slightly faulty or the officer misread the radar indication as sixty-five miles per hour. The sociocultural method of resolving this interpreted violation is the same as if it actually occurred. In the second example, consider that a drunk fell against you and as you lost your balance, you accidentally struck your date. This occurred in the middle of a heated argument and no one else in the sociocultural unit saw the drunk. The sociocultural unit would interpret such behavior as an actual violation of its expectancies. Overcoming these interpreted violations is an arduous task with a great deal depending on your past reputation as a member of the unit and the significance of any contrary evidence that you may produce. Each of the sociocultural unit expectancies may also be viewed from the perspective of each individual making up that unit. Thus, one may not only violate the unit expectancy but also violate each individual member's expectancy. Of course, individual expectancies are far more numerous than sociocultural unit expectancies.

INDIVIDUAL VIOLATIONS

Let's consider an individual expectation that is violated. You see the world about you and feel that this person likes you and that person doesn't like you. We have a strong tendency to make such judgments. What would the reaction be if the person that didn't like you started coming to you for advice on personal problems? You would be shocked. Why were you shocked? Because you had an expectancy of that person's behavior toward you based upon your social identity. You believed that he or she thought of you as a worthless individual and suddenly he or she is coming to you for advice.

In much the same manner as sociocultural units operate, each individual operates on the assumption that others know and understand expectancies and will conform to them. Thus, violations of individual expectancies may also be either actual or interpreted.

For example, if you were a newly hired manager and walked in to meet the staff on the first day, and they treated you like a laborer, your expectancies may have actually been violated. Or as a student you were expecting to be treated as a student, but you were treated as an equal when seeing your professor, that also may have been an actual violation.

Your social identity can be violated. We've already indicated some examples of this. If people that you like suddenly attack you verbally, this is not expected behavior based on all their previous cues about who they think you are. All our past experiences can be violated. If you were to release a pencil and it rose instead of dropped, your expectancies would be violated. Your idea of consistency would be violated because you've learned that when you release something that isn't filled with helium or hot air, it's going to fall. If you're driving down the street, and you turn your steering wheel to the left, you fully operate on the expectancy that the car is going to turn to the left. If it doesn't and turns to the right, your expectancies have actually been violated. The same thing works in your personal experiences. If you have a particular opening line to ease into the conversation when meeting others, and you've used it a number of times in the past successfully, you fully expect it to be successful again. When it's not successful it has violated some idea of consistency.

There are going to be many things that can cause an interpreted violation. An interpreted violation is one that really is not a violation, but perhaps because of a situational index, perhaps because at that particular point in time you're concerned with a particular need, you might well misinterpret the communication cues. You might come home from school really exhausted one day. You're tired. You're angry. You had a heated disagreement with your instructor. The first thing your roommate or spouse says is, "I'm going out to play cards tonight." You were expecting to get a little sympathy, a little warmth, a little understanding, and pow, your mate is gone. You might fully misinterpret this as, "He (or she) doesn't love me anymore." And you are going to react as if this were actually the case. Remember, interpreted violations are real to the person doing the interpreting.

REACTIONS AND RESOLUTIONS OF
EXPECTANCY VIOLATION

The reactions and resolutions of expectancy violation vary with the degree of impact or importance of the expectation. In addition, the circumstances surrounding the violation may affect reactions and resolution methods.

Since the sociocultural unit plays a major role in interpersonal communication transactions, we will discuss its method of handling expectancy violation separately from individual methods.

THE SOCIOCULTURAL UNIT

With governmental sociocultural units there is typically a clarification period when one may have the opportunity to address the interpreted versus the actual violation issue. However, in social units, such a clarification period rarely exists. Typically, the resolution method is put into effect immediately (that is, all the guys in the group, when seeing your hand contact the girl's face, violently strike you). Only with the passage of time does the typical social unit acknowledge alternative explanations for observed behavior.

Five predominant resolution methods are used by sociocultural units when people violate expectancies. Governmental units may utilize the concept of probation. Social or work units also may instigate warning followed by a probationary period when daily activities are under constant scrutiny. Usually this resolution method takes into account that you may be ignorant of the sociocultural expectancy of your minor infraction.

A second resolution method typically associated with minor violations is to penalize you in some way so as to reduce the probability that you will violate the expectancy in the future. The governmental unit may impose monetary fines, for instance. The social and work units have a number of penalties, including monetary fines, but also they include demands on behavior. Social fraternities and sororities are known for the strange behavior required of members who violate the units' expectancies. But let's look at a less structured social unit, such as a group of friends. When you commit a faux pas, the group sits in judgment and, in a sense, declares a new set of expectancies for your specific behavior if you are to remain in that social unit.

The third and perhaps major reaction-resolution method is that of ostracism from the social unit. Governmental units use jails and deportation procedures. The social and work units utilize the cold shoulder, the avoidance technique, and occasionally come right out and tell you, "We do not want you as a member of our group." The latter is found in the blackball system of some fraternities and sororities. It may also be put into effect by employers or educators.

The fourth reaction-resolution method is to accept the violation with reluctance. This is how change in the unit's expectations occurs. Consider the case of long hair on males. In the past, long hair on males severely violated sociocultural expectancies about normal male behavior. Yet in the late 1970s, it raises little furor. The expectancies were altered by the existence of three factors: (1) the number of times the violation occurred in conjunction with the number of people doing the violating, (2) the exposure given to the violations, and (3) the persistence of the violation over time. Women's and men's liberation groups have been involved in this procedure for some time and are beginning to affect the sociocultural unit's expectancies of male and female sex role behavior.

Perhaps two major problems are faced by potential changers. Changers must be willing to pay the price of initially violating the unit's expectancies, because such violations will result in one of the above-mentioned resolution methods before anything approaching acceptance with reluctance will occur. The second and perhaps major problem is time. The larger units are traditional and very comfortable with that which they expect. To introduce change is to disrupt that comfort. To make the uncomfortable and insecure into the comfortable and secure does not occur overnight. The initial changers do grow older and do enter into other sociocultural units where quite often the penalty for violation is much more severe (long hair in the college unit may be resolved by strange looks and social avoidance, while long hair on the job may be resolved by lack of pay raises or business avoidance through the act of firing the violator). Thus, the mere passage of time and the extended responsibilities and altered circumstances associated with time progression are barriers to reaching this method of violation resolution.

Last, but not least, is a resolution method termed happiness. While sociocultural units have positive expectations of its members' behavior, they also have negative expectations. When a negative expectation is violated, the unit may rejoice in happiness at the surprising behavior of its members. Perhaps this is intertwined with some initial disbelief and bewilderment, but it ultimately moves to happiness and a new set of positive expectancies. The national sociocultural unit has undergone this process. Following the riots of the 1960s and early 1970s, it is an understatement to indicate that this unit had negative expectancies of college students' behavior. During the year of 1974, the bewilderment and happiness resulting from the "streaking phenomena" was evident. College students were still violating expectancies, but to a much lesser degree and to the exclusion of more dreaded expectancies. During 1975 and 1976, even these violations disappeared. The college student is gaining the reputation of being a sensible, rational human being as a result of the violation of negative expectancies.

THE INDIVIDUAL

Because the expectancies of both a sociocultural unit and an individual may be violated by another, the violator may find that the principle of double jeopardy is not operative in the interpersonal world. The individual may find that both a sociocultural unit and another person will exert punishment for a violation of expectancies.

Regardless of whether the violation was actual or interpreted, remember that the individual will operate on the assumption that a violation actually occurred.

The following material will probably be more meaningful to you if you would attempt to recall several instances when your friends were pleasantly surprised at your behavior and several instances when they were unpleasantly surprised. Try to focus on their reactions to your behavior in terms of the verbal and nonverbal communication cues they emitted to you. What was the effect of both types of instances on the state of your relationship with the people involved?

Because we have a positive-negative perspective on events occurring in our life space, we can have either positive or negative reactions to violations of our expectancies. If a positive expectancy is violated, we generally react in a negative fashion (that is, frustration, depression, or anxiety). If a negative expectancy is violated, we generally react with suspicion or distrust initially. If the new behavior is repeated over time and is interpreted as reliable, we shift in a positive direction (that is, warmth, happiness, or joy). There are exceptions to this latter statement, but we are concerned primarily with the general orientation.

Assume that friends talked you into a blind date. You've committed yourself; called the other person on the phone and said, "Yes, let's go out to dinner, to a movie, and then we'll go dancing." Then your friends start in, "Wait until you see who we've got you fixed up with. You won't believe this person. We really put one over on you." This may or may not violate your expectancies of your friends' behavior toward you, depending on how weird your friends are. If you were negatively affected, you may react with anger or perhaps depression. If it were interpreted as a playful love stroke, you may be inwardly pleased. Let us assume, though, that you believe in keeping your commitment, that you feel you must go through with this date, and that you are a male. Your expectancies toward the evening have become established as nothing less than horrible. Regretfully, you must meet. She comes down the stairs and she is utterly beautiful. Expectancy violated! Or, if you are of the opposite sex, your date meets you at the door with a bouquet of roses, would pass for Robert Redford's double, and carries on an intensely interesting conversation. Expectancy violated! Your negative expectancies were violated.

We can react with happiness to the violation of our expectancies.

But because we're really confident people and operate on the basis that we have truth, the vast majority of our expectancies of ourselves and others are positive. This results in negative reactions to numerous violations during the average day. The reactions can include a variety of things. They could include anger, frustration, and/or depression. Assume you and another person have established a substantial relationship and have reached the point of friendly insults. "Hi, dummy!" is not an unusual greeting. You're out on a date at an expensive restaurant. Your friend comes into the restaurant, walks over to the table and says, "Hi, ya, dummy!" Pow! Your friend slaps you on the back and begins roughhousing with accompanying obscenities. Your expectancies of this friend's behavior in that context were indeed violated. One just might react with anger, frustration, or depression.

Or consider that you have been dating a girl or a guy for a long time and believe that you're in love with the other person and that person is in love with you. You're out one night and the other person says, "Gee, I think we ought to break this off. I've got to get some more experience here in college before we really settle down." That can surely be frustrating. You certainly had your expectancies violated. It could be depressing. You can become intensely angry. You will react and make psychological or physical effort to resolve the inconsistent state of having your positive expectancies violated. The following chapter will detail the various psychological and physical adjustments we tend to utilize. It will point out the negative consequences of such activity.

CHAPTER SUMMARY

One of comedian Flip Wilson's favorite lines is, "What you see is what you get." In this chapter, we suggest that what you get is not only a function of what you see but also a function of what you expect. Indeed, human expectancies affect interpersonal communication to an inordinate extent. And we would all do well to periodically remind ourselves of this fact.

Remember, our expectancies result from primarily five sources of communication: (1) sociocultural units, (2) the past, present, and projected future, (3) our perceptions of our individual identities, (4) our relationships, and (5) our interpersonal need states. Also, remember that expectancies actually may be violated, or we may perceive they have been violated when this is not necessarily the case.

THINK ABOUT IT

IN GENERAL

Complete the exercises given under Think About It: In General at the end of Chapter 1.

IN EDUCATION

1. Think back to a time when your expectancies about a teacher and class were violated severly. What was the source of your expectancies (for example, course description, academic advisor, or friend). How did your expectancies influence your communication behavior during the beginning stages of the class? What changes in your communication behavior took place as a function of your expectancies being violated? Did the experience teach you anything about the way expectancies can serve to accent the positive or negative in a given situation? If so, how do you plan to use this information to become a more skillful interpreter of what is communicated to you by sources of information in the educational environment?

2. Assume the role of a new high school teacher. The school principal tells you that your students will be the troublemakers and underachievers that populate the school. The principal also informs you that you should expect the worst from your students. How might this information bias you toward your new students? How might this information affect the ways in which you communicate with your students? Do you think teachers who are skilled in communicating with their students place much value in what sources external to the classroom say about students? Why or why not?

IN THE ORGANIZATION

1. You've been given an interview for an important position with a corporation with a highly conservative image. You expect the interview to be very formal, with the interviewer sitting behind an expansive desk. You enter the office, the personnel director greets you, and suggests that the interview be conducted in a conversational area in the corner of the office. Totally unexpected, moreover, the personnel director is a female. Your expectancies have

been violated and you must regroup your thinking almost instantaneously. What would the skilled communicator look for and how would he or she handle the situation?

2. Assume you are at a meeting being conducted by the vice president in charge of sales for the company in which you're employed. As other employees have told you, the vice president is not fond of personnel who challenge his policy decisions. Even so, you feel one of his recent policy decisions will negatively affect both sales personnel and the company as a whole. Are you going to challenge him by speaking out on the matter? How might you do so without severely violating the expectancies of everyone involved?

IN YOUR RELATIONSHIPS

A long and trusted friend discloses to another person information about you that you confided to the friend in complete confidence. Your expectancies about the friend have been shaken severely. You meet with the friend and want to discuss the issue. At the same time, you do not want to undermine the relationship further than it has already been undermined. How are you going to communicate your feelings to this friend, and what outcomes do you want to follow this transaction?

SUGGESTED READINGS

Rosenthal, R. *Experimental Effects in Behavioral Research.* Appleton Century Crofts, New York, 1966.

Although this book is research oriented, it provides excellent examples of how human expectancies can influence the outcomes of human behavior. The advanced reader may want to examine the examples and apply them to interpersonal communication settings.

Rosenthal, R., and L. Jacobson. *Pygmalion in the Classroom.* Holt, New York, 1968.

This book focuses on the impact of teacher expectations of their students. Although its rather sweeping conclusions have come under attack recently, one of the points has received empirical support. Teacher expectancies about students influence the ways in which teachers communicate with their students.

Chapter Eight
Resolving Violated Expectancies

Distortion Perceiving and communicating things in ways other than how they really are.

Denial of reality Failing to accept the fact that an expectancy has been violated.

Rationalization Creating a seemingly logical reason for the violation of our own or other's expectancies.

Identification Imitating the positive traits, attitudes, or behavior of others.

Attribution Placing blame or responsibility on others rather than on ourselves. Also, incorrectly placing blame or responsibility on people.

Regression Psychologically retreating from a negative situation in the present to a positive situation in the past and adopting the communication behaviors that accompanied it.

Reaction formation Communicating an exaggerated opposite of how one actually feels.

Emotional insulation and apathy Not getting involved with others and convincing yourself that you don't really care about them.

Swallowing but remembering Temporarily placing violations in the back of your mind, but storing them up until they reach major proportions.

Avoidance Refusing to communicate verbally or nonverbally with another.

Displacement Letting loose our emotional reaction to a violation on someone other than the actual violator.

Verbal aggression Verbally attacking one who has violated your expectancy.

Physical aggression Physically attacking one who has violated your expectancy.

Identity alteration Changing expectancies by altering self-perspective.

Derogation Inferring negative qualities of some aspect of another's identity.

Have you ever gotten angry when a friend purposely misunderstood what you were attempting to communicate? While you were communicating with another, have you ever felt that person was "off in space" and not paying attention? Have you ever uncovered another lie in a series of what seemed to be bald lies? Have you ever known someone who had an excuse for everything? Have you ever met anyone who seemed to not care about anybody? Have you ever let things build up inside you until you exploded at a friend? Have you ever put someone else down hard for no apparent reason?

We feel that you will have responded yes to many of the above questions. Few, if any, of us can go through a day without having an expectancy violated, but we behave as if the violations do not occur or are not recognized. As a result, we use many methods of handling situations to allow us to operate at an individual level of psychological comfort. Unfortunately, many of these methods of avoiding or handling expectancy violation are nothing more than lies — lies that allow us to manipulate ourselves or others, lies that are predominantly subconscious efforts to fool our conscious thinking processes. Most of these methods are psychological in nature, and each has tremendous impact on our interpersonal communication behavior.

In this chapter we will discuss some of the more common ways people cope with the violation of their expectancies. Consider the impact of each method on your interpersonal communication behavior and its ultimate impact on your relationships. A relationship that is founded on manipulation, deceit, and lies may temporarily satisfy one's needs. However, in the long run it will fall far short of what it potentially could have been.

We strongly suggest that you make each example come alive for you in your life space. Minutely examine its impact on your communication and the type of relationship it leads to.

It is important that you keep in mind that we provide examples for each of the techniques that are purposely isolated. In the real world of interpersonal communication, we rarely use just one technique but rather all that seem available at a given moment. So it is not unusual to have difficulty in classifying your behavior or that of others.

TYPICAL COPING STRATEGIES

DISTORTION

This method of resolving violations contains two primary orientations — fantasy and compensation. *Fantasy* is escaping from reality by temporarily entering an unreal world. Individuals who think highly of themselves and because of circumstances find themselves employed in an utterly boring job will often fantasize during the work day in an effort to resolve the inconsistency. When a person regards himself or herself as bright and promising, it is boring to work at a meaningless task. By fantasizing, the day goes faster, but the root of the violation remains. Little effort is expended to alter the state of affairs. Instead, efforts are expended simply to make them bearable. A husband or wife who thinks well of his or her ability to attract handsome or beautiful people may be married to a person not so handsome or pretty and may begin to fantasize that the sexual partner is a famous movie star. While on the surface this may result in psychological comfort, such comfort is only temporary and certainly is not shared by the sexual partner. It may lead to dissolution of the relationship should a slip of the tongue become evident during more intimate communication activities of the relationship.

Compensation is the substitution of positive traits for negative traits either in ourselves or those around us. Someone may say, "You know, you really are an obnoxious loudmouth." Instead of personally reflecting upon your past behavior in the presence of this individual to see if indeed you have been communicating in such a manner, you may internally compensate for this apparent deficiency by focusing on your behavior that is representative of warmth, consideration, and kindness. We substitute in ourselves positive aspects to replace or overcome the negative aspects.

Or consider our orientation toward friends. Generally, we do not have friends who have immensely negative traits and instead of focusing on the negative ones, we focus on the positive ones. We substitute, in a sense, positive traits for the negative traits, thus ignoring them. This, of course, contributes to the halo effect discussed in Chapter 6. Another example of individual compensation would be to put all energy into becoming successful in an occupation when one's home life is relatively unhappy. The positive aspect was substituted for the negative one. Instead of really getting involved in the home scene and trying to resolve those problems, such people remain "covered." Success in business compensates for failure in the home. Perhaps even more tragic today is the drug scene. If a person is failing at one particular aspect of life, the positive state of euphoria brought on by hard drugs may psychologically compensate for that deficiency. This person may be compensating internally the positive aspects of life for the negative aspects of life. The case histories of drug addicts indicate that at the point of initiating heavy drug use they were not in a valid positive state.

Divorced or separated parents may attempt to compensate for the missing relationships with their children by bringing armloads of huge expensive toys and games or artifacts on an infrequent visit. The parent may be trying to compensate. This may be a process of making up to others for having violated their expectancies. What we don't often realize is that this has a selfish motivation in that it allows us to resolve our violation of our own expectancies. It involves some communication behavior designed to make the other individual and ourselves forget or overlook violations. They typically arise from a feeling of guilt and on the surface appear to be saying, "I'm sorry. It was inconsiderate and unkind of me to have done so. Please understand that I'm apologetic and will not do so again." Underneath, such people are saying, "Maybe if I do this you will forget and overlook what an inconsiderate, unkind person I am." Behavior that truly represents the former statement is quite desirable, but when we simply use it as a cover or as a momentary technique to persuade ourselves or others that we're really a nice person, the phrases become cliches that ultimately will tear down our relationships as well as ourselves.

DENIAL OF REALITY

Denial of reality is often termed *repression* or *blocking*. Sometimes rather than face violations of our expectancies, we protect ourselves by denying their very existence. We quite simply do not recognize that which will be painful. In a husband and wife situation, one spouse may think the spare money ought to be spent one way and the other thinks the money ought to be spent another way. Rather than trying to get together and work out this problem, they simply try to pretend that it doesn't exist. Sometimes families that have a distinctive problem — an alcoholic parent or a child who is on hard drugs — deny that the problem exists. You may also find this in an opposite sex interaction — boy-girl, man-woman. One person may really love the other and think that the other loves him just as much. The other person may start to give leave-taking cues — not exactly like closing your books near the end of class, but similar. The perspectives of the relationship level are far apart. The second person may say to the other, "I really think that we're getting too serious. I'm not ready for marriage yet, and it's really time to start meeting other people." Because of the first person's love for the other and the anticipation of love in return, that individual many distort totally what the other person says and make it into a love stroke rather than a slap in the face. How many marriages today are still operative where one person does not want to be married to the other and the other person goes on saying, "Gee what a great thing we've got together"? They're distorting reality, distorting the violation and repressing their failure.

You do not realize you're denying reality, and it takes something of major impact to break through the distortion. Some people become so involved in their distorted reality that they can't break back through. Think of the number of mental illness cases. Many cases consist of a distortion of reality, a repression of the way things are. Quite often they combine this with a fantasy and instead of just daydreaming the fantasy, they distort reality to fit the fantasy world. They become totally obsessed with attempting to avoid negative states of reality. Consider the situation of college students who are getting all D's and F's. They may go along denying that they are getting these grades and say, "I can go out with the guys or the girls for a beer. I've got plenty of time to study later." They deny the negative state of the world.

RATIONALIZATION

The next resolution system is called rationalization. This is basically a way of explaining failure, rejection, or disappointment, or perhaps even a violation of society's expectations. It's a way of explaining when you become involved in what you feel is a negative state by providing a logical, rational reason for doing something that is really illogical. Have you ever justified cheating in class by saying that the information you are supposed to learn wasn't really important anyway, or that everybody cheats a little bit? What about those pens and pencils and paper you took from work? Do you rationalize that on the

"I don't care what your three witnesses say. My children didn't steal anyone's bike."

basis of, "It's a big company and they'll never miss them"? Are those the real reasons or just excuses for expectancy violations — rationalizations on your part? Have you ever rationalized hurting somebody's feelings by saying, "He deserved it"? Or have you ever shrugged off being hurt by a friend by saying, "Aw, he or she's just drunk and didn't realize what was done"?

We can find other examples of the rationalizing process. There is the example of the husband who comes home from work and starts snapping at his kids. The wife might say, "I understand how you feel, honey, but the kids didn't do anything wrong." And the husband responds, "Well, they deserved it for what they did yesterday. You can't tell me they weren't thinking about doing it again." Yes, we rationalize our way out of negative states.

One of the primary differences among these three closely connected techniques is method. They are all psychological ways of resolving a violation. Compensation is a substitution method whereby we substitute a good quality for a bad quality. The denial of reality method is to deny the existence of an expectancy violation. We don't substitute for the violation, we simply say it does not exist. In the rationalization method, we acknowledge that it exists, but we provide an excuse for its existence, which appears logical and consistent to us. Blaming is a type of rationalization that involves excusing oneself from negative feedback by shifting the cause of the problem to someone else. If a person needed to lose weight and if during interaction with others, the seat of the person's pants ripped, blaming would involve placing the fault with the manufacturer for using cheap material. Or when a guy is late for a date, he may shift the blame to his roommate for not waking him in time. Can you recall those instances where you have violated someone's expectancies (which is a violation of your own expectancies) and as you were approaching that person, you went over in your mind all the plausible reasons you could give. That's rationalization. Trust is an extremely important expectancy in forming close interpersonal relationships. Violation of those trusting expectancies are severe; hence, we tend to rationalize by shifting the burden of responsibility. These communications are obviously detrimental to the relationship.

IDENTIFICATION

The fourth method of resolving violations of our expectancies is through introjecting or identifying with our environment. Basically, this method involves incorporating what seems to be the desirable traits of others into our personal identity. In order to avoid negatives from others, we may hide our true feelings by imitating the feelings of those around us. The problem with identification of this sort is that it produces artificiality. We get so involved in being like someone else that we can't respond to a situation genuinely as ourselves. Instead, we react as our hero would react.

Occasionally, an imitated feeling or behavior becomes a part of our ideal identity. In our efforts to reach the ideal, we may tend to confuse reality. Most of us have a notion of the ideal family unit or the ideal marriage. Having conjectured as to the ideal spouse, we integrate those notions into our behavior. Sometimes after being married, we realize that our expectancies are being violated — we do not have that ideal marriage — and instead of backing off and examining the reasons for failure, we simply continue playing the role of the ideal spouse in the same manner we have since being married, perhaps even identifying with more traits from "Father Knows Best."

During the developmental years, identification is operative in forming an individual's conception of identity. It provides a means to determine what traits are desirable. We find further instances of such behavior late in life with individuals imitating the clothes and mannerisms of respected others. Friends moved from the North to the South. Within two years they had acquired a distinctive southern accent. Whenever we move to a new area, we are under pressure to gain acceptance. The tendency to yield to that pressure and to accumulate as parts of our identity the behavior or customs of those around us is very strong and not necessarily undesirable. The problem centers on the cutoff point. When do we stop being ourselves and become simply an imitation of our blended environment?

Identification does have it good points. One response to the question, "If I don't care much for who I am, how do I change?" lies in an area related to identification. If I really think I'm a hateful or spiteful person, and I really don't want to be that way, I may start by communicating like a warm, sensitive person. Typically this will be followed by extensive positive reinforcement from the environment indicating, "You're starting to act like a human being. You'll meet your belongingness and love needs a lot easier than before." Thus, one continues such loving behavior and ultimately the internalized notion that "I am a horrible person" will be replaced by the notion that "I am a loving person." This is only one way that identity may be altered, but it does provide a positive claim for the use of identification.

However, problems do develop when good attributes are altered through this process to become negative. This possibility contributes to some parental concern regarding a child attending college or an impressionable youngster "falling in with the wrong crowd." The primary concern we have with this technique is that of using it as a crutch instead of delving into the problem. We would suggest this is negative in terms of developing sound interpersonal relationships. Imitations are not the real thing.

ATTRIBUTION

Attribution involves shifting unacceptable or unpopular personal identity items or communication behaviors associated with them to someone else. How many loudmouths have you heard complaining about the loudmouth across the hall? How many gossips have you heard making derogatory remarks about other people gossiping? Think of this situation. You've been dating a person for some time and are asked to go on a weekend camping trip. You respond, "Gee, I'd really love to, but I have a big midterm examination coming up next week and I have to study." While there are many logical reasons for not going on the camping trip, including that you don't want to go, the situation has been resolved by attributing your decision to the need to study for a test rather than to what you really feel. Attribution is considered negative because it involves us in inconsistencies at an internal level. Specifically, it involves lies of varying degrees or at least the withholding of truth. As such, the lie can occasionally become the truth for the user. You see it in family quarrels and

business discussions. "Damnit! You're the one who's being unreasonable!"—
when the entire argument started with an unreasonable demand from the
person saying the above statement. And were you to ask the person later, odds
are the above statement would be repeated. Thus, this person's perspective of
the other individual was influenced by his or her own shortcomings and the
resultant attribution. Attribution of this nature does not do many positive
things for the development of stable interpersonal relationships.

REGRESSION

Regression is often related to the idea of dependency. It involves psychologically retreating from a situation to a prior period of our lives that involved
positive states. Most typically, it involves a period of our lives when we were
relatively helpless and dependent on someone else's assistance. Sometimes,
rather than admit that we don't want to do something, we convince ourselves
and others that we can't do it or that we just aren't ready yet to try it.
Regression also involves stereotypic communication behavior representing
earlier periods of our life, such as crying, not understanding, and general states
of overemphasis (that is, depression or happiness). In much the same way that a
child learns to manipulate parents through using this behavior, adults learn to
use similar behavior to manipulate others and themselves when confronted
with a violation of their expectancies. Out of fear of rejection, a fellow may
never approach a girl for a date and use the regression method of resolving his
violation of his own expectations. "Gee, I sure ought to ask her out, but I'm
just not ready to date yet." The employee may continually turn down offers for
promotion with additional responsibilities by saying, "I'm not sure I can
competently handle that job. I'm not quite ready for it yet." An individual
may regress in breaking off a relationship by inferring that "we just aren't
ready to settle down yet." The person who didn't keep a date and said, "I just
didn't understand that our date was Tuesday; I got all mixed up," may really
have cut out because of a last minute call from an old flame and may have been
using regression. Another example would be the person who cries over the
slightest incident.

   We can see extreme examples of regression in our mental institutions when
adults who cannot handle and get to the root of violations of their expectancies
regress totally to childhood. They go around sucking their thumbs, crying,
and performing all the behavior of the infant. In a sense, they are demanding
dependency — that someone take care of them. While the extreme cases tend
to repulse us, many of us use this technique to a lesser degree. Is it any
healthier, however? We strongly suggest that you make efforts to determine if

friends in need (either physical or psychological) truly are in need or if they're just copping out through regression. The former deserves all of your assistance; the latter all of your understanding.

REACTION FORMATION

Reaction formation is acting in a way that is an exaggerated opposite of how you really feel. Have you ever known someone who played the role of the life of the party — always laughing, always making jokes — but who really is unhappy? He's laughing on the outside, crying on the inside. Both males and females may handle a violation of their identity that concerns opposite sex attractiveness by collecting as many dates and sexual conquests as possible.

Most of us have experienced the blind date jitters. A friend may fix us up, we reluctantly accept, and unfortunately, the date is unsuitable. We feel horrible and wish we were somewhere else. Yet we continue to give off communication cues that we're having a great time — even to the extent of kissing goodnight. Sometimes we find ourselves trying to meet other's expectancies of us so hard that we become lost in the morass of roles. Employer's expectancies and typical reactions often fall into the category of reaction formation. Workers who are expected to "live in the style appropriate for a person in this position," involve themselves in the acquisition of material possessions. Wives who are expected to be good housekeepers often perform that function to extravagance while really preferring to develop occupations.

Some individuals who have had their belongingness and love need unsatisfied for some time (thus violating their expectancies of themselves) may completely give in on all personal values and communicate the exact opposite value or attitude. Sometime during a life, most people run across someone who is totally agreeable — not just on a few things but on everything. This may be the result of a reaction formation and involve an effort to act in an exaggerated opposite of the person's true feelings.

EMOTIONAL INSULATION AND APATHY

Often, rather than face an unpleasant situation, people will avoid being hurt by not getting involved or by pretending that they don't care. Probably the most common example of emotional insulation is that of the person who after developing a strong attachment to someone and then breaking up, refuses to become involved again because the pain is so great. In other words, he or she becomes removed and unapproachable. Other times persons who are hurt insulate themselves by becoming apathetic, by saying that they don't care about whoever hurt them. The sad thing about emotional insulation and apathy is that they prevent the person using them from doing anything about dealing with the cause of the problem. As long as such people say, "I don't care about dating" (but they really do), they can't go out with anyone, because this would be inconsistent with their artificial identity. As long as I don't admit that I care about you, our relationship has little chance of growing. This is a very difficult resolution to recognize in yourself and very difficult to change. It happened to us when we first started teaching this course. We didn't realize the openness of the teaching method involved in interpersonal communication courses. We didn't know how much an orientation toward learning instead of teaching would open one up to possible hurt from the student. A typical resolution was, "I don't care about students and all of this 'try to relate' nonsense," which was simply a way to try to get over what was experienced that wasn't expected. Luckily, we recovered as the warms outweighed the colds.

This type of resolution is found throughout the college and work environments. You blow a test: "I don't really care about grades anyhow." You don't get the promotion: "I didn't really want all the responsibility anyway." You get stood up on a date: "I don't really care about that person." You insulate yourself. The thing that you should remember is that you may convince yourself that this is an item in your personal identity. You may talk yourself into not caring. Then you believe that you don't care. To care would be inconsistent and we are striving not to be inconsistent. So once we start not caring, we tend to continue acting that way.

SWALLOWING BUT REMEMBERING

This resolution method involves putting the violation into the back of your mind and proceeding as if it didn't happen; yet remembering and storing all the violations until a point of explosion is reached. You may be in a small group situation when your friend puts you down or perhaps you're introducing someone new to your friend when he puts you down. Because you don't want an argument in this situation, you may cover it up, swallow it. But you really don't forget. You remember it and you stash it back in your subconscious. As the violations start to build up, the little stack of things back there gets higher and higher, and eventually the negative aspect of your friend's violation of your expectancies becomes so high that it begins to shift out of being a swallowed item and explodes into a huge confrontation. We would strongly suggest that this resolution procedure, while allowing one to overcome small immediate violations, ultimately results in negative implications for the relationship.

AVOIDANCE

This resolution method does not alleviate the immediate problem caused by the expectation violation, but does insure that the individual will not violate your expectancies again. By the same token, however, it literally destroys any potential to ever resolve the existing problem and certainly destroys any potential to further the relationship. Think of the last time you got angry with a fellow worker or student. Did you avoid that person by refusing to talk to him or her? Did you make sure that you stayed out of the same room? Did you go out of your way to avoid meeting on the street? We have seen the stereotyped fight between lovers when each refuses to answer the phone. Luckily, movies and television find some way to get them back together, but real life is not like the movies and television. Totally destroying the potential for communication destroys the potential for the relationship. Time is too short to spend it not in communication with our loved ones.

DISPLACEMENT

When our expectancies are violated, typically we become frustrated and wish to strike out, either physically or psychologically, at the individual who committed the violation. Many factors can prevent us from doing so. Thus, the frustration or hostility may be kept inside until someone who is in a less dangerous position becomes available. Then we take out our anger on this relatively innocent person. *Displacement* is the process of letting loose our emotional reaction to a violation on an individual other than the one who did the actual violating.

We often see this in business. When a manager has had a deal fall through that was expected to be successful, this violation of expectancies may often be handled by taking it out on the employees. If this is not appropriate or available, it may well be taken out on the spouse or children that evening.

Most of us have been snapped at by a friend for what appeared to be an innocent question or behavior. Most of us have done some snapping ourselves. Basically, this type of behavior is an effort to reduce the impact of a previous violation of expectancies. Unfortunately, in itself it may be a violation of our friend's expectations.

VERBAL AGGRESSION

This is one of the more popular techniques and consists of verbally attacking the person who has violated your expectations.

Have you ever watched a discussion grow into an argument? Part of the reason behind this turn of events is that one or both parties began to experience a violation of personal or social identity expectations. "I am losing this discussion and I'm not the kind of person who loses" or "I believe my fellow workers are perceiving me as losing this discussion and I am not the kind of person who loses." Given this violation of expectancies the individual may begin attacking and continue to accelerate that attack as the other individual responds in a similar manner. Thus, both parties may elect to handle the violation in the same way. It would seem evident that the verbal aggression technique will move the relationship in a negative direction.

PHYSICAL AGGRESSION

Quite often this is combined with verbal aggression or grows out of failure to reduce the violation through the verbal aggression technique (which is a violation in itself). It consists simply of physically attacking the violator.

Consider the friendly insult phenomenon. Some people have a tendency to literally insult their friends, expecting the insult to be taken as a stroke rather than a slap. "Hi there, Dummy!"; "What's happening, Fatso?"; "Hey, Turkey!"; and "Man are you ugly!" are examples. Occasionally, however, a friend does not realize the situational limitations of friendly insults. If physical aggression follows verbal aggression, the relationship may well terminate.

IDENTITY ALTERATION

With so many potential violations being associated with our identity factors, it is not unusual for a particularly major violation or a series of minor violations to be handled by altering facets of our identity and thus altering future expectancies. If a person thought of himself as a likable individual and over a period of time was continually unsuccessful in acquiring dates, he may handle this violation by shifting that personal identity item from likability to nonlikability and simultaneously shifting his expectations of other people's reaction to them.

Obviously, the inverse situation would produce a shift from an identity item of nonlikability to likability. Thus, we have another method of handling violations of our expectations that may have a positive result relative to the establishment of strong positive relationships.

"You don't listen, do you . . . !"

DEROGATION

This is closely associated with identity shift. However, instead of derogating oneself and thus ultimately shifting that personal identity item, one derogates the violator. When we have violated our expectancy of ourself, we may utilize blaming, but when others violate our expectancies, we tend not to question the expectancy or our perception, but to immediately infer negative qualities about the other individual's personal identity. This, of course, creates an image of the other that is not conducive to furthering the interpersonal relationship. Sometimes we swallow but remember and sometimes we utilize verbal aggression. Derogating another's intelligence, personality, or family heritage will likely lead to a violation of his or her expectations. That person may, in turn, utilize this technique in rebuttal. Then there is another round of you, then the other, and so forth, until the potential to understand approaches zero — and so does the relationship. Consider that one's personal identity includes the notion of being physically attractive and one's social identity is similar. If one of our friends were to remark, "Putting on a little weight these days, aren't you?" a violation of our expectancies would occur with the violation handled by a verbal attacking response such as, "Well, you don't exactly look like body beautiful yourself!" Obviously, this method of reduction does little to enhance the relationship.

EFFECTS ON COMMUNICATION BEHAVIOR

The impact of the resolution methods discussed thus far are detrimental and will detract from communication fidelity. All of the methods result in mental images that are not representative of an accurate perception of self or others. These incorrect mental images will later affect communication behaviors you engage in while attempting to establish interpersonal relationships. Some techniques are communication behavior in themselves — verbal and physical aggression, derogation of others, reaction formation, displacement, and avoidance. Such communication behaviors will in all likelihood be interpreted by others in such a way as to produce negative evaluations of the person using them. As other techniques are used at a psychological level, they tend to produce verbal and nonverbal communication cues that are representative of the new cognitions. Rationalization, for example, may occur internally to produce internal comfort, but would that be enough if friends did not understand your reasoning? Probably not. You would tend to communicate that rationalization to others. When one imitates the attitudes and values of others (identification), one cannot help but also communicate those changes to others. While attribution occurs internally, self-comfort is further enhanced by communicating it to others and receiving agreements.

In summary, mental activity in the form of resolution of expectancy violation becomes associated with the behavior in which one engages. That behavior is viewed by others as communication cues representing the type of person you are. On that basis they utilize the perception variables of attribution and causality to form an idea of your identity. In all likelihood that picture will not be consistent with the picture you maintain. We have discussed at length the complexities of fidelity communication in light of the importance of identity confirmation. The utilization of communication behaviors associated with these reduction techniques can only be detrimental to the achievement of actual consistency between the way an individual sees him or herself and the way that others see that person.

If this chapter has been read from the perspective of your life space, many of the manipulative techniques were probably absorbed with a negative impact. Just casual observation of ourselves and others will bring out numerous instances of their use. We do not suggest you spend your interpersonal communication time in analyzing everything you and others may say. We admit to having painted a rather bleak picture of the interpersonal communicator, but there is a bright side. There is an answer to the question, "Well now that I'm aware of all these negative aspects, what do I do about it?" The answer lies in a three-step process.

AWARENESS OF NEGATIVES

Much can be written on all the negative aspects of humanity, and we have only skimmed the surface of generalized techniques. The variety of ways and situations in which those techniques are applied is endless, and being aware requires a great deal of effort. Being aware means understanding those techniques and introspecting (looking into yourself) in many different situations to determine if your subconscious is utilizing them. There are so many aspects to merely existing that most of our mental activity is habitual and not known by the self to be operative. Self-awareness occurs through slowing down mental activity and examining your decision-making process. The complexity of one's existence and the continual shifting nature of the self makes this a long-term, if not endless, process.

DESIRE TO CHANGE

In the process of becoming aware, one may discern aspects of identity that one may think would have been better left unknown. The motivation to become aware and to change is produced by the potential expectancy of more comfort resulting from such efforts. If one does not expect a more comfortable existence, then such activity may well be detrimental. This is a decision that may be made only by an individual. In a sense, this book attempts to provide the awareness of another alternative to the present state of affairs oriented toward immediate but temporary comfort. A lifestyle consisting of manipulation of the self and others must be compared to a lifestyle of openness and fidelity. The decision, of course, is yours.

ACTION

Assuming one has engaged in becoming self-aware and desires to reduce the utilization of negative resolution methods, all that remains is to do so. Action consists of actively altering one's psychological and physical behavior. We must recognize that we do not psychologically or physically behave in a random manner. We decide how we are to behave. Admittedly, much of the decision-making process does not occur consciously; nor is each physical behavior preceded by an extensive review of evidence and projected alternatives and consequences. But somewhere in our development each of us decided on all controllable behavior. Decisions can be changed. New decisions can be made. Action involves behaving in such a way that over time actual changes in identity and communication representing that identity occur.

It is not easy and does take time and effort. The last method we offer for handling violations of your expectancies provides a means to change behavior both physically and psychologically.

UNDERSTANDING THROUGH INTERPERSONAL COMMUNICATION

This method of handling violations is one that produces positive behavior oriented toward moving an interpersonal relationship forward. It consists of verbalizing and describing the expectancy, its violation, and one's reaction to the individual who did the violating. These efforts will increase awareness and understanding between individuals in the relationship. Communicators using this method will have relationships with a solid, honest foundation. As such, the relationship will last longer and produce a higher level of satisfaction and comfort for both individuals. Individuals who have taken personal action regarding their psychological and physical behavior must realize that the vast majority of others have yet to do so. Thus, each will in a small sense be a teacher. One will quickly realize that not everyone will like the real person and in turn will discover that not everyone else is likable. But that is not bad, for when attraction does occur, it will be founded on truth rather than deceit and manipulation. Thus, interpersonal communication is a double-edged sword. On one edge is temporary satisfaction based on manipulation and on the other is long-term happiness based on fidelity between communicators.

CHAPTER SUMMARY

It's not easy for any of us to meet an actual or perceived violation of one of our expectancies head on. Perhaps this is why we commonly resort to coping strategies like distortion, rationalization, or regression. It's extremely important, however, that we realize such strategies amount to little more than kidding ourselves about the actual or perceived nature of things.

While it may be much more difficult to open up honestly to ourselves and others when expectancies have been violated, we believe such a process is far more desirable than some of the negative strategies discussed in this chapter. Painful as such a process may be, ultimately it may change us or the people we care for in a positive direction. That possibility, we think, makes the risk of pain worth taking.

THINK ABOUT IT

IN GENERAL

Complete the exercises given under Think About It: In General at the end of Chapter 1.

IN EDUCATION

Think back to a time when you used the process of either rationalization or attribution to resolve a violation of one of your expectancies about school. What do you think you gained as a function of employing these two intrapersonal means for resolving expectancy violations? What might you have gained if you would have communicated the violation to the person(s) involved? What communication skills (for example, trying to empathize) are necessary in situations where you try to communicate that an expectancy has been violated?

IN THE ORGANIZATION

1. Assume you and your spouse (or date) go to a party attended by those with whom you work. These coworkers are in a position to influence your career, and they are rigid in their thinking about the corporate image one's spouse (or frequent relational partner) communicates.

Perceiving this to be a stressful situation, your spouse (or date) indulges in too much alcohol and begins telling off-color jokes. This not only violates the expectancies of your coworkers, but also violates your expectancies about the role your relational partner should play in furthering your career. As a skillful communicator, how are you going to resolve this matter, that is, in terms of communicating with both your coworkers and relational partner?

2. Your company is involved in sensitive negotiations with the air force about an important defense contract. In the company of your superior, you meet with several air force officials to discuss your company's product and its features as compared with those of your chief competitor. Your superior comes across as extremely aggressive and pushy. This violates the expectancies of a majority of the officials, and you lose the contract. At a later date, you learn that your superior has told higher-ups in the company that the contract was lost because you were passive in the discussion. First, what might you have done as a communicator to resolve the violation in expectancies committed by your superior? Second, how are you going to communicate the violation to your own expectancies that your superior committed by attributing his own ineptitude to you? Finally, how are you going to communicate about this violation with those who have learned that your superior attributed his failure to you?

IN YOUR RELATIONSHIPS

At a social function you are introduced to a person who begins to disclose very intimate information. This violates your expectancies about communication during the acquaintance process. Should you communicate the violation? Why or why not? If you believe you should, how would you communicate but not offend this person?

SUGGESTED READINGS

Bennis, W. G. et al., eds. *Interpersonal Dynamics: Essays and Readings on Human Interaction.* The Dorsey Press, Homewood, Ill., 1973.

For the advanced students, this book of essays and readings explores a full range of human emotions as they relate to interpersonal relationships. Of particular relevance to this chapter are the essays in Part 1 and 11 that deal with emotions and the strategies for coping with them.

Lindgren, H. C. *Psychology of Personal and Social Adjustment.* American Book Company, New York, 1959.

Every chapter in this book is relevant to what we've just discussed. Chapter 5, which deals with patterns of defense and escape, should prove to be an invaluable supplement to the information that we have provided.

Part Three
Interpersonal Communication in Process

In Part 1 and Part 2 we demonstrated the interdependencies that exist between our interpersonal communication behavior, the personal and interpersonal needs we experience, and our individual identity systems. At this juncture, we shift our focus to questions concerned with the process by which humans develop, nurture, and maintain their associations through what they do and say.

Chapter 9 overviews self-disclosure and the process by which people gain access to their respective identity systems. Chapter 10 focuses on variables that influence us prior to and during our initial encounters with people, including interpersonal communication skills that can make our initial encounters more rewarding. Chapter 11 extends this information to the process by which people begin to define formally the nature of their associations, including their potential depth. Chapter 12 discusses intimate communication and intimate relationships, and details both the consequences of intimacy and the communication behavior that will sustain it. Chapter 13 addresses relational deterioration in terms of contributive and preventive communication. In the final chapter, we speculate about the future as it will relate to our relationships and the communication behaviors that will characterize them.

Chapter Nine
Revelations: Self-Disclosure and Identity Penetration

Self-disclosure Information we both intentionally and unintentionally reveal about ourselves.

Identity penetration The process by which we try to gain access to the public, private, and intimate information about another's identity.

Identity exchange The process by which people exchange information about themselves through purposeful, and usually, equitable self-disclosures.

Social exchange theory A theory that suggests that when person A gives something to person B, person B will return something of equal value.

Trust A special kind of expectancy about the probability of another person, who is in control of the risks we take, minimizing them for us.

Double blind Conflicting verbal and nonverbal messages.

On the surface, our relationships with other people seem to grow and deteriorate for unknown reasons. When pressed, for example, most of us find it difficult to explain in a less than superficial manner why we were either attracted or repulsed by a certain individual or group. Maybe that's why we so commonly resort to cliches, such as, "they're just beautiful people" or "we just don't seem to relate," in the effort to explain our interpersonal behavior.

Although all human processes seem to have their mystical side, interpersonal relationships are systematic, with phases that characterize the beginning and middle stages of a relationship and phases that signal that a relationship is about to end. These phases can be identified and distinguished from one another on the basis of interpersonal communication behaviors that characterize a relationship. In this chapter, we want to discuss what many have come to regard as the cornerstone of interpersonal communication and the development of interpersonal relationships: self-disclosure and identity penetration. These two terms refer to the process by which we reveal and gain access to our respective identity systems. Aside from their importance to the whole question of interpersonal communication, self-disclosure and identity penetration seldom are understood completely.

First, therefore, we will talk about the nature of self-disclosure, and second, we will address the question of why we need to disclose. Next, we will examine the concept of trust as it relates to disclosure, and then consider variables other than trust that influence disclosive messages. Finally, we will roughly sketch the process by which we reveal and gain access to our mutual identity systems and then briefly discuss some potential consequences of this process.

THE NATURE OF SELF-DISCLOSURE

Although self-disclosure has been studied for nearly three decades, to the communication theorist it is a relatively new area of inquiry. As a result, there is no universally accepted definition of self-disclosure nor is there widespread agreement as to what it does or does not involve. Thus, to begin with, realize that our discussion of its nature is not based on absolutes. Also, realize that self-disclosure appears simple on the surface. Nowhere is this more apparent than in some of the ways in which self-disclosure has been defined. For example, Cozby defines it as "any information about himself which person A communicates verbally to a Person B,"[1] while Wheeless and Grotz define it as "any verbal message about the self that a person communicates to another."[2] Don't let these definitions deceive you. Self-disclosure is not simply you revealing yourself to someone or vice versa. Self-disclosure is one of the most complex and elusive concepts with which scholars and students of communication are faced. And this is reflected by the fact that while self-disclosure frequently is talked about in books on interpersonal communication, it is seldom pinned down to a single, all-encompassing definition. Rather than attempting to define self-disclosure in a dictionarylike manner, consequently, we will describe some generalizations concerning its nature, specifically, in terms of its typical depth, where it is most likely to occur, and how it fits in with the notion of reciprocity.[3]

THE QUESTION OF DEPTH

Children are remarkably honest when it comes to opinions, emotions, and even self-concepts. If you ask children what they think of themselves, you can count on honest responses. As children grow older, however, they begin to learn that while honesty may be the best policy, it is not always adhered to when it comes to people revealing themselves. As R. D. Laing suggests, they learn to provide others with an "edited" version of themselves.[4]

Adults are experts at providing people with shallow and edited versions of themselves. What this means is that while we are revealing ourselves constantly by what we do and say, we are revealing very little concerning what we

---

[1]P. Cozby, "Self-Disclosure: A Literature Review," *Psychological Bulletin,* 35 (1970), 3.

[2]Lawrence R. Wheeless and Janis Grotz, "Conceptualization and Measurement of Reported Self-Disclosure," *Human Communication Research,* 2 (1976), 338.

[3]W. Barnett Pearce and Stewart M. Sharp, "Self-Disclosing Communication," *The Journal of Communication,* 23 (1973) 407–425.

[4]R. D. Laing, *The Politics of Experience,* Pantheon, New York, 1967.

are truly like. Self-disclosure most frequently concerns the superficial facets of our individual identities and infrequently concerns the deeper-seated facets of our identity systems. Thus, the first conclusion we can draw about the nature of self-disclosure is that it is shallow in relation to most of the people with whom we come in contact.[5]

THE QUESTION OF WHERE

In his book on dyadic communication, William Wilmot convincingly argues that the potential for intimate communication is much greater between two people than three or four.[6] Disclosures, therefore, concerning the deeper-seated facets of our identities most likely will occur when we are communicating with only one person. Generally speaking, third parties appear to inhibit self-disclosure. As Pearce and Sharp point out in their review of self-disclosure, this seems to be especially true when third parties are not directly involved in the communication transaction.[7] The second conclusion we can draw about the nature of more than shallow self-disclosures, then, is that they most likely will occur in dyads, that is, between two people.

THE QUESTION OF RECIPROCITY

In Chapter 3, we emphasized that, above all, the skilled interpersonal communicator is mindful of the idea of reciprocity. In terms of self-disclosure, we can look at the notion of reciprocity in one of two ways. One way of looking at it is in terms of safety.[8] When we disclose sensitive information about ourselves to a person, the person frequently may interpret the disclosure to mean we feel safe. In turn, this disclosure will be viewed positively and also make this person feel safe in our presence. Feeling secure in our presence, this person probably will reciprocate our initial disclosure by revealing information to us.

The second way we can look at reciprocity as it relates to self-disclosure is through social exchange theory.[9] This theory suggests that relational partners

[5]Pearce & Sharp, p. 5.

[6]William W. Wilmot, *Dyadic Communication: A Transaction Perspective,* Addison-Wesley Publishing Company, Reading, Mass, 1975, pp. 13–16.

[7]Pearce and Sharp, pp 417–418.

[8]Sydney M. Jourard, ed., "To Be or Not to Be — Existential Psychological Perspectives on the Self," University of Florida Monographs, Social Sciences 4, University of Florida Press, Gainesville, 1967.

[9]W. Worthy, A. Gary, and G. M. Kahn, "Self-Disclosure as an Exchange Process," *Journal of Personality and Social Disclosure,* 13 (1969), 59–63.

tend to exchange things of equal value. Thus, if you reveal something about yourself to a relational partner, he or she will return something to you that he or she perceives to have the same worth, for example, a revelation similar to the one you disclosed.

So far we have said that self-disclosure most frequently is shallow in depth, is more likely to occur in dyads than groups of three or four, and can be tied into the idea of reciprocity in one of two ways. Keep these generalizations about the nature of disclosure in mind, as we now turn to a question all of us have considered.

WHY DISCLOSE?

As we've already implied, we learn at an early age that the more intimate the information another possesses about us, the greater the pain this person can inflict upon us. It's unfortunate but not uncommon for people to use information that has been revealed to them as a psychological weapon during times of duress, for example, during an intense argument or when one of their expectancies has been violated severely. Remember the couple in Tom Wolfe's article who used information about each other as a form of one-upmanship? Why, then, should we tell people who we are or, more accurately, who we think we are? Why should we run the risk of having this information turned against us?

SO WE MAY KNOW

In *The Transparent Self,* the late Sydney Jourard seemed to say that we may have no way of knowing the motives of humankind unless we ask, and we have no right to ask unless we are willing to reveal. To Jourard, who was one of the pioneer researchers in self-disclosure, revealing oneself was a way of tuning into the environment and its people. But even more than that, Jourard felt that self-disclosure was a way of tuning in and understanding one's self. For example, any time we communicate with someone there will be portions of the person's identity of which we are not aware or that are hidden from us. While that may be perfectly obvious, there also will be facets of our own identities of which we are not aware. Joseph Luft and Harry Ingram have visualized this situation for us in what they call the "Johari Window."[10]

As can be seen in Figure 9-1, there are four quadrants in the "Johari

[10]Joseph Luft, *Group Processes,* National Press Books, Palo Alto, California, 1970, p. 15.

FIGURE 9-1
JOHARI WINDOW

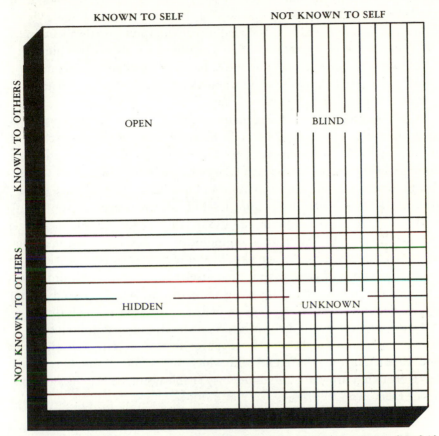

Reprinted from *Group Processes: An Introduction to Group Dynamics* by Joseph Luft, by permission of Mayfield Publishing Company (formerly National Press Books). Copyright © 1963, 1970 by Joseph Luft.

Window." These quadrants are designed to illustrate what is known or unknown about an individual in relationship to other people. The first quadrant consists of facets of our identity that are known to the self and to others. The second quadrant is a blind area, comprising identity items and behaviors that others are aware of in us although we are not (for example, pulling our earlobe while talking). The third quadrant is made up of identity items and behaviors of which we are aware but keep hidden from the person with whom we are communicating. Finally, the fourth quadrant is composed of deep-seated identity items of which we as well as others are not aware.

When one of these quadrants changes, it will affect changes in the remaining three. Further, the four quadrants may expand or contract depending on the nature of the interpersonal relationship. For example, two people who are in the process of becoming acquainted usually know very little about each other and may keep a great deal of information about themselves hidden. Thus, we would expect quadrant one to be quite small and quadrants two, three, and four to be large. Also, we would expect the fidelity with which these people communicate to be relatively low.

As people progress from the acquaintance stage of a relationship to friendship, the four quadrants depicted in the Johari Window will undergo changes, if the people engage in purposeful disclosures in the effort to increase the accuracy of their interpretations of each other's identity. In such a case, we would expect quadrant one to increase and quadrants two and three to decrease. Knowing more and keeping less hidden from each other, the fidelity with which the parties communicate also should increase. Beyond increasing the fidelity with which the parties communicate, however, purposeful disclosures should increase each person's knowledge of self. As we become friends, it is not uncommon to gain insight into ourselves as a function of our friend's communication behaviors. This seems to be the case whether friendship is established on the job, at school, or the places we live. At the very least, then, self-disclosure is a way of knowing. On one level, purposeful disclosures between people enable them to better approximate their respective identities and, thereby, increase the fidelity with which they communicate. On another level, though, purposeful disclosures may enable people to gain new insights about their own identities.

INTENTIONALIZING COMMUNICATION

As we pointed out in Chapter 2, our verbal and nonverbal communication behavior is disclosive whether or not we intend it to be. The instant people become aware of us, they begin to evaluate and make inferences about us on the basis of clues they find in our communication behaviors. Since our communication behaviors are not always intended to provide people with clues about our identities, they may misinterpret our behaviors or mistakenly attribute certain characteristics to our identities. For instance, most of us have been in situations where, unbeknown to us, a person has made a negative judgment about us as a result of our unintentional communication. Had we been aware of what we unintentionally disclosed to this person, no doubt we would have attempted to change the person's judgment. On yet another level, purposeful disclosures may diminish the probability of people misinterpreting each other's communication, or inappropriately assigning certain characteristics to their respective identities.

NEEDS

At this point, you probably know all too well that the probability of satisfying your needs depends on how skillfully you communicate in the effort to satisfy them, and how well your communication behaviors assist other people in satisfying the needs that they experience. For the most part, however, people are not completely aware of communication behaviors in which they engage to tell others that they are experiencing certain needs. Few of us are in the habit of saying, "By the way, Susan, I'm currently experiencing a strong need for social inclusion. Can I come over?" By the same token, most of us would not know how to react if a person were to communicate in a similar fashion to us. In effect, this means that most of us rely on the interpretive abilities of others to decipher the needs our communication behaviors represent and vice versa.

But is it really wise to put our faith solely in the interpretive skills of other people, considering that these skills vary from person to person and from relationship to relationship? Might it not be wiser for us and the people with whom we come in contact to communicate about our needs more explicitly? Certainly there are outer bounds regarding what needs we should communicate explicitly to other people. Within these bounds, however, wouldn't you agree that the probability of your needs, as well as those of your relational partner, being satisfied would increase as a result of purposeful disclosures?

Along the same lines, think about the issue of need compatibility. How often do people make inappropriate judgments about the degree to which their needs are compatible or incompatible as a result of failing to bring their respective needs out into the open? While we are unaware of specific research in this regard, we would speculate that the number is quite high. You'll recall from the first part of this book that need compatibility is something that people will negotiate and renegotiate throughout the life of an interpersonal relationship. But how can people realistically negotiate the extent to which their needs are compatible unless they purposefully disclose their needs to each other?

As you can see, purposeful disclosures involving needs may serve two highly useful ends. First, purposeful disclosures of needs may increase the likelihood of these needs being satisfied. Second, such disclosures also may assist people in negotiating the degree to which their respective needs are compatible.

CONSISTENCY

The psychological need for consistency is a strong motivational force. And this is particularly true with respect to our personal, social, and ideal identities. The process of self-disclosure is one of the primary ways people attempt to maintain or achieve consistency within their individual identity systems.

To illustrate this point, we offer the case of Max Black, a friend and long-time colleague. For some time, Max has provided communication training to supervisors employed by federal, state, and local governments. During one of these training sessions, Max noticed a person who appeared to greet everything he said with some measure of disbelief. Although this person didn't say anything orally, the person's nonverbal communication behavior strongly suggested that he regarded Max as anything but credible. Given Max's own belief that he was good in such training seminars (personal identity) as well as the positive feedback he perceived he had received from participants in previous sessions (social identity), this person's communication behavior was causing him to experience psychological inconsistency.

Rather than ignore the person, which would accomplish little in the way of restoring consistency to his identity system, Max approached this person during a coffee break and disclosed his feelings. In turn, the person disclosed some highly incorrect perceptions about Max. Specifically, the person told Max that given his young age, dress, and position in life he could tell he was born with a silver spoon in his mouth, welched off mom and dad through college, and had never gotten his hands dirty as a result of manual labor. Max set the record straight, pointing out that he was reared in a middle-class family, worked throughout his undergraduate career, and was supported by an assistantship in graduate school.

From here on, the two were able to communicate with each other in an effective manner, and Max's former picture of himself was restored. Had Max failed to engage in purposeful disclosure, though, the situation in all likelihood would have deteriorated, and Max would have continued to experience inconsistency. That is, unless the other person, who was experiencing inconsistency as a result of being trained by someone he regarded as incredible, took the initiative and disclosed to Max.

There are good reasons for people to engage in purposeful self-disclosures. In addition to helping us maintain psychological consistency, purposeful disclosures: (1) provide us with a way to know others as well as better know ourselves; (2) can assist us in minimizing the impact of unintentional communication; (3) aid in the satisfaction of needs or determining the extent to which they are compatible with those of our relational partners; and (4) potentially increase the fidelity with which we communicate.

TRUST: JUST BETWEEN YOU AND ME . . .

If we were forced to choose the single most important factor that influences self-disclosure, we would say it is the concept of trust. When it comes right down to the bottom line, the degree to which people feel safe in purposefully revealing themselves to each other depends on the degree to which they trust each other. What does the concept of trust really mean?

A SPECIAL KIND OF EXPECTANCY

Trust is an expectancy about another person. Morton Deutsch, a leading scholar in the area of conflict, defines trust in the following way:

> An individual may be said to have trust in the occurrence of an event if he expects its occurrence and his expectation leads to behavior which he perceives to have greater negative motivational consequences if the expectation is not confirmed than positive motivational consequences if it is confirmed.[11]

According to Deutsch, then, we trust other human beings when we engage in risks of which they are largely in control and we expect them to minimize the risks involved in the behavior with which we engage. Your instructor, for example, might want you to pair off with a classmate and participate in an exercise that demonstrates what is being suggested. This exercise involves being blindfolded and led around various parts of the campus that are replete with obstacles. While there are risks involved and your partner largely is in control of them, you should expect your partner to minimize them for you. In other words, if you engage in the exercise, you will have to trust your partner.

THE EFFECTS OF TRUST

Given the obvious relationship between trust and self-disclosure, you would think a great deal of research has been conducted in this area. This has not been the case. What research has been done, however, has produced some surprising and interesting results. While trust seems to be necessary for self-disclosures, trust doesn't necesssarily guarantee self-disclosure.[12] It appears to depend on the conscious intent of one's self-disclosures as well as one's attitudes toward self-disclosure.

As you can well imagine, much of what we disclose to others is unintentional and vice versa. Evidently, trust is not too important in this respect. In terms of self-disclosures that are based on conscious intent, though, trust

---

[11]Morton Deutsch, "Trust and Suspicion," in *Interpersonal Communication: Survey and Studies,* ed. D. C. Barnlund, Houghton Mifflin Company, New York, 1965, p. 422.

[12]Wheeless and Grotz, pp. 338–346.

appears to be essential. It is this latter finding that is most important to interpersonal communication and the development of interpersonal relationships. This is because, as we stressed earlier, one of the things purposeful disclosures can assist us in is intentionalizing our communication behavior.

Finally, not all people share the same attitudes about disclosure. Some people may characteristically disclose as a function of their attitudes, whereas others may disclose little as a result of their attitudes. Women, for example, seem to engage in much more self-disclosure on a regular basis than men.[13] While this may mean women are more trustful of others than are men, more research on the subject is needed. In any case, remember that trust is highly significant when it comes to purposeful self-disclosures.

BUILDING TRUST

Unfortunately, there are no cookbook strategies for people to follow in the attempt to establish mutual trust. To be certain, a good measure of plain old common sense won't hurt in this regard. And it is in this light, that we present the following guidelines.

Honesty It's only natural for humans to try to convey the best possible image of themselves during initial transactions. For example, if we interview for a job we desperately want, we will attempt to verbally and nonverbally communicate (for example, by dress) in a way that we perceive will aid us in landing the position. By the same token, we engage in similar communication behaviors on first dates or when trying to gain favorable acceptance from a desirable social group. Such behaviors are certainly understandable.

The issue that needs to be addressed, though, is whether it is ethical to misrepresent our identity through what we do and say in the effort to gain acceptance from a potential employer, mate, or social group. It seems to us that we have a responsibility to disclose an accurate picture of our identity to those we meet. Deception and misrepresentation have no part in interpersonal communication. What's more, when we employ such communication strategies, we are fooling no one but ourselves. While deception and misrepresentation may work to our advantage during an initial encounter, our false front inevitably will be discovered in subsequent encounters. Of course, any trust present in the relationship also will be destroyed as a result of our deceit.

How can I put this? In addition to being honest about ourselves, we need to be as honest as we can about our feelings toward others when we meet. At an

---

[13]James C. McCroskey and Lawrence R. Wheeless, *An Introduction to Human Communication,* Allyn and Bacon, Boston, 1976.

all-day bridge tournament several years ago, a noon luncheon was served with ice cream for dessert. About four o'clock in the afternoon, a couple approached our table. One individual had a medium-sized red beard. In the lower left corner of his beard was a glob of ice cream. Imagine, the people at the bridge tournament had allowed this gentleman to circulate for four hours unconsciously sporting ice cream in his beard. He was slightly embarrassed but more than grateful when informed of his noon meal error. The moral of this story is, For crying out loud, don't let your friends walk around with ice cream in their beards. If they are doing something subconsciously that others may be misinterpreting, let them know about it, not to rub it in or make them feel bad, but for the purpose of letting them know that others may be misinterpreting a particular set of communication cues.

Along these lines, it might be to your benefit to sit down with a trusted friend and exchange information about your communication cues in different situations in light of the possibility that others may misinterpret them. A former student engaged in this disclosure activity and gained valuable insight into herself. As a part of her personal identity, she believed she was a friendly person who always took time to be with other people. She sat down with a girl friend and spent about half an hour trying to get her friend to disclose whether she had any "ice cream in her beard." Finally the friend realized that she was trying to improve the fidelity of her communication and opened up. It seemed that several girls had been talking about how she always was on the go and never really seemed to have time to sit and talk with people who were supposed to be her friends. Our student was, of course, astounded. After careful and minute examination of her behavior, she and her friend realized that she had developed a habit of playing with her keys. She would carry them in her hand and jingle and twist them without being aware of it. Apparently her friends attended to this as a purposeful communication cue and interpreted it as an indication she had somewhere better to go. This, of course, was entirely wrong, yet the people attributed an air of superiority to her. If it had not been for the brief but honest disclosure session, that identity error and the erroneous communication cue would probably still be operative today.

Honesty, albeit in concern with ourselves or others, is fundamental to the establishment of mutual trust. And this holds true for relationships on the job, at school, and the places where we live. Honesty also is communicated through the consistency between what we disclose and how we actually behave.

BARRIERS TO TRUST

Just as we need to be mindful of the factors that facilitate the establishment of mutual trust, we also need to be mindful of the factors that can lead to its erosion once it has been established. Again, a large measure of common sense is involved in trying to avoid barriers to trust.

Expectancy Violations Since we've already discussed the negative consequences of expectancy violations, we want only to re-emphasize here that trust is a highly special kind of expectancy — an expectancy that is based on the perception that relational partners will assist each other in minimizing the risks they take in relationship to each other. On occasion, people will violate this special expectancy. Recurrent violations in this regard, though, will erode the foundation on which people have built their perceptions of trust.

The Double Blind A second barrier to trust is the double blind, a specific communication problem that consists of one person emitting simultaneous communications that are in conflict — saying one thing verbally and the opposite nonverbally. The parent who tells a child how much he or she is loved while slapping the child with a belt is committing a double blind. This causes confusion on the part of the attender as to what the other really means and ultimately what the other person is really like. We see numerous expressions of this in interpersonal communication situations. For example, in rejecting an invitation, it is not uncommon for us to say one thing verbally and something quite different nonverbally. In telling Jack that she thought he was extremely nice and she was sorry she could not accompany him, Cheryl avoided his stare and discreetly increased the distance separating them. Usually the double blind is viewed as an inconsistency and brings about frustration and anxiety. This lack of clarity regarding the other's intended meaning brings about an aura of distrust as the person is unable to establish and verify positive expectations.

Communication Denial Our expectancies about each other periodically need a shot in the arm. That is, they periodically need to be reaffirmed through what we do and say. Once we have established mutual perceptions of trust with someone, there is no guarantee it will be maintained. One of the more obvious ways we can chip away at mutual perceptions of trust is simply to avoid the communication behaviors that gave rise to them in the first place. Let's face it, few of us ever feel so secure in a relationship that we do not need a little reassurance once in a while. When we deny trustful communication to someone, we also deny the person this kind of reassurance.

CONCLUDING REMARKS ON TRUST

Earlier in this chapter, we emphasized the fact that purposeful self-disclosures are necessary for the initiation, maintenance, and growth of our interpersonal relationships. We added that trust is fundamental to purposeful self-disclosures. Self-disclosure and trust, consequently, also reflect the idea of reciprocity as it relates to interpersonal communication.

BEYOND TRUST: OTHER INFLUENCES

Important as trust is to purposeful self-disclosures, it is not the only factor that influences disclosive messages between people. Other important factors that have an impact on self-disclosure are: (1) prior experience and risk, (2) assumptions about time, (3) and the transactional components we discussed in Chapter 2.

PLEASE DON'T HURT

Just how much we engage in the process of self-disclosure depends in part on our past experiences and the degree to which we perceive that risks are involved. If our past revelations to people seemed to promote growth in ourselves and in our relationships, we most likely will have positive attitudes about self-disclosure in the present and future. On the other hand, if we revealed ourselves to others and they used this information to hurt us, we will be cautious and reluctant to disclose ourselves. Most of us have had both kinds of experiences. Most of us have experienced situations in which a disclosure assisted us to gain insights into ourselves or to improve the relationship with the person who received the disclosure. Then again, most of us have been in situations where a revelation to someone was exploited.

Self-disclosure involves some element of risk. Whenever we tell others about ourselves, we run the risk of rejection, ego deflation, or other negative communications. Perhaps this is one of the primary reasons that self-disclosure most frequently is shallow. But life is full of risks that are necessary to take. To achieve fidelity in communicating or to maintain need compatibility, self-disclosure is a necessary risk. Thus, the real question is not whether people should disclose, but when should people disclose. The ability to discriminate in this regard is not acquired easily. Most of us have trouble in objectively weighing the potential risks that self-disclosure involves against the potential rewards that can result from self-disclosures.

TIME

In order to become skilled at making decisions about appropriate or inappropriate situations for self-disclosures, we must recognize the importance of time. In our discussion of the Johari Window, we suggested that as people spend more time with each other, they will keep less about themselves hidden.

Self-disclosure is an incremental process.[14] This means that the more we reveal to others about ourselves, the more we can expect these others to reveal to us. Even so, the probability of self-disclosure depends on how safe we feel in doing so. How many people do you feel safe with when it comes to more than shallow disclosures? How much time did you spend with these people prior to feeling safe in disclosing more than shallow information to them?

One of the more common mistakes people make in their initial transactions is to rush self-disclosures. While it is all right to disclose a lot of information during initial transactions, people have expectancies about the level of self-disclosures in such situations. During initial transactions we expect to learn a great deal of superficial information about someone, for example, major, course load, academic rank, present or intended occupation, home town, and so forth. However, we do not expect people to tell us that they have severe doubts about their emotional stability, like to be tied up, or prefer to drink champagne from a spike-heeled shoe. By the same token, the people with whom we are just becoming acquainted do not expect such revelations from us.

Time allows people to make more accurate assessments about each other. At a minimum, it enables them to determine more accurately the extent to which their needs are compatible and their identities are similar. In turn, these more accurate assessments enable people to decrease the potential errors that they are prone to make in their initial transactions.

Of course, there are exceptions to what we are suggesting here. Some people seem to immediately hit it off, reveal intimate information about themselves, and build a thriving relationship. Such cases, though, are rare. Generally, people need time to make sound judgments about the appropriate depth of their disclosures.

TRANSACTIONAL INFLUENCES

In Chapter 2 we discussed the fact that communication is transactional, that it involves our triparte perceptions, simultaneous encoding and decoding, and the environment. Disclosive messages also involve these three factors.

Direct, Meta- and Meta-meta-perspectives   You'll recall from Chapter 2 that how we view someone is called a direct perspective. This may have a significant influence on self-disclosive behavior. Whether we view a person as trustworthy or untrustworthy, for example, may have little impact on our

[14]Pearce and Sharp, p. 421.

unintentional disclosures. When it comes to purposeful disclosures, which we regard as essential to relational involvement, our direct perspective concerning trust is of major consequence.

When we begin to communicate with people, we develop a picture of how they view themselves on the basis of what they disclose to us. You'll remember we called this your meta-perspective. Again, how we think people view themselves influences our purposeful disclosures, but just what influence our meta-perspective has depends on our intentions in relation to them.

Finally, decisions concerning self-disclosure also are affected by what we think that other people think about our feelings toward them that is, our meta-meta-perspective. Here, it is important to recognize that our meta-meta-perspective will vary in terms of accuracy. As a result, the confirmation of it can be achieved only if we view the person as trustworthy enough to reveal intentionally what we think he or she thinks we feel.

Simultaneous Sending and Receiving Even as we engage in verbal self-disclosures, we attend to what is being disclosed nonverbally by the other person. On the basis of these nonverbal disclosures, we make inferences about another's feelings toward us and adapt our verbal behavior accordingly. During a job interview, for instance, we are forced to disclose information about ourselves. However, as we disclose this information we will search for clues in the interviewer's behavior that may cause us to adapt our disclosive messages.

Environments The environment does or should influence the pattern of self-disclosure between people. In Part 2, we discussed behavioral sets and situational identity based on the situational index. We suggested that certain situational identities are appropriate in some but not all environments (for example, assuming the role of child at work). So it is with respect to self-disclosure.

Just as people have expectancies about the relationship between time and self-disclosure, they also have expectancies about what should be disclosed in certain environments. It is important, therefore, that we learn what these expectancies are prior to running the risk of disclosing inappropriately. If these expectancies are consistent with our own, we will have little difficulty in abiding by them. Then again, if they are inconsistent with our own, we may want to change ourselves or work for constructive change in others.

CONCLUDING REMARKS

Stripped to the barest of essentials, interpersonal communication concerns the meeting and merging of identities. Such a meeting and merger would be impossible if people were not willing to reveal their identities to each other. Thus far in the chapter we have attempted to describe self-disclosure in terms of what it is and what it involves. Toward that end, we have said that self-disclosure is primarily shallow in a majority of cases, most likely to become less than shallow in dyadic relationships, and that it is inseparably tied to the idea of reciprocity. We indicated the necessity of purposeful disclosures between people and discussed its relationship to a very special kind of expectancy — trust. Finally, we examined factors other than trust that affect the timing of our disclosive messages. Given this framework, we will now roughly sketch the process by which our identities meet and merge, and discuss some of the potential consequences of this process.

IDENTITY PENETRATION

As we have said, the identity system is comprised for four parts: core identity, ideal identity, personal identity, and social identity. It is also composed of public, private, and intimate levels of information.[15] The questions we want to address at this point seemingly are simple: How do people reveal and gain access to these various levels of information which comprise their respective identities, and what are the potential consequences of this process?

THE IDENTITY SYSTEM: GAINING ENTRANCE

Figure 9-2 approximates the identity system to show that it is comprised of public, private, and intimate levels of information. You will note that the area in the center of the circle is labeled intimate information and is bordered by private and public information.

Think of the figure as the identity system of another individual. Try to imagine that you are standing outside the circle and desire to gain entrance. You approach the outermost periphery of the system, labeled public information, and find that it is highly permeable. Gaining entrance, you move forward into the public facets of the individual's identity, periodically stopping to evaluate your progress. As you approach the area labeled private information, you begin to notice that it's more difficult to move ahead.

[15]Irwin Altman and Dallas A. Taylor, *Social Penetration: The Development of Interpersonal Relationships*, Holt, Rinehart, and Winston, New York, 1973.

FIGURE 9-2
IDENTITY SYSTEM FROM AN INFORMATION PERSPECTIVE

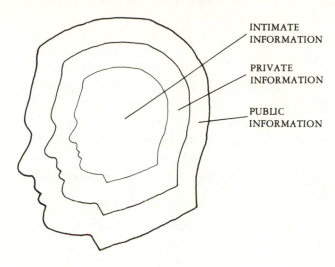

INTIMATE
INFORMATION

PRIVATE
INFORMATION

PUBLIC
INFORMATION

Nonetheless, you gather your strength and, eventually, reach the perimeter of the area that houses private information about the person. You try to gain entrance, but find that the perimeter is highly impermeable — impossible to penetrate. You back off and decide to explore the perimeter in its entirety, reasoning that you may find a point of entrance along the way.

As you move along the perimeter that fences private information about the person, you are distracted by items of public information that were heretofore unknown to you. Puzzled, you stop to familiarize yourself with each of these items of information, temporarily losing sight of the perimeter shielding private information about the person. But once you have become familiar with these new items, your attention again returns to the next perimeter and what lies beyond. This time the perimeter appears more permeable and the private information it protects more accessible. Your perception proves correct. You gain entrance and access to private information about the individual and the process begins anew.

As we said in our summary of self-disclosure, interpersonal communication basically concerns the meeting and merging of identities. What we have described here is simply the process by which one individual attempts to gain entrance to the exceedingly resistant facets of another individual's identity system. In reality, of course, the penetration of identity systems is a reciprocal one. People in a relationship exchange identities as a function of their needs, time, and purposeful self-disclosures. These exchanges begin with the superficial, nonintimate areas of their respective identity systems.

PUBLIC INFORMATION

The facet of our individual identities that appears to be most visible and most permeable is comprised of the things that make us public people, for example, the way we look, the way we dress, and even the way we talk in various environments. As we described the process, gaining entrance to the public side of our identities is relatively easy because the information that makes up this part of our identity system is visible to anyone who happens to attend to us in a given situation.

But you should not think that the public facets of identity are without consequence simply because they are accessible to most anyone. Decisions about initiating communication are largely a function of how people perceive public information as it relates to an individual's identity. If people decide to communicate on the basis of public information and the communication is sustained, they may very well exchange deeper-seated facets of their identities, that is, information of a more private nature. As long as these exchanges serve to satisfy their mutual needs, there is a good chance that the people will share the information comprising their respective identities even further.

However, this does not necessarily mean that identity exchange will be in the direction of private or intimate information. While people may move in this direction at this stage of their relationship, there is no guarantee that identity exchange will continue toward the center of the identity system. Instead, their exchanges may focus on items of public information that they have yet to reveal to each other, for example, items of public information that may be relevant in some social context other than the present one.

We have visualized this situation for you in Figure 9-3. The arrow indicates the depth of identity penetration. The area that is shaded represents the amount of public information that they have exchanged. As you can see, each person has penetrated deeply into the area of identity concerned with public information. But they have exchanged only small amounts of public information about themselves, that is, public information that is relevant in social contexts other than the present one.

At work, for example, people may penetrate deeply into their respective public selves as these public selves relate to the work environment. Assuming their public selves vary with the environments in which they find themselves, though, some public information would remain unknown. When we say public information is readily accessible, therefore, we mean it is accessible as it relates to a given environment at a given point in time. As a result, the penetration and exchange of public information in one, two, or even three

FIGURE 9-3
PUBLIC INFORMATION

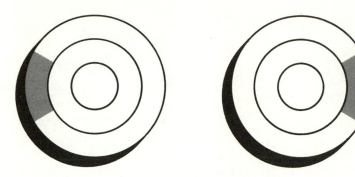

contexts does not mean that identity penetration and exchange will move from public to private information.

PRIVATE INFORMATION

When placed in the context of public information, identity penetration and exchange is more accidental than intentional. It simply comes about as a function of two people attending to one another. When placed in the context of private information, however, identity penetration and exchange become more intentional as a result of purposeful self-disclosures and penetrating questions.

As stated earlier, adults are quite skilled at revealing edited versions of themselves. They seem instinctively cautious about revealing or allowing other people to penetrate the private information concerning them. Remember Christine Chubbuck. None of the people she worked with felt that Chris had ever been above board with them about what she really thought of herself. Perhaps she was overly cautious because she was afraid that she only would be hurt further by revealing private information about herself. Maybe, to a certain degree, this is true of all of us.

In most instances, we would not expect simple acquaintances to penetrate the private information of each other's identity system. But if a relationship serves to satisfy mutual needs, has evolved over a significant span of time, and sufficient amounts of public information have been exchanged, the participants may begin to penetrate and exchange private information. Initially, the depth of this penetration will be quite shallow, and it will give the participants in the relationship a chance to evaluate the impact of this first exchange. If they evaluate the initial exchange positively, they may make private information about themselves even more accessible to each other. As was the case with the exchange of public information, this new accessibility may be reflected in

FIGURE 9-4
PRIVATE INFORMATION

terms of the depth of identity penetration or in terms of the amount of private information they've exchanged.

In Figure 9-4 we show what the identity systems of two people might look like during this stage of their relationship. You will note that the people have revealed approximately the same amount of private information about each other and penetrated the private side of each other's identity to approximately the same depth. You may also note, however, that the areas of private information that have been exchanged are different. This indicates that private information revealed during the exchange process need not correspond identically. For example, one person may reveal private information that pertains to attitudes about masculine and feminine roles, whereas the other person may reveal private information pertaining to attitudes about premarital sex or extramarital affairs. Thus, the items of private information exchanged would be different, but similar in the sense that they reflect private thoughts in relation to their respective identity systems.

Once people penetrate and exchange private information, decisions are made about further identity penetration and identity exchange. While the people may judge the relationship sufficiently rewarding to engage in deeper identity penetration, the reverse also may be true. That is, the people in the relationship may decide that the relationship for the time being has gone far enough. This in no way means the relationship is less than it should be. If the people feel that further identity exchange is not warranted at present, it simply means that they feel comfortable with the existing state of their relationship. This feeling may be sustained throughout the life of the relationship, or it may change as a function of need satisfaction and need compatibility, time, and purposeful self-disclosures.

INTIMATE INFORMATION

That facet of our identity system kept most secret from other people is comprised of intimate information about ourselves. Intimate information may

FIGURE 9-5
TWO RELATIONSHIPS WHERE IDENTITY PENETRATION HAS REACHED THE SAME
DEPTH

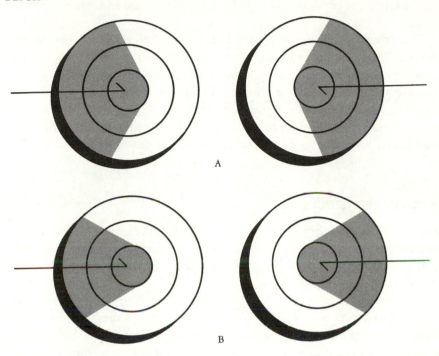

A

B

concern things like psychological insecurities, hang-ups, and fantasies ranging from realistic to absurd. The penetration and exchange of private information occurs in only a handful of relationships because of the potentially volatile
nature of such information.

Figure 9-5 depicts two relationships. While the depth of identity penetration is the same for both relationships, the amount of information exchanged
at each level of identity is different. In the first relationship (A), the principals
have exchanged large amounts of public and private information. In the second
relationship (B), however, the principals have exchanged a great deal less
public and private information.

The latter situation can be looked at in several ways. First, the principals
may have consciously provided each other with skillfully edited versions of
themselves in the attempt to accelerate identity penetration. Second, they may
have narrowed the focus of their relationship to specialized private and
intimate information that both perceive necessary to reach some goal.

The first perspective suggests the principals engaged in deception and
misrepresentation for some self-serving end, for example, gaining temporary
sexual favors. This practice has been termed by John Daly, a friend and
colleague, "instant intimacy." The second perspective, however, suggests that

the process of identity penetration and exchange intentionally was accelerated, but for some common goal, for instance, completing an assigned task at work that required the exchange of limited amounts of private and intimate information.

Thus, the first relationship depicted (A) is apt to be an enduring one because the principals have spent sufficient time at each level of identity to make accurate judgments about the potential of the relationship. Depending on the underlying motivations of the principals in the second relationship, we would expect their relational ties to be temporary or limited to a specific context like the work environment. As is the case with most of the interpersonal processes we discuss, however, there occasionally are exceptions to this conclusion.

POTENTIAL CONSEQUENCES

As the identities of people merge, there are a number of potential outcomes that are positive in nature. Since this chapter is intended as an overview, we will discuss a number of potential consequences briefly and expand or add to this discussion in the remaining chapters.

Uncertainty Reduction When people meet for the first time, they experience a high degree of uncertainty, because they have little information about their respective identity systems and because they are not sure about the outcome of their meeting.[16] As people learn more about one another through revealing and gaining access to their identities, this uncertainty and the anxiety that accompanies it will begin to disappear. Since anxiety can undermine our interpersonal communication skills, this also means that the potential for communication error will diminish as people come to better know each other.

Communication Fidelity Our abilities to interpret each other's messages as they are intended to be interpreted are limited to what we know about each other's experiences and feelings. When we first meet people, these abilities are restricted severely. As we learn more about the experiences and feelings of people we meet, our abilities to accurately interpret their messages increase and vice versa. Of course, this learning process occurs as a function of identity penetration and exchange.

Need Satisfaction and Compatibility Need satisfaction depends on interpersonal communication skills. We've already said that our skills in deciphering the real meaning of another's messages increases as we learn more about the person. Also, the ability of people to determine the extent to which their needs are compatible will reflect how much they know about one another.

Identity Maintenance and Change Confirmation of what we think about ourselves is provided by communication behaviors of those with whom we come in contact. As long as our interpretations of behavior are consistent with our feelings about ourselves, our present identity will be maintained. In discussing the Johari Window, however, we pointed out that self-disclosure sometimes provides us with new insights about our identities. On occasion, these insights will cause us to experience inconsistency, and we will change our identities for the better in order to restore consistency. Thus, identity penetration and exchange also are the means by which our identity is maintained or altered.

Expectancies Finally, people's expectancies about each other are only as accurate as the information on which they are based. The probability of people possessing accurate information about each other increases as they exchange knowledge about each other. It follows, then, that identity penetration and exchange should increase the validity of people's expectancies about each other.

CONCLUDING REMARKS

As the preceding discussion suggests, the meeting and merging of identities tends to be orderly and sequential. The exact order and sequence, however, depend on a host of factors beyond needs, time, and purposeful self-disclosures. Beginning with the next chapter, we will bring some of these factors into focus.

CHAPTER SUMMARY

In this chapter, we provided a broad overview of interpersonal communication in process. This overview includes a discussion of self-disclosure, which is the cornerstone of interpersonal communication and interpersonal relationships. We described three generalizations concerning the nature of self-disclosure and suggested that purposeful self-disclosures are important for many reasons. Following this, we emphasized the importance of trust to purposeful disclosure and described a number of other important factors that affect disclosive messages. We also provided a rough sketch of the process by which we reveal and gain access to our respective identity systems, and discussed potential consequences of this process. In the next chapter, we will elaborate on this process in terms of what affects initial interpersonal communication encounters and the skills that are involved.

THINK ABOUT IT

IN GENERAL

Complete the exercises given under Think About It: In General at the end of Chapter 1.

IN EDUCATION

1. We have suggested that purposeful disclosures reduce uncertainty and potentially can increase the fidelity with which people communicate. Since high uncertainty and low fidelity will hinder learning, what should be expected in the way of purposeful disclosures between teachers and students? At what level of their identities (that is, public, private, and intimate) should students and teachers engage in identity penetration and exchange?

2. Your school work is being hindered by severe problems at home. While your teachers should know this, you are reluctant to disclose this information because of its private nature. How does trust come into play in this regard, and how would a skilled communicator broach the subject with teachers?

IN THE ORGANIZATION

1. In working with organizational personnel, we consistently have found that line personnel distrust management. First, why do you think this is the case? Second, if you are or plan on a career in management, how might you use the information in this chapter to establish a climate of trust between line personnel and management?

2. Alcoholism rapidly is becoming a major problem for corporate executives. Assume you work for a highly conservative and image-conscious corporation. You begin to notice that a coworker and friend's drinking is beginning to undermine his or her work. Your options are many. You can confront the person and disclose your concerns; confront the person's most significant relational partner and disclose your concerns; or confront a higher-up and disclose your concerns. Full knowing that people with a drinking problem are

aware of it and may be excessively defensive, how are you going to manage this problem? What interpersonal communication skills are necessary in this situation?

IN YOUR RELATIONSHIPS

We have suggested that relational partners should communicate their needs more explicitly. How does one communicate that a relational partner is failing to assist in the satisfaction of an important need without making the relational partner defensive?

SUGGESTED READINGS

Johnson, D. W. *Reaching Out.* Prentice-Hall, Englewood Cliffs, N.J., 1972.

Chapters 2 and 3 discuss the concepts of self-disclosure and trust. Examples and exercises are given that would tend to assist in making the material more meaningful to you.

Jourard, S. *Self-Disclosure: An Experimental Analysis of the Transparent Self.* Wiley-Interscience, New York, 1971.

This text is a collection of the research efforts of Jourard, his peers, and his students in the area of self-disclosure. It will be helpful to those students who wish to learn or pursue a scientific approach to information gathering about the process and effects of self-disclosure.

Jourard, S. *The Transparent Self.* D. Von Nostrand Co., Princeton, N.J., 1964.

An outstanding paperback book stressing the idea that deceiving oneself, while popular, is not beneficial to psychological health and meaningful relationships. In addition to discussing the psychological importance of disclosure, Jourard also discusses the importance of authenticity and inspiration.

Luft, J. *Group Processes* 2d rev. ed. National Press Book, Palo Alto, Calif., 1970.

For a detailed explanation and application of the Johari Window, you should read this book. While not concerned exclusively with this perspective, the first chapter provides a detailed explanation of its basic principles.

Stewart, J. and G. D'Angelo. *Together: Communicating Interpersonally.* Addison-Wesley Publishing Company, Reading, Mass., 1975.

Chapter 4 of this basic textbook discusses a concept termed "negotiation of selves." While this concept was not distinctly included in our text, the chapter does provide a good discussion of the relationship between time and self-disclosure.

Chapter Ten
Beginnings: Initiating
Interpersonal Communication

Interpersonal attraction Perception concerning how physically desirable a person is as well as how desirable a person is in social or task environments.

Perceived similarity Perceptions of the degree to which another person's appearance, background, attitudes, and values are like your own.

Social style Perception of a person's characteristic ways of behaving based on verbal and nonverbal communication behaviors.

Affiliative behavior Verbal and nonverbal behaviors that indicate how attentive a person is to someone.

Responsiveness Verbal and nonverbal behaviors that indicate how concerned a person is with someone.

Ingratiation Verbal and nonverbal behaviors designed to gain favorable acceptance from someone.

Immediacy The physical and psychological distance that separates people.

Uncertainty The inability to predict accurately future events.

Tolerance for uncertainty How well one can cope with his or her inability to predict future events.

Authenticity The degree to which one's communication behaviors provide others with an accurate picture of identity; or, spontaneous as opposed to planned communication.

Machiavellianism The tendency to characteristically manipulate others.

Professor (thinking to herself): "Looks like a group of eager and bright faces. Maybe this will be a good semester."

Student (thinking to himself): "Certainly younger than I expected. Maybe I'll be able to feel comfortable asking questions or expressing myself. That would be a change!"

Job Applicant: "I'm Jim Smith, Ms. Hughes. I've been looking forward to meeting you and interviewing for this position. Mind if I smoke?"

Ms. Hughes (thinking to herself): "No doubt about this one's confidence in his ability. Smoke? Sure . . . feel free to take off your shoes if you like."

Male: "I know this will sound foolish given our differences in age, but I was wondering whether you'd like to join me for a drink?"

Female: "I know this will sound foolish given our differences in age, Professor Jones, but I would love to join you for a drink."

How is it that some people who are strangers succeed in establishing the kind of rapport that will enable them to satisfy the needs they experience while others fail? For example, why do some teachers consistently hit it off with their students while other teachers fail? Similarly, why do some people have little trouble in landing a job, while other qualified people blow it in the process of being interviewed? Finally, why do people say yes to one stranger's invitation to socialize and no to another's? To answer these questions, we will discuss first encounters and interpersonal communication in its earliest stages. We will include a brief assessment of two of the important motivations that lead to first encounters, an examination of the factors that influence this process, and a consideration of the communication skills that are necessary if our first encounters are to be successful.

FIRST ENCOUNTERS: WHY?

NEEDS

At the heart of first encounters are the personal and interpersonal needs we all experience. In a lonely airport terminal, on a cross country bus trip, or while waiting in a long line, it is not uncommon for us to initiate communication with a stranger or vice versa. These initiatory attempts typically reflect interpersonal needs like belongingness or social inclusion. But first encounters do not always reflect these kinds of needs nor do they always take place in social settings. Many of us enjoy working in certain environments because it serves to satisfy needs like self-esteem or behavior control, that is, the need to be perceived as competent and responsible. What happens, however, if the position in which we find ourselves fails to satisfy these important and frequently job-related needs? Might not this situation cause us to seek work elsewhere? Might we not seek a job interview, which is a special and highly formal type of first encounter, because our present position no longer satisfies our esteem needs or our need to be perceived as competent and responsible?

In addition to these psychological needs, we sometimes find ourselves in positions where our safety or sense of security are perceived to be in jeopardy. In the effort to restore or achieve a new sense of security we may seek out what appears to be a sympathetic face and try to strike up a conversation. Sometimes, what starts out as an attempt to achieve safety (for example, finding your way around a large city) may develop into something unexpected — a new acquaintance.

STIMULATION

Small children have a very short attention span. Rare is the young child who can sit quietly through a movie, a six-course dinner, or even an extended conversation. We adults are really not very different. Although our attention span is certainly greater than that of small children, we too can become bored and restless with the overly familiar or from the simple lack of stimulation. This fact is reflected in statements like "familiarity breeds contempt," "variety is the spice of life," and the favorite of a former professor of ours, "I like steak, but I wouldn't want to eat it every night."

Indeed, human beings like new and unique sources of stimulation. As Murray Davis puts it, "humans are *stimulotrophic* in the same way that some plants are heliotropic": they continually orient themselves toward a source of stimulation in the same way certain plants continually orient themselves toward the sun.[1] This helps to explain why some humans seem compelled to seek out unusual situations, for example, flying a hang-glider off a mountain side, hurdling a formula- one race car through the streets of Monaco, or even swallowing a tablet of questionable composition and origin. Most of us, however, have neither the inclination nor the ability to stimulate ourselves in these ways. As a result, we seek out perhaps the most intriguing source of stimulation in existence — other people. And here is one of the better explanations for first encounters: people accost people because they need to be stimulated.

In addition to fulfilling the needs we've talked about extensively, therefore, people seek out other people to be stimulated. This holds true whether they are at work, in a crowded saloon, or seated next to one another during a transcontinental flight. First encounters are not without rhyme or reason.

FIRST ENCOUNTERS: AGENTS OF INFLUENCE

What happens once we are motivated to initiate communication with a stranger or once a stranger is motivated to initiate communication with us? What factors come into play, and how do they affect the probability of people achieving superficial but immediate rapport with each other? The answers to these questions depend on our mutual perceptions and the environment in which we find ourselves. It also depends on what happens to the high level of uncertainty that characterizes initial transactions. Let us turn our attention,

[1]Murray Davis, *Intimate Relations,* The Free Press, New York, 1973, p. 31.

therefore, to some of the factors that influence our decisions about persons with whom we would like to communicate, as well as factors that influence what takes place once communication has been initiated.

THE DIMENSIONS OF INTERPERSONAL ATTRACTION

Our decisions to try to initiate a first encounter result from our perceptions of other people and the clues we find in their communication behavior. This also is true of our decisions to respond or not to someone attempting to initiate communication with us. Interpersonal attraction, which is comprised of three aspects, is exactly the kind of perception we are talking about.[2] In fact, decisions about communicating with a person for the first time are, to an inordinate extent, based on how interpersonally attractive we perceive the person.

Physical Attraction When you have finished reading this chapter, pick up a magazine and thumb through its advertisements. Following this, go back and concentrate on those ads depicting people engaged in some activity. Whether they are admiring a new car, sipping Harvey's Bristol Cream, or debating over which brand of bathroom tissue maxes out on the softness continuum, we'd be willing to bet on one thing: most of the people in each ad are, at the very least, semi-beautiful. So what else is new? The fact that our society seems possessed with physical beauty probably comes as no surprise to you. And just because society is preoccupied with statuesque women and golden Greeks does not mean that you are too. But the research strongly suggests that on the whole, perceived physical attraction is the single best predictor of two people communicating for the first time. More than that, the research also suggests that men and women who are perceived as physically attractive generally will be more successful in their initial encounters with people than people perceived as unattractive, regardless of the sex of the persons doing the perceiving. Moreover, this appears to be true also for nonsocial settings like a job interview.

This is not to say that perceived physical attraction is the only perceptual factor that influences first encounters and the acquaintance process. Rather, we are saying that putting all other factors aside, the probability of two people conversing for the first time or hitting it off will increase significantly if they

---

[2]James C. McCroskey and Thomas A. McCain, "The Measurement of Interpersonal Attraction," *Speech Monographs,* 41 (1974), 261–266.

perceive each other to be physically attractive.[3] As one of our colleagues puts it, the research leading to this conclusion supports one of her long-held beliefs: "Beauty may be only skin deep, but Americans are only interested in skin."

Social Attraction The second dimension of interpersonal attraction is social attraction. When we perceive someone to be socially attractive, this usually means we enjoy this person's company in a variety of social contexts, for instance, parties and casual get-togethers.

Social attraction also may influence first encounters. Sometimes we are in close proximity with people we really don't know. At a party we may find ourselves in a position where we can listen to the verbal communication of relative strangers as well as observe their nonverbal communication. It is not uncommon for us to then make judgments about the social attractiveness of these people. Carrying it one step further, we also may decide we would like to know a particular stranger as a result of these observations. Thus, in this instance, it would be our perception of social attraction that motivated us to seek out a person for purposes of communicating.

However, social attraction seems to be most important following our first encounters. Things like extreme physical attraction may tend to overpower other factors when we meet someone for the first time in a social setting. And we may secure a second meeting with a person solely on the basis of the strong physical attraction we feel toward this person. During the second meeting, however, we may regain our senses and realize that the gorgeous creature seated across the table from us is a social moron. Thus, in this case, the initial physical attraction that we felt for this person might be severely undermined by also perceiving that the person is socially unattractive. We'll have more to say about this following our discussion of task attraction, the third aspect of interpersonal attraction.

Task Attraction If you are currently working, or have worked in the past, you probably know that we do not have identical feelings about all the people with whom we work. In most working situations, we usually find a person or persons with whom we enjoy working on mutual tasks.

Task attraction concerns the degree to which we perceive another person to be a desirable coworker. When we perceive someone as highly task attractive, we tend to believe working with that person will prove both productive and enjoyable. Like social attraction, task attraction seems to be most important

[3]James C. McCroskey & Lawrence R. Wheeless, *An Introduction to Human Communication*. Boston: Allyn and Bacon, 1977, pp. 106–109.

following our first encounters with people. Frequently, we have little choice about working with a particular person. If we are new on the job, we also have little to go on with respect to the person as an individual or as a coworker. Once we have had the opportunity to engage in some mutual task with the person, however, we usually are in a position to gauge whether the experience was pleasant or unpleasant. If our initial experience is pleasant, we will tend to believe future experiences with this person also will be pleasant. And if this belief is borne out, we will come to perceive the person as interpersonally attractive on the task dimension.

Finally, it is quite common for people to generalize task attraction on the job to social contexts. In effect, we say to ourselves, "Sharon is dynamite on the job, so why shouldn't she be great at a party, at dinner, or on the town?" While these generalizations do not always hold up, they can serve as a base for a new acquaintance in a new social context. In our own cases, for example, we were first colleagues and then friends. And this book is a reflection of the fact that we perceive each other to be interpersonally attractive on both the task dimension and social dimension. Like physical and social attraction, then, task attraction can do more than influence decisions about first encounters.

While it is quite true that perceived physical attraction is the most influential aspect of the three in terms of initial or first-time communication encounters (particularly as the encounters relate to social settings), it seems to be of lesser importance as an interpersonal relationship evolves. This is because once we've penetrated beyond the exterior, public side of a person, we begin to appreciate and place value on the very stuff of which that person is made. For example, we begin to appreciate a person's wit, a person's intelligence, and a person's sense of humanity. In the long run, consequently, it is the remaining two aspects of interpersonal attraction that influence more than first encounters.

THE DIMENSIONS OF SIMILARITY

In all candor what do you think: Do "birds of a feather flock together" or do "opposites attract"? People have struggled with these questions and heatedly debated the theme. This is interesting because the answer to both of these questions is "all of the above." It simply depends on the context in which the question is addressed. If we were talking about mass communication, for instance, we would suggest that public opinion leaders most frequently are people whom we perceive to be moderately dissimilar from us, particularly in terms of their competence and background. But we are not talking about mass communication. Rather, we are talking about factors that influence both first encounters and the process by which people become acquainted. And while perceptions of moderate dissimilarities may enhance perceptions of opinion leadership, the opposite holds true for first encounters and the process by which people become acquainted. Stated simply, the more similar we perceive another person, the more likely it is that we will attempt to initiate communication with the person, or respond favorably to that person's attempts at initiating communication.[4]

Like interpersonal attraction, perceived similarity is multidimensional.[5] Also like interpersonal attraction, the dimensions of perceived similarity serve as qualifiers and assist us in making decisions about communicating with people. As a result, we'd like to explain first each of the dimensions of perceived similarity, and then discuss how they work together to influence our encounters with people.

Appearance The first dimension of perceived similarity is appearance. Consistent with our declaration above, we are more likely to communicate and become acquainted with people whom we perceive to appear similar to us than with people whom we perceive to appear dissimilar to us. If you doubt this, try to form a mental picture of some of your closest friends of the same sex. Now think about how close you are in age to your friends, how similar your length and style of hair is, and the degree to which you dress in a similar style.

When asked to engage in this task, our students concluded that they are very similar in appearance to those people they regard as close friends. We suspect that you too arrived at a similar conclusion.

Background A second dimension of perceived similarity is background, meaning things like place of origin ("So, you're from Ames, Iowa, too"), ethnic heritage ("I was beginning to think I was the only Chicano in this city"), and education ("It's good to talk to someone who also went to junior college before going on"). Generally, we feel more at ease communicating with a person when we perceive that the person shares a background similar to ours. We also tend to perceive that such people are similar to us in other attributes. Oregonians, for example, perceive other Oregonians as generally being more similar to them than Californians, blacks perceive other blacks as being more similar to them than whites in a majority of attributes, and policemen are likely to perceive other policemen as being more similar to them than nonpolicemen. Thus, when people perceive that they share similar

[4]McCroskey & Wheeless, pp. 109–113.

[5]James C. McCroskey, Virginia P. Richmond, and John A. Daly, "The Measurement of Perceived Homophily in Interpersonal Communication," *Human Communication Research,* 1 (1971), 323–332.

backgrounds, they are likely to also perceive other similarities between them. This, of course, will increase the ease and effectiveness with which they communicate with one another.

Attitudes and Values The final two dimensions of perceived similarity concern attitudes and values. It should not come as any great shock to you that we tend to communicate much more comfortably with people when we think that they share our attitudes and values. Most of us simply are not in the habit of surrounding ourselves with people whose attitudes and values are highly discrepant with our own. And most of us would find it quite difficult to talk civilly with a person who challenged each and every attitude and value that we expressed. As was the case with appearances and backgrounds, consequently, we are much more likely to initiate and sustain communication with people whom we perceive share our attitudes and values.

Given the preceding framework, we'd like to discuss how each of the dimensions of perceived similarity influences decisions about communicating with new people. First, there is the question of similar appearances. As we pointed out in our discussion of nonverbal communication, we infer a great deal about people on the basis of their appearance. By appearance, we mean not only what a person looks like physically but also the way the person is dressed — including accouterments like jewelry, make-up, or any object the person might be carrying.

On the basis of a person's overall appearance, we make inferences about a person's age and personal tastes. We also use this information to judge how similar the person is to us on a very base level. But more than that, we sometimes make predictions about a person's background on the basis of the person's overall appearance. Remember the case of Max Black? One of the things that was disclosed to him by the person he confronted was a perception of extreme dissimilarity between their backgrounds on the basis of his appearance.

Just as we sometimes predict a person's background on the basis of his or her overall appearance, we sometimes predict a person's attitudes and values on overall appearance. This was particularly true during the 1960s. The length of a person's hair, the manner in which the person was dressed, and his or her accouterments were treated commonly as evidence of the person's politics, attitudes toward social mores, and general set of values. While people today are somewhat more reluctant to make these kinds of inferences solely on the basis of appearance, we think it still happens.

So what are we saying here? First, people will make decisions about the desirability of communicating with someone on the basis of perceived similarities in appearance. Second, people will make judgments about whether their backgrounds are similar to another person on the basis of perceived similarities in appearance. Finally, people also will make inferences about how similar their attitudes and values are with those of another person on the basis of the two preceding judgments. The only way we have of knowing whether our inferences about the degree to which a person is similar or dissimilar to us is to actually communicate with that person. Again, however, the probability of doing just that will depend on our initial perceptions of how similar the person is to us.

But let's assume we perceive ourselves and another person to be similar. Let's further assume that we initiate communication with the person and a conversation ensues. What is likely to happen? Most likely we will engage in communication behaviors that are designed to confirm or disprove our initial perceptions. If we find that our initial perceptions were correct, we probably will pursue the possibility of becoming better acquainted. On the other hand, if our initial perceptions prove to be false, little is likely to result from our initial encounter.

To review, perceived similarity is important to first encounters and the acquaintance process in three ways. First, when we perceive that a person is similar to us we are more likely to approach the person and initiate communication. Second, when we find out by way of talking to the person that he or she is, in fact, similar to us, we are more likely to pursue the possibility of becoming acquainted with the person. Lastly, the research suggests that communication between people who perceive themselves as similar is more effective than communication between people who are dissimilar.

NONVERBAL ELEMENTS

Other factors that influence decisions about first encounters are nonverbal communication variables. Specifically, we would like to talk about impression formation as a function of social styles, discuss the relationship between immediacy and propinquity to communicate, examine the influence of environments on first encounters, and focus on how people use nonverbal objects as a means to initiate encounters.

Social Styles   Some people are quick to make inferences about others, perhaps too quickly. We've already talked about appearances and the inferences people make about people on the basis of this class of nonverbal communication variables. Now let's examine the nonverbal communication behaviors that people exhibit and the resulting social style that we attribute to them on the basis of these behaviors.[6] That is to say, nonverbal communication behaviors

---

[6]Albert Mehrabian, *Silent Messages,* Wadsworth Publishing Company, Belmont, California, 1971, pp. 57–72.

that cause us to label a person as egotistical, extroverted, or introverted even though we have never talked to the person.

Albert Mehrabian, an expert in the area of nonverbal communication, suggests that there are four primary elements of style: (1) affiliative behavior, (2) responsiveness, (3) dominance-submissiveness, and (4) ingratiation.[7] Judgments about these four elements of social style are based on both verbal and nonverbal communication behaviors. However, we will concentrate on nonverbal behaviors that contribute to a person's general social style.

To begin with, decisions about the desirability of communicating with someone frequently are influenced by our observations of another's affiliative behavior. Affiliative behavior concerns things like how much time a person spends looking at a relational partner, frequency of gestures, and the tone of the person's voice when communicating with a relational partner. The more a person looks at a relational partner, the more the person gestures, and the more pleasant the tone of voice, the more affiliative the person is said to be. Generally, people who are perceived to be affiliative also are perceived to be desirable relational partners. Thus, the more affiliative that we perceive people or the more affiliative that they perceive us, the more likely it is that an initial communication encounter will take place.

Responsiveness also is an important element of social style. We tend to judge people more positively when they seem genuinely concerned with the communications of their relational partners. Mehrabian has found that people who are high in responsiveness tend to reflect concern for others in their facial gestures, tone of voice, and rate of speech.[8] Observation of these nonverbal behavior patterns, consequently, also may lead to inferences about the desirability of first-time communication encounters.

In our discussion of the interpersonal need for behavior control, we emphasized that there are times we must make decisions as well as times when we must accept the decisions of others. Another way of looking at this interpersonal need is in terms of dominance and submissiveness. Depending on the environment and the situation in which we find ourselves, there will be times that require us to assume a dominant or submissive role. We tend to more positively perceive people who are capable of assuming either position than people who assume one or the other characteristically. Here too, the nonverbal behaviors people exhibit are rich in clues concerning dominance and submissiveness. A person who tends to relax in the presence of someone who appears tense clearly holds the higher or dominant status of the two. Given sufficient time to observe these two people in a number of social contexts (for example, a meeting, at lunch, or at a party), we may be able to determine whether they are

[7]Mehrabian, pp. 73–88.
[8]Mehrabian, pp. 73–88.

characteristically dominant or submissive. Further, we may use this information to make judgments about initiating or responding to communication.

The final element of social style we shall discuss is ingratiation. While this element most easily is discerned by things like the amount of flattery and praise in which a person engages, there is a corresponding set of nonverbal behaviors. A male who characteristically tries to ingratiate himself, for example, is likely to nod his head excessively in agreement or exhibit other kinesic behaviors that mirror the sentiments of his relational partners. While ingratiation may facilitate liking during an initial encounter, it may lead to perceptions of insincerity as a relationship progresses. It may, in other words, come to be viewed as a communication technique void of authenticity. Thus, if we observe someone who constantly exhibits ingratiating behaviors in an environment like work, we are not likely to try to initiate communication or respond favorably to communications that the person directs toward us.

People have little or no control over the nonverbal behaviors that contribute to perceptions of their general social style. Also, realize that the four elements of social style we've discussed vary with people and environments. While a person may appear affiliative and responsive to coworkers, this does not mean the person appears this way in the home or certain social settings. Finally, realize that all of us have a social style that is judged on both our verbal and nonverbal communication behavior. Just as it is important for us to learn about the elements of social style in relation to others, it is important for us to learn about these elements in relation to ourselves. For example, are you affiliative, responsive, and capable of both dominance and submission? Think about it.

Immediacy   There are at least two ways we can look at immediacy since it concerns perceived distance. First, we can look at immediacy in terms of physical distance or proximity. As a general rule, the probability of two people engaging in communication with one another increases as the physical distance separating them decreases. When we are in extremely close proximity to another person, in fact, it is next to impossible not to communicate.

On a crowded plane, for example, we commonly find ourselves sitting next to a stranger. More often than not, we also feel uncomfortable as a function of being in such close proximity with this stranger. The question is why? One explanation is that our discomfort is attributable to not knowing anything about this stranger. Put another way, it is the uncertainty we feel as a function of being so close to someone whom we do not know that causes us to feel ill at ease. One way we can decrease the uncertainty characterizing the situation and thereby reduce the discomfort we feel is to find out something about the stranger. In order to do so, however, we must initiate communication. It is important to note that the stranger probably feels much the same as us. Thus, pressure to communicate comes from the discomfort that we feel because we are close to a stranger and the discomfort that the stranger feels because he is close to us.

Fortunately, this discomfort that we feel as a function of our close proximity with an unknown person can work toward a positive end. Assuming we or the stranger initiates communication, the possibility of a new acquaintanceship arises. And even if the transaction while in the air doesn't result in a new acquaintance, the possibility exists that our life will be enriched because of our brief exposure to a new identity.

The proximity rule we've talked about works in a host of different environments. People who work in close proximity usually talk, students who sit next to each other in class usually become acquainted, and even sports fans sitting close to one another in a stadium typically exchange a few words. In a very real sense, then, proximity can be a significant catalyst for first encounters.

We also can look at immediacy, however, in terms of psychological distance.[9] In the typical interview setting, for example, we can expect to be seated in front of a large desk that communicates the status relationship that is operant and a sense of territory. Such a setting also suggests that the person conducting the interview is aloof — psychologically distant from us. It decreases rather than increases immediacy and tends to make us cautious and even unauthentic in terms of our representation of self.

On the other hand, if we found ourselves being interviewed in a conversational area of an office and the interviewer appeared relaxed and at ease, immediacy would be increased. Under these circumstances, moreover, the communication encounter would be more authentic, even though it was an initial one.

The preceding also is true for first encounters in social settings. Relaxed postures and the absence of well-defined territories increase immediacy and decrease perceptions of psychological distance. The research also suggests that such settings facilitate self-disclosure.[10] If a first encounter is to result in something more, a sense of immediacy between people is essential.

Environments   Our decisions to communicate with someone for the first time reflect more than just our perceptions of social style or immediacy. Put simply, our decisions to communicate reflect our perceptions of social style, immediacy, and the overall environment in which we are situated.

In Chapter 3, for example, we talked about two people meeting for the first time in what we implied was a singles bar. Generally, people go to such places expecting that they may meet someone new. And to a large extent, owners of

---

[9]Mehrabian, pp. 101–107.

[10]P. Ekman and W. V. Friesen, "Nonverbal Leakage and Clues to Deception," *Psychiatry,* 32 (1969), 88–106.

such establishments try to create an environment that will be conducive to first encounters. Thus, when one person decides to approach another person in such an environment, the decision will not only reflect his or her perception of the other person but also reflect his or her perception that the other person expects such confrontations.

One type of environment that may serve to facilitate first encounters, therefore, is an environment specifically created for people meeting each other. This includes, of course, more than singles bars. Parties, organized social gatherings like church picnics or fellowship meetings, and joint functions between fraternities and sororities are frequently structured so that people can meet and become acquainted with relative ease.

Just as there are environments where people fully expect to make new acquaintances, there also are environments where the last thing in the world a person expects is to be approached by a stranger. For example, when was the last time you struck up a new acquaintance in an elevator, a public bathroom, or the library?

The point, then, is a simple one. That people are sensitive to their environment and take it into account when making decisions about communicating is inherent in the idea that human communication is a transactional phenomenon. Thus, it only stands to reason that first encounters are influenced by environments.

Objects Whether visiting an art gallery, strolling through a park, sipping wine in a sidewalk cafe, or sitting under a tree on campus, there are usually people around we might like to meet. More often than not, these people are in close proximity to some nonverbal object or holding on to the object itself. Like so many other nonverbal variables, these objects may serve to facilitate first encounters. Instead of assisting us in making decisions about whether we should attempt to communicate with another person, however, these nonverbal objects very often assist us in determining how we should initiate communication with another person. At a minimum, we can use these nonverbal objects as openers. For example:

Speaking to a person viewing a painting in an art gallery, "Interesting technique, don't you think?"

Speaking to someone in a park, "I haven't flown a kite since I was a kid, mind if I watch?"

Interrupting someone seated near by in a sidewalk cafe, "Excuse me, but isn't that *Zen and the Art of Underwater Macrame* you're reading?"

Catching the attention of a photographer on campus, "Hey, that's some camera you've got there. How do 'ya pronounce it — NICKON?"

In addition to serving as openers, these nonverbal objects may prove to be ingratiating topics of discussion. For example, in the art gallery a full-fledged discussion of pointillism may follow the opening comment about the artist's technique; in the park, the escapist qualities of kite flying may be brought up; and on campus, the photographer may feel compelled to correct the accoster's pronunciation of Nikon and point out the camera's superior features.

As you can see, the encounter process is influenced by a host of nonverbal factors. Social styles, immediacy, environments, and the nonverbal objects within a person's immediate environment may serve to facilitate first encounters and eventually, the process by which people become acquainted. Try to remain sensitive to this fact as we turn from the skeletal features of first encounters and begin to look at the substance of our communication transactions with people.

GETTING TOGETHER: WHAT HAPPENS AFTER "HELLO"

At this point, let's try and tie some loose ends together. In Chapter 9, we said that stripped to the barest of essentials, interpersonal communication concerns the meeting and merging of identities and that this process is systematic and reciprocal. By this, we mean that there is a pattern to the process by which one individual tries to gain access to another's identity, and ideally this pattern involves a give-and-take attitude on the part of the people engaged in this process.

In this chapter we've discussed factors that influence decisions about trying to gain access to another's identity and touched upon some more of the important factors that guide our decisions about initial communication transactions. Now we will discuss the factors that affect the probability of an encounter succeeding or failing once communication actually has been initiated. Our thoughts in this regard have been influenced in no small way by the developmental concept of Charles Berger and Richard Calabrese, two leading researchers in the area of interpersonal communication.

Becoming Familiar In addition to having a low tolerance for inconsistency, people have a very low tolerance for uncertainty. Nothing, in fact, can arouse anxiety as much as not knowing what is going on or what is about to happen. Frequently, for example, the anxiety that results from not knowing what is going to be asked on an upcoming exam, how someone will react to us on a date or during an interview turns out to be about ten times as great as the anxiety we feel while taking the exam, while on the date, or during the interview. Because we have such a low tolerance for the unknown, we typically engage in behaviors that are designed to make future events less anxiety producing. For instance, we will ask a teacher about what we can expect in the way of questions on the exam, we will consult a friend who knows quite well the person we are about to date, and we will attempt to learn about the company that will interview us. By engaging in such behaviors we are better able to predict what the future event will be like and plan our behaviors accordingly. By asking the teacher what is likely to appear on an upcoming exam, we can better predict what will, in fact, be on the exam and plan our study time around our prediction. By consulting with a friend, we also can better predict what our date finds pleasurable or unpleasurable and make plans accordingly. And by learning as much as we can about the company that is interviewing us, we can better predict the company's personnel needs. In addition to assisting us in making predictions about future events, these behavior patterns will assist us in reducing the uncertainty that characterizes the situation, and, in turn, this will help us to reduce the anxiety that we feel. Put simply, then, uncertainty gives rise to anxiety, and this anxiety motivates us to engage in behaviors that will allay it.

Once we've made a decison to communicate with a stranger, we can't help but feel anxious. We know little about the stranger — that is, aside from what we can determine on the basis of the stranger's appearance — and know even less about what is likely to transpire once we have initiated communication. Therefore, communication during the encounter phase of a relationship will serve three important functions. First, it will reduce the uncertainty that characterizes the situation. Second, it will serve to assist us in making more accurate predictions about how the stranger is likely to respond to what we say. Finally, communication will assist us in adapting as a result of either confirming or disproving our predictions about the stranger.

Uncertainty Among other things, high degrees of uncertainty influence verbal and nonverbal communication, the intimacy of communication content, and information-seeking behavior. In addition, the amount of uncertainty that characterizes a communication encounter is affected by the degree to which communicators perceive that they are similar.[11]

In the effort to reduce high uncertainty during most first encounters, we aim our communication behaviors at gaining information about the other person, that is, above and beyond the information we've been able to gain as a result of the person's appearance and our immediate surroundings. We will, for example, invite the other person to disclose information, and we will voluntarily disclose information about ourselves, fully expecting the other person to reciprocate.

[11]Charles R. Berger and Richard J. Calabrese, "Some Explorations in Initial Interaction and Beyond: Toward a Developmental Theory of Interpersonal Communication," *Human Communication Research,* 1 (1975), 99–112.

Since uncertainty also influences the intimacy of communication content, this means that questions and self-disclosures during the initial phases of an encounter will be concerned with nonintimate facets of our respective identities. We may reveal and exchange the name of our home towns, present or intended occupations, and reasons for being in a particular environment, but it is not likely we will reveal and exchange less shallow facets of our respective identities.

Likewise, we seem to be intuitively cautious about our nonverbal communication behavior when uncertainty is high. During first encounters, people engage in little affiliative behavior. By this we mean that people sustain eye contact for briefer periods of time, exhibit fewer facial expressions that communicate emotion, and exhibit fewer affiliative gestures.

By revealing and exchanging even superficial characteristics, however, people begin to reduce uncertainty. This exchange, for example, frequently assists people in determining the extent to which they are similar. Since perceived similarities serve to reduce uncertainty, the establishment of such similarities will tend to promote communication not specifically targeted at gaining information. Also, affiliative behavior begins to increase as uncertainty decreases. And when uncertainty has sufficiently decreased for the communicators, corresponding decreases will begin to take place in their information-seeking behavior.

The probability of people experiencing a successful first encounter largely depends on what happens to the uncertainty they initially felt. If uncertainty is not decreased as a result of communication, the encounter will achieve little. Moreover, if uncertainty increases, it may lead to feelings of dislike because liking between people decreases as uncertainty increases.[12]

What can we learn from this discussion as it relates to first encounters? It seems rather evident that the probability of an initial encounter succeeding depends on how well our communication behaviors assist others in decreasing the uncertainty that they feel. When interviewing for a job, we must try to reduce the uncertainty an employer is bound to have about us. In the attempt to make an acquaintance, our obligation also would appear to be similar. Toward this end, though, we must keep in mind the information presented in Chapter 9 and put it to good use.

The uncertainty that characterizes first encounters will not disappear during a single meeting. On the contrary, some degree of uncertainty is likely to be present throughout the life of a relationship. And this is because our relationships are continually changing. In effect, then, communication assists us in reducing uncertainty to a point where we can tolerate it during our initial transactions. Furthermore, communication will serve to keep the uncertainty within tolerable limits as the relationship continues to evolve.

[12]Berger and Calabrese, "Some Explorations in Initial Interaction and Beyond: Toward a Developmental Theory of Interpersonal Communication," pp. 99–112.

Predictions As the uncertainty present during the beginning stages of a first encounter decreases, our ability to predict accurately how a person will respond to us increases dramatically. At the outset of a first encounter, we know very little about the other person. Therefore, our predictions about how the person will respond to us are based on the most general of information, for example, what the person looks like and the degree to which we perceive the person to be similar to us.

Once we have gained access to even the most peripheral aspects of the person's identity, however, we become increasingly sophisticated in predicting how a person will respond to us. It only stands to reason that if we know something about a person's geographical origins, attitudes, pattern of interacting, and past history, we are in a better position to predict the person's behavior than if we knew nothing about the person.

So what is the payoff? Well, if we can predict with reasonable certainty how a person will respond to what we communicate, we can structure our communication behavior in such a way that it is not likely to offend that person or elicit a negative reaction. As a case in point, imagine that you just met someone and, in the process of reducing uncertainty, learned that this person was deeply religious. Now, would you predict that this person would respond favorably to indictments of organized religion or listen to x-rated jokes? Of course not. And you probably would take this prediction into account in your communications with the person.

The ability to predict how a person will respond to what we communicate also assists us in avoiding comments that might misrepresent our true beliefs and feelings. As we pointed out earlier, we cannot help but reveal a sample portion of our identity during our initial transactions. And the person with whom we are communicating will form a picture of us on the basis of this sample portion and make judgments about us accordingly. One of the potential consequences of this process is that even the most innocent of our comments may be misconstrued or distorted. For example, in talking with a stranger we may make what we perceive as a harmless comment about a political candidate. Unknown to us, however, the stranger has very strong convictions about this political candidate. As a result, the stranger may make a whole string of negative inferences about us on the basis of this single comment. And some, if not all of these inferences, may be highly inconsistent with our true beliefs and feelings. Already having made the faux pas, we probably wouldn't be given a chance to set the record straight. The point is that this situation could have been avoided altogether had we known the stranger's feelings toward the specific candidate or, perhaps, had we known something about the stranger's political attitudes in general. If we had been supplied with such information, we probably could have predicted the stranger's reaction to our comment and refrained from making it.

As we spend more time communicating with a person, we are bound to learn more about the person's significant attributes. This information not only will serve to further reduce the uncertainties in our relationship with this person, but it will also assist us in making more accurate predictions about how this person will respond to our communication behavior. Beyond what we've already said, therefore, the ability to predict another's response to us is likely to increase the fidelity of our communication transactions with this person. That is, the accuracy of our interpretations of the person's communication behavior as well as the appropriateness of our responses to this behavior are likely to increase. When you generalize this conclusion to people you meet at school, at work, and in more socially oriented environments, its importance cannot be minimized.

Confirmation Finally, there is the role that communication plays in confirming or disproving our predictions and expectancies about another person. To begin with, the decision to try to initiate communication reflects an expectancy on our part that the person will respond favorably to our invitation to communicate. Communication, then, assists us in either confirming or disproving this initial expectancy.

Of more importance to us, however, is the role communication plays once we've made contact with a person and the communication transaction has begun. As we have already said, our predictions about the other person will become more accurate as we gain information about the person, and these predictions will assist us in formulating appropriate communication behaviors. But there is a bit of "Murphy's Law" in every new encounter. And that law, as applied to first encounters, states that if anything can go wrong when we meet someone for the first time — it will! For example, since we can't possibly learn all there is to know about a person in a single meeting, chances are that at least some of our predictions about the person will be wrong. This means that at least some of our communication behaviors also will be inappropriate. Fortunately, though, communication assists us in adapting to such situations. If we judge one kind of communication behavior to be inappropriate on the basis of a person's response, we are likely to abandon the expectancy and prediction that gave rise to the communication behavior. We also are likely to abandon related expectancies, which probably will motivate us to return and build on a set of expectancies and predictions that already have been confirmed. Thus, communication not only serves to reinforce expectancies that have been confirmed, but also serves to extinguish those expectancies that have met with an unintended response.

In this section we have shown that our initial encounters with people concern uncertainty reduction in which communication plays a significant role, for it helps us to make predictions about how a person will respond to us and to adapt to the situation once our predictions have been confirmed. Of course, the probability of being successful in our initial encounters involves more than knowing what preceded the encounters and what is taking place. It also involves knowledge of some of the behaviors that can serve to undermine a potential relationship as well as some of the skills that can facilitate the growth of the relationship. Therefore, we can now turn to the more common mistakes people are apt to make in their initial encounters and to some of the skills necessary for a relationship to grow.

APPROACH WITH CAUTION

One could spend a lifetime trying to catalogue all of the little factors that can work against two people meeting and eventually becoming acquainted. We will discuss three specific obstacles that you should be aware of before and during your first transaction with someone: misinterpretation of nonverbal cues, violation of expectancies, and failure to listen.

MISINTERPRETING NONVERBAL CUES

We noted that our decisions to communicate with a stranger are based largely on nonverbal communication variables. One of the more commonly misinterpreted nonverbal variables is eye behavior. To review, when a person makes and sustains eye contact with us, we tend to predict that this person would enjoy communicating with us. If this person is of the opposite sex, moreover, we may predict that he or she is sexually attracted to us, since sustained eye contact frequently does indicate sexual attraction.

The trouble is that people stare. In particular, they do so when in confined and crowded quarters, for instance, at parties in a home, in a crowded restaurant, or in a small night club. What we predict, then, is that a desire on the part of another person to communicate with us is just as likely to be an innocent and unintentional stare. And, as a result, our initial attempt to communicate with this person may be greeted with a polite hello, indifference, or something a bit stronger. Thus, eye behavior is commonly misinterpreted and should not be regarded as sufficient evidence of a person's desire to communicate with us.

The same can be said about environments. We may make an inaccurate prediction about a person prior to engaging in communication with him or her on the basis of the immediate environment. For example, no matter what the owner of a singles bar would like us to think, people who frequent such places are not always in search of Mr. or Ms. Goodbar. If we assume otherwise, however, our initial attempts to talk with a person may offend rather than ingratiate. By the same token, if we are successful in initiating communication, but continue to behave on the basis of the preceding prediction, the outcome will be the same.

What we are suggesting, then, is that we can ill afford to make hasty decisions about communicating with people on the basis of nonverbal variables. If our decisions and the predictions leading to them are faulty, the communication behavior we exhibit will in all likelihood prove to be highly inappropriate. As a result, our attempts to initiate a potential relationship also will be unsuccessful.

VIOLATING EXPECTANCIES

Closely aligned with the problem of misinterpreting nonverbal cues is the problem of violating expectancies. Obviously, if we misinterpret the nonverbal cues that we associate with someone, the probability is that we will develop an inappropriate set of expectancies about another's reaction to our initial attempt to communicate. This, in turn, will serve to increase the possibility that we will violate the other person's expectancies about what normally takes place during first encounters.

Beyond the preceding, our ignorance or insensitivity to unit expectancies may work against us making contact with a person. The Ugly American syndrome illustrates our point. During the 1960s, most Americans experienced a new-found affluence. This increased their mobility — particularly with respect to travel abroad. The problem was that some Americans had little or no knowledge about the cultures of the countries in which they were traveling. Edward Hall, one of the pioneers in nonverbal communication, relates one of his own experiences that demonstrates how easily an American abroad can violate the expectancy of a European when the American is unaware of nonverbal expectancies.[13] As the story goes, he was standing outside an open apartment door talking to a young woman inside. The apartment door served as entrance for not only the young woman but also a German artist who occupied part of the dwelling. Looking inside, Hall could see the artist conversing with friends and, in turn, the artist could just barely see him. Hall kept his voice low while talking, so as not to disturb the conversation some fifty or so feet inside the apartment. Suddenly, the artist appeared at the door and shoved the young woman away. In an outraged manner, the artist challenged Hall to explain why he felt it was okay to enter his home without permission. Hall had based his behavior on the American assumption that one is not inside a house unless he is standing in the house proper. Such an assumption apparently has no basis in Germany.

So it was with many Americans who traveled in foreign countries during the 1960s. Unknowingly they violated many of the more important unit expectancies in these cultures. As a consequence of these violations, Europeans, Asians, and Latins came to regard American tourists as insensitive — even vulgar. This was reflected in the treatment that they gave to American tourists. What we are contending, therefore, is that we need to thoroughly familiarize ourselves with the unit expectancies operating in an environment before running the risk of violating them through our communication behavior.

FAILING TO LISTEN

The most common obstacle that people confront in their initial transactions is failure to listen. When people meet for the first time and begin to communicate, they are very concerned with how they are perceived. While this concern is quite natural and not to be condemned, it can work against people making optimum use of their initial transactions. To illustrate, we would like to introduce a new word to your vocabulary — *duologue*. This word, which was introduced to us by a good friend and colleague, Tom Young, was created because there seemed to be no existing word for a behavior people frequently engage in when they first meet. So, what does duologue mean? Well, let's first review the meanings of two other words: monologue and dialogue. A *monologue* usually refers to a speech delivered by one person. A *dialogue* usually refers to a conversation between two or more people. The word *duologue* combines the meaning of monologue and dialogue and refers to a person engaged in an intrapersonal monologue at the same time he or she is engaged in an interper-

[13]Edward T. Hall, *The Hidden Dimension,* Doubleday & Company, New York, 1966.

sonal dialogue. For example, when we meet someone for the first time we may get caught up in trying to intrapersonally evaluate the impact of what we have said or are about to say, without really listening to the other person's response. This intrapersonal monologue reflects our preoccupation with questions about how we are being perceived. At the same time, however, we act as if we are paying the closest of attention to every word the person emits.

Since what takes place during our initial transactions with someone is likely to dictate what follows (including a second meeting), it is extremely important that we make optimum use of what is initially said. But that is not possible unless we actually hear and process what is being said. Thus, it is extremely important for us to try to overcome our preoccupations with self during initial transactions. Acknowledgment of a person's communication behavior is not the same as understanding the substance of a person's communication behavior. The former is passive behavior, whereas the latter involves a total sensorial commitment. Be mindful of this conclusion as we now turn to some communication skills that not only will facilitate successful first encounters but also will facilitate fidelity communication throughout the life of an interpersonal relationship.

ESSENTIAL SKILLS

In addition to the preceding obstacles, communicators should try to avoid interpersonal communication behavior that may elicit defensiveness. Interpersonal communication should assist people in becoming more aware of their needs and feelings. It should not put people on guard, ready to defend their individual identities at the drop of the hat. Let us examine some important interpersonal skills that we all should practice in the attempt to minimize defensive communication postures.

Nonevaluative Statements Perhaps because of our high need for closure, we have a tendency to evaluate and judge everything with which we come in contact. This is particularly true with respect to the people we meet. Even though the potential for error is quite high in our initial evaluations of people, we continue to make evaluations. More often than not, they are reflected in our verbal and nonverbal communication behavior.

The trouble is that none of us like to be evaluated and pigeonholed as this or that type of person. When we perceive that a person is engaging in such behavior — by how and what he or she is communicating — we may become defensive.[14] Our defensive communications may be perceived as offensive by

---

[14]Jack R. Gibb, "Defensive Communication," *Journal of Communication,* 11 (1963), 142–148.

the person, and the first thing we know, a full-scale disagreement may result. It is of the utmost importance, therefore, to avoid evaluative-laden statements in our transactions.

Democratic Communication When discussing the interpersonal need for behavioral control, we discussed autocrats. You'll recall that autocrats like to make all the decisions and exert absolute control over their immediate sphere of influence. In contrast to autocrats, we suggested that democrats were willing to share in responsibilities and decisions.

Just as people don't like to be judged and pigeonholed, they are not particularly fond of people who always try to control them. Nothing, in fact, can be quite as frustrating as knowing someone who is trying to control our behavior and who is communicating for us rather than with us. In addition to avoiding evaluative communication, therefore, we should strive to become democratic communicators.

Authenticity In Chapter 9, we said that deception and misrepresentation have no business in the business of interpersonal communication. We also suggested that we have some responsibility to communicate an authentic picture of our identity to the people we meet. While Machiavellianism — the tendency to manipulate — may work in business and politics, little good can come from it in communicating interpersonally and in developing interpersonal relationships. Most people do not like to be manipulated. When they find out they've been the focus of a manipulative communication strategy, they will immediately assume a defensive posture. A skill we need to develop, then, is to communicate in an authentic manner.

Equality   In Chapter 11, we will discuss some types of relationships in terms of upward and downward patterns of communication. At this point, however, we would like to suggest that people customarily do not appreciate being communicated down to. As a case in point, consider those teachers you've had who talked as if you were incapable of taking on responsibilities or making intelligent decisions. Now compare those teachers with ones who have taken the opposite view of you and other students. Need we say anything more in the effort to justify equality in communication?

Openmindedness Finally, we should always try to keep an open mind whether we are involved in a first encounter or any other communication transaction. To put it another way, we should avoid communicating in absolutes. Few things are truly black or white, including the attitudes, beliefs, and values that are revealed as people communicate. Not only should we recognize this when we communicate, we should respect it.

CHAPTER SUMMARY

We have presented a picture of what precedes and takes place during our initial encounters with people, as well as some of the factors that influence, facilitate, or interfere with our attempts to establish new relationships. In review, we reaffirmed our belief that human relationships evolve systematically and that human communication is the medium in which human relationships are spawned and nurtured. Toward that end, we explained some of the more important perceptions that influence decisions about communicating, highlighted three functions communication serves as we try to become familiar with someone, and mentioned three obstacles that we should keep in mind in our initial transactions with people. Finally, we presented some skills that can assist us in these endeavors. We hope that you can relate our discussion to your experiences and will apply our suggestions to situations you have yet to experience.

THINK ABOUT IT

IN GENERAL

Complete the exercises given under Think About It: In General at the end of Chapter 1.

IN EDUCATION

Perhaps one of the sadder commentaries on the process of instruction is that students in the same class seldom meet, much less become acquainted. Pair off with someone in your class whom you don't know. Face each other and observe appearances. Maintaining silence, write down what you predict the other person is like and have the other person write down predictions about you. Reveal your predictions and have your partner reveal his or hers. Discuss the accuracy of these predictions as well as their base in terms of what we've said about first encounters.

IN THE ORGANIZATION

1. We've stated that the interview setting is a special form of first encounter. We've also suggested that during first encounters we have some responsibility to reduce the uncertainty that characterizes the situation. Finally we indi-

cated that success in first encounters often is dictated by how well the communicators reduce uncertainty. Assume you are being interviewed for a job that is ideally suited to your career goals. In light of the information we've presented, what factors are you going to pay careful attention to in the effort to reduce uncertainty? How will you put these factors to use, that is, in terms of your actual communication behavior?

2. Reverse the above roles. In light of our discussion of immediacy, what are your plans for interviewing potential employees? What is the justification for these plans?

IN YOUR RELATIONSHIPS

In class, generate a list of sentences that not only reflect what people talk about during first encounters but also will increase the potential for defensive communication postures. Following this, generate a corresponding set of statements that would minimize defensive postures. Discuss the two lists.

SUGGESTED READINGS

There are a variety of sources that should be valuable supplements to the information provided in this chapter depending on how technical or advanced you would like your reading to be. We offer the following:

Berger, C. and R. Calabrese "Some Explorations in Initial Interaction and Beyond: Toward a Developmental Theory of Interpersonal Communication." *Human Communication Research,* 1 (1975), No. 2, 99–112.

This article, though somewhat advanced, deals at length with questions of uncertainty reduction and predictions during our initial transactions with people. The axioms posited by the authors not only make good sense but also are supported by the research on initial interactions. In addition, they are easily related to most of our experiences with first encounters.

Newcomb, T. *The Acquaintance Process.* Holt, Rinehart, and Winston, New York, 1961.

Newcomb's book has become a standard in the field of interpersonal dynamics and interpersonal communication. While this book is very data-oriented, concentrating on research findings, it is a good one and should assist you in more thoroughly understanding the process by which people come to know other people.

Chapter Eleven
Interpersonal Communication and Relational Definition: What Happens Now

Rituals, activities, and pastimes Communication behaviors that are not designed to provoke or offend those with whom we are casually or formally acquainted.

The status norm A shared perception concerning appropriate and inappropriate communication behaviors when people believe they are similar or dissimilar in status.

Symmetrical communication Communication behaviors that stress the equalities exisiting between communicators.

Asymmetrical communication Communication behaviors that accentuate dissimilarities between communicators.

Solidarity The degree to which people perceive themselves as being close to or remote from one another.

Although interpersonal communication is largely predictable, it is not completely predictable. You would think, for example, that we could predict accurately the evolution of an interpersonal relationship on the basis of how successfully the participants communicated with each other in their initial encounter. Yet, how many times have you found yourself in a situation where you have had a successful first encounter with a person, developed a positive set of expectancies about a long-term association, and come away from a second meeting wondering why on earth you were attracted to the person in the first place? In contrast, how many times have you failed to see eye-to-eye with someone in an initial encounter, but later developed a long and rewarding association with that person?

In Chapter 10, we were concerned with variables that influence our initial encounters and the communication behaviors that serve to make such encounters more rewarding. Although we suggested that these variables and behavior patterns are not tied to any specific context, the examples we used were most applicable to extended encounters occurring in social environments. In this chapter, we examine factors that influence what takes place following both extended and abbreviated encounters in task-oriented rather than socially oriented environments. An inordinate amount of communication in task-oriented environments falls within the three categories of rituals, activities, and pastimes. These behavior patterns, we will show, are not as meaningless or directionless as many books on communication suggest. We will discuss also two communication-based norms affecting the way people begin to define the nature of their association and influencing the conclusions that they draw about the potential depth of their association. Lastly, we will discuss three communication skills that bear directly on these two norms.

RITUALS, ACTIVITIES, AND PASTIMES

In the attempt to make students more aware of the rewards that can be derived from more than shallow relationships with people, we sometimes lose sight of the fact that a great many of our communication behavior patterns are not intended to invite close interpersonal ties. Instead, they are designed to assist us in our day-to-day business without provoking or offending the people with whom we come in contact, and at the same time, satisfying their needs to be recognized and provided with psychological strokes; that is, verbal and nonverbal communications that make people feel good about themselves.[1] Such communication behaviors can, and very often do, assist us in easing into conversations with people we know from an extended but single encounter or hardly know from frequent but extremely abbreviated encounters.

RITUALS

Although we're not accustomed to thinking about it this way, many of the communication behaviors we exhibit in the course of a day are ritualistic.[2] Such behaviors range from simple recognition, as when two people nod their heads in passing, to formal and synchronized kinds of greeting like those exhibited by an employer to an employee. We engage in these kinds of ritualistic behaviors with people with whom we are formally acquainted as well as people whom we have frequently encountered but to whom we have never been formally introduced. Ritualistic communication behaviors are designed to let people know that they are aware of each other's identity and to stroke each other psychologically. Although not designed to stimulate extended conversation, such behaviors may have that result.

During the course of a day, for example, how many times do we inquire about the physical and psychological well being of someone we know only by sight? How many times do we respond to similar inquiries from people who know us only by sight? Probably many more times than we would think. Yet, when we make such inquiries or when we respond, typically we do not think about their actual meaning or possible implications. Although we do not give much conscious thought to them, these frequent rituals can, and sometimes do, motivate us to formalize an acquaintance or make a date to pick up where we last left off with a person we've already met. However superficial it may seem, ritualistic communication, whether on the job, at school, or in more relaxed social settings, is not altogether insignificant. At the minimum, it

[1]Eric Berne, *Games People Play*, Grove Press, New York, 1964.
[2]Muriel James and Dorothy Jongeward, *Born to Win: Transactional Analysis with Gestalt Experiments*, Addison-Wesley Publishing Company, Reading, Mass., 1975, p. 57.

assists people in satisfying their need to be recognized and acknowledged; also it provides people with a convenient medium by which they can engage in psychological stroking. At the maximum, it can be an interpersonal catalyst, motivating us to formalize a passing acquaintance or extend an acquaintance that already has been formalized.

ACTIVITIES

Aside from being ritualistic, many communication transactions following an extended or a series of mini-encounters are activities centered.[3] When we enter a new work environment, for example, normally we are afforded only a brief initial encounter with those with whom we will be working. Shortly thereafter, we are likely to find ourselves in the position of having to communicate with coworkers about assigned tasks or work-oriented activities. Frequently, this activity-centered communication reduces uncertainty to the point where we and our coworkers feel comfortable about discussing nonjob related topics. While they are not necessarily intended to assist coworkers in becoming more formally and thoroughly acquainted with one another, these activity-centered communications frequently do just that.

PASTIMES

Finally, much of the communication that transpires following initial encounters is designed to pass the time.[4] No matter how brief or extended a first encounter, people seem to be instinctively cautious about the content of their messages on subsequent encounters. By this, we mean that people will try to avoid generating messages that may prove to be offensive. As a result, they pass the time by communicating about relatively innocuous subject matter, for example, a football game, the weather, or superficial facets of their biographies.

Pastime communication behaviors may appear to be superficial and of minimal consequence to an association that has yet to take on a high degree of definition, much less one between friends. True, they are superficial. But at the same time, such communication behaviors enable people who are becoming better acquainted to do so in a nondefensive communication environment and enables those already acquainted to communicate about matters that do not overly tax their respective identity systems.

---

[3]Muriel James and Dorothy Jongeward, pp. 57–58.
[4]Muriel James and Dorothy Jongeward, pp. 57–58.

CONCLUDING REMARKS

Given the importance that is placed on topics like purposeful self-disclosures, authentic communication, and the like, we sometimes overlook a simple truth: very few of our day-to-day communication behaviors on the job, at school, or places where we go to relax, are directed toward development of deeply involved interpersonal relationships. In the process of overlooking this simple truth, we tend to demean the role that these kinds of communication behaviors play in our day-to-day interpersonal experiences. Also, we need to point out that these kinds of behaviors do not disappear once people move beyond the acquaintance phase of an interpersonal relationship. Even the best of friends engage in ritualistic behavior or activities-centered communication and discuss innocuous subjects in passing their time together. In the final analysis, then, it makes little sense to dismiss such behaviors as being unimportant. We should strive to become more conscious of both their meaning and implications to our day-to-day experiences and, where appropriate, put them to constructive use.

INTERPERSONAL NORMS AND RELATIONAL DEFINITION

Of greater impact on the way we begin to define a relationship or the conclusions we draw about its potential depth than the rituals, activities, and pastimes just described are such factors as need satisfaction and need compatibility, time, self-disclosure, and communication fidelity. Since we already have spent a significant amount of time discussing these factors, we will discuss two norms that not only affect our conclusions about these factors but also have a tremendous impact on relational definition and relational depth. Roger Brown, who is one of the most respected social psychologists, calls these two norms *status* and *solidarity*.[5]

STATUS

At one time in this country, a person's position was evident in his or her dress, circle of friends, and even leisure time activities. Among other things, for example, sports like golf, sailing, and tennis were primarily associated with the aristocracy; that is, the elite. While this largely is no longer the case, status lines still exist within our society and affect our relationships with people. For example, the degree to which people perceive they are similar or dissimilar in

[5]Roger Brown, *Social Psychology*, The Free Press, New York, 1965, pp. 71–100.

The way people position themselves frequently communicates status.

status still has a significant impact on the way they define the nature of their association. This is because there are norms concerning similar or dissimilar status, such as appropriate and inappropriate communication behaviors. For example, once two people have become formally acquainted, the degree to which they perceive similarities or dissimilarities in status can influence (1) the equality of language they use in addressing each other, (2) the degree to which their communication transactions are symmetrical, (3) the amount of communication in which they engage, and (4) the way they spatially situate themselves. In turn, such communication behaviors affect both the definition of their association and the conclusions about its potential depth.

Equality of Address For the moment, think about the ways you address people whose status you perceive to be higher than your own. Would you say that the way that you address these people is different from the way that you address people with similar or lesser status than your own? If you're like us, your answer would have to be yes. Okay, what about situations where you perceive your status is higher than someone else's? Do you expect inequality in the way you address each other?

Put simply, people who share similar status generally use language that is roughly equitable when addressing one another. If one person uses the other's first name, the other probably will reciprocate. When people are nonequivalent in status, however, the language they use in addressing one another usually is anything but egalitarian. It may be perfectly all right for a professor to address a male student by his first name, but as you well know, the professor might react negatively to the student reciprocating this behavior.

Symmetrical Communication The degree to which people perceive themselves as being similar or dissimilar in status also affects the degree to which their communication behavior is symmetrical or asymmetrical. As we are using the terms here, *symmetrical* concerns messages that imply the communicators are equals, whereas *asymmetrical* means that the messages imply one communicator is superior to another.[6] As you would think, persons of similar status do not adopt postures in which one person customarily communicates downward (for example, "Get that dossier for me right away, Hamblin") while the other customarily communicates upward (for example, "Yes sir, Mr. Jones — right away"). Among people who are not nonequivalent in status, though, such asymmetrical communication behavior may be the norm.

Amount of Communication Given what we have already said, it should come as no surprise that people who are dissimilar communicate less frequently than those who are similar in status. As we pointed out in Chapter 10, perceived similarities have a significant impact on decisions about communicating. This also is true with respect to status once a relationship has gone beyond the encounter stage.

Spatial Relations As the story goes, a famous producer-director, whose stature was not quite that of the leading men in his pictures, had the desk and chair in his office elevated more than two feet off the floor. Why? So he could make sure his leading men well knew who was boss.

What the movie tycoon intuitively realized has a sound empirical base. The degree to which people are similar or dissimilar in status is reflected in the way they spatially situate themselves. Both territory and personal space, for example, clearly are affected by status. People who share equivalent status can be expected to abide by their respective spatial needs. More to the point, people who are perceived to have higher status than our own, are given certain liberties regarding our territory and personal space. Simply stated, we not only may allow people of higher status to infringe upon our spatial needs but also may expect these invasions.

[6]Roger Brown, pp. 71–73.

SOLIDARITY

One of the things we've stressed is that interpersonal communication concerns the meeting and merging of human identities. In order for this to occur, people must try to reduce the psychological distance that initially separates them. You will recall from the last chapter that one of the ways people can do this is by engaging in nonverbal communication behaviors designed to increase immediacy.

Like immediacy, the solidarity norm is concerned with the degree to which people perceive themselves as being psychologically close or remote, but it is far more encompassing. According to Roger Brown, people can begin to define the nature of their association and make judgments about how distant or close they are from one another on the basis of any one of five categories. These categories concern: (1) personal characteristics, (2) spatial relations, (3) sentiments, (4) behavior, and (5) symbols.[7] Given these categories, associations that are characterized by at least some degree of solidarity would be those that meet at least one of the following criteria:

1. Similarities in personal characteristics, such as attitudes and values, exist.
2. Close proximity or immediacy is maintained.
3. Sentiments like affection, respect, and trust are held mutually.
4. Interaction behavior is high.
5. Symbols or symbolic behavior that is indicative of closeness are present.

Brown suggests that associations meeting at least one of the above criteria are both solidary and symmetrical.[8] It logically follows, moreover, that solidarity and symmetry increase as the number of criteria an association meets increases. Conversely, associations that fail to meet any of the above criteria are asymmetrical and cannot be regarded as solidary. Like status, consequently, the decisions we make about an association are influenced by our perceptions of how close or distant we are from people on one or more of the preceding criteria. Also like status, these perceptions will influence our judgments about appropriate and inappropriate communication behavior with certain people.

THE INTERACTON OF STATUS AND SOLIDARITY

It should be clear that status and solidarity affect relational definition and relational depth. It is important to recognize, moreover, that people take both

[7]Roger Brown, pp. 71–73.
[8]Roger Brown, pp. 71–90.

these norms into account as they begin to define the nature of their association and make projections about its potential depth. Like so many other concepts we've discussed, status and solidarity are interdependent rather than dependent. This means judgments about status affect judgments about solidarity and vice versa.

Associations that are both socially oriented and characterized by a high degree of solidarity are most commonly those in which the relational partners share equivalent status. On a social dimension, in fact, it is doubtful that two people could form a rewarding association and thereby achieve some degree of solidarity unless their status was roughly equivalent. But does this mean people who are dissimilar in status can neither become associated nor achieve at least some facsimile of solidarity in their lives?

While status differences may undermine solidarity on a social dimension, this need not be the case on a more task-oriented dimension. When you enter the work environment, for example, you are going to be confronted with people whose organizational status is dissimilar from your own. This is because status frequently is part of the system of rewards in organizations. Even though status differences are built in to the organizational environment, you may be able to achieve some degree of solidarity with people of higher or lesser status as a function of:

1. Sharing similar personal characteristics other than status
2. Working in close proximity with these people on tasks for which you hold some degree of mutual responsibility
3. Mutually held sentiments like trust or respect
4. Finding yourself in a position where you must frequently interact with them
5. Using symbols or engaging in symbolic behavior that identifies you with these people

Whether or not we achieve some degree of solidarity as a function of meeting one or more of the above criteria, however, is dependent on our own interpersonal communication skills as well as the skills of those with whom we work. And it is in this direction we would like to now turn your attention.

ACHIEVING INTERPERSONAL SOLIDARITY

As you can well imagine, many factors influence the probability of people achieving interpersonal solidarity. For example, the achievement of interpersonal solidarity is influenced by:

1. Self-disclosure and identity penetration
2. Need satisfaction and need compatibility
3. Time
4. Interpersonal attraction and perceived similarity
5. Expressiveness-responsiveness
6. Dominance and submission
7. Uncertainty reduction
8. Expectancies
9. The degree to which an extended or abbreviated encounter is perceived successful

Beyond the preceding factors, which we discussed at length in Chapters 9 and 10, the achievement of interpersonal solidarity also is affected by the context in which people become acquainted. The way we achieve interpersonal solidarity on the job may be highly variant from the way we achieve it at school or in an informal social setting. Regardless of the context in which people become acquainted, however, we believe there are certain communication skills that can assist people in achieving interpersonal solidarity, that is, communication skills we may have mentioned but not discussed thoroughly. These skills concern status, the ability to accurately process the messages of another, and the ability and willingness to adapt to people where appropriate.

MINIMIZING STATUS DIFFERENCES

Read the following two conversations and see if you can pick out the most striking dissimilarity between them:

> Mr. Wash: I think you'd do well to study these points I've underlined.
> Mr. Peters: As you say, sir.
> Mr. Wash: I don't mean just read them either Peters. I mean study them 'til your contacts wear out if you have to.
> Mr. Peters: Oh . . . you can rest assured, Mr. Wash, I'll study them. I wouldn't want my performance to reflect badly on you in any way.
> Mr. Wash: Your performance reflecting on me, my dear boy, is distinctly impossible!

> Mr. Starke: Hey Jonee, did you get that brief typed for tomorrow's hearing?

Ms. Greer: Not yet, I'm still working on Redford's deposition. Speaking of getting things done, what about my raise, Bob?

Mr. Starke: On Friday, I promise.

Ms. Greer: Seein' is believin'.

Mr. Starke: What ever happened to that timid young secretary whose motto was "Blessed are those who ask for nothing, for they will not be disappointed?"

Ms. Greer: She became indispensible to a successful attorney who couldn't find his way to court without her!

As you no doubt picked up on, the above conversations concern people in superior and subordinate positions. However, the status differences so evident in the first conversation are missing from the second.

In Chapter 10, we suggested that communication should be democratic or, to put it another way, egalitarian. In this chapter, we suggest that equality of language reflects the degree to which people are similar or dissimilar in status. To the extent that people are similar in status, we usually can expect them to communicate equitably. But what about situations where there are very real status differences between people, for example, the organizational or school environment? Assuming some degree of interpersonal solidarity is desirable in these environments, what can we do to minimize any negative effects that might result from status differences or language that serves only to accentuate these differences?

Supervisors, managers, and teachers frequently find themselves in a dilemma when confronted with this question. While they may want to increase interpersonal solidarity between themselves and subordinates or students, many believe they can't because it would serve to undermine their authority. This need not be the case. In task-oriented environments, a supervisor's or teacher's ability to influence people is determined largely by how competent these people perceive the supervisor or teacher to be. It is to the supervisor's or teacher's advantage, therefore, to communicate in a manner that will maintain perceptions of competence. To the extent that they do not interfere with the maintenance of this perception, people in superior positions can communicate with subordinates in a more equitable fashion. Of course, egalitarian language will minimize rather than accentuate status differences. In turn, this will increase perceptions of solidarity and alter the way in which people in subordinate roles define the nature of their association with a superior.

Ideally, status differences should never undermine the fidelity with which people communicate. The simple truth is, however, that whether real or imagined, status differences undermine both perceptions of interpersonal solidarity and communication fidelity. Yet, if we are aware of real or imagined differences in status, we can do something about them. Specifically, we can minimize their effects by communicating with people, rather than talking down to them.

INFORMATION PROCESSING ABILITIES

How competent we are as interpersonal communicators largely depends on how well we actually hear what someone says to us and how appropriately we respond to what someone says to us. By the same token, the degree to which we are able to reduce the distance separating us from people in task- or social-oriented environments largely rests with these same two skills.

When we talk about a person's ability to process information, we are really talking about one's ability to engage in empathic communication.[9] Empathic communication encompasses, among other things, one's ability to:

1. Assume the role of someone else
2. Identify and be sensitive to the needs of others
3. Accurately interpret the authentic emotions of others on the basis of what they do and say
4. Block out extraneous intra- and interpersonal sources of interference that can impair our abilities to listen[10]

Needless to say, it is not easy to become skilled in empathic communication. Not only does it require egalitarian communication, it demands also that we be expressive and responsive with people, encourage and reciprocate interaction behavior like self-disclosure, and overcome our tendency to get caught up in how we are being perceived by the people with whom we communicate. If we are to be successful in reducing the distance that separates us from our superiors and subordinates or those with whom we become socially acquainted, we must acquire at least minimum competencies in this regard.

ADAPTATION

By the time we reach eighteen to twenty years of age, most of us have adopted customary patterns of communication. These patterns reflect our individual

[9]Norman N. Foote and Leonard S. Contrell, Jr., *Identity and Interpersonal Competence*, University of Chicago Press, Chicago, 1965. See also, Arthur P. Bochner and Clifford W. Kelley, "Interpersonal Competence: Rationale, Philosophy, and Implementation of a Conceptual Framework," *The Speech Teacher*, 23 (1974), 281–301.
[10]Bochner and Kelley, pp. 281–301.

identities, prior successes and failures in attempting to establish bona fide relationships, and resulting expectancies. While we have stressed the need for people to keep open minds as they consider developing an interpersonal relationship, we have said little about the need for people to be flexible and willing to adapt in their transactions.

Nothing can be quite as frustrating as confronting a person who is in a position of authority and, at the same time, is unwilling to adapt to your individual needs. People who are unyielding and inflexible cannot help but increase perceptions of interpersonal distance as a result of what they do and say. What does this suggest to you, as an individual communicator and as a person who would like to reduce the interpersonal distance that separates you from other people? We hope that is suggests and demonstrates the need for people to exercise "behavioral flexibility."[11] That is, people should have both the ability and willingness to: (1) recognize behavioral alternatives, (2) relate to people in ways with which you are unfamiliar, and (3) identify as well as abandon inappropriate communication behavior.[12]

CONCLUDING REMARKS

We've suggested that the way we define our associations as well as the conclusions we draw about their potential depth depend on our perceptions of status and interpersonal solidarity. Further, we've suggested that our perceptions in this regard will affect us in a full range of environments. Finally, we have suggested or implied that the preceding skills, in conjunction with those we have already discussed, have an immeasurable impact on status and interpersonal solidarity. Assuming that the achievement of at least some degree of interpersonal solidarity is important in a majority of communication environments, we would hope that you not only keep these skills in mind, but, along with your colleagues, discuss their implications for your present or future careers and relationships.

CHAPTER SUMMARY

Interpersonal communication does not always concern people meeting and becoming deeply attached to one another. On the contrary, it probably most

[11]Bochner and Kelley, p. 291.
[12]Bochner and Kelley, pp. 281–301.

frequently concerns salespersons and clients, teachers and students, and supervisors and subordinates conducting their day-to-day business in as amiable an atmosphere as possible. Even so, the principles that apply to more socially oriented relationships also apply to relationships that evolve in task-oriented environments. This is what we're communicating in this chapter.

We have said that once people become casually or formally acquainted, they will engage in ritualistic, activity-centered, and pastime communication behavior. Rather than dismissing this behavior as being superficial and without purpose, we suggested it may assist people in (1) satisfying their need for recognition, (2) providing one another with psychological strokes, and (3) formalizing their relationship. We discussed two norms, status and solidarity, that influence factors like needs and relational definition and depth. We also introduced three additional communication skills that can assist people in further reducing the interpersonal distance that separates them.

THINK ABOUT IT

IN GENERAL

Complete the exercise given under Think About It: In General at the end of Chapter 1.

IN EDUCATION

1. Frequently, little or no interpersonal solidarity exists between teachers and students. In class, discuss communication behaviors that teachers are prone to engage in that promote perceptions of interpersonal distance rather than interpersonal solidarity. Afterwards, generate a list of communication behaviors that teachers might employ to increase solidarity with students, but which wouldn't undermine student perceptions of the teacher's competence.
2. Without realizing we may be doing so, both our verbal and nonverbal behaviors in the classroom may lead others to think we are aloof or guard ourselves as being superior — a form of status. Take time to analyze your customary verbal and nonverbal behaviors in the classroom. Do you think they promote or undermine interpersonal solidarity with your classmates? Why or why not? Communicate with someone in class about your analysis to see if he or she shares the conclusions you've drawn.

IN THE ORGANIZATION

1. Assuming status differences are potentially a problem in the organizational
setting, how might a supervisor or manager attempt to lessen the importance
of status differences between him or her and subordinates? In contrast, what
communication behaviors might subordinates engage in as they attempt to
minimize status differences between themselves and their superiors?
2. How do you think competition affects interpersonal relationships among
subordinates when they find themselves in a position where promotion to a
supervisory role is at hand? How might the skilled interpersonal communicator try to attain this role without alienating his or her coworkers? In
class, generate a list of interpersonal communication skills in this regard.

IN YOUR RELATIONSHIPS

1. Have you ever felt excessively defensive when communicating with someone of higher status than you? If you have, attempt to locate the source of your
feelings of defensiveness and any resultant communication behavior. Then, see
if you can identify any skills that would have made your communication
behavior less defensive in this situation.
2. Have you ever made someone defensive as a result of accentuating rather
than attenuating status differences, for example, with a waiter or waitress,
grocery clerk, or new acquaintance? If you have, place yourself in the person's
shoes and try to ferret out the communications that prompted the defensive
reaction. Is there anything to be gained from accentuating status differences?
Justify your response.

SUGGESTED READINGS

Bochner, A. P. and C. W. Kelley. "Interpersonal Competence: Rationale,
Philosophy, and Implementation of a Conceptual Framework." *The Speech
Teacher*, 23 (1974), 281–301.

This article not only details the kinds of skills that will serve to increase
solidarity between people but also discusses teaching strategies that should
facilitate the acquisition of these skills. It would be to your advantage,
therefore, to read this article and discuss it with people in your class.

Brown, R. *Social Psychology*. The Free Press, New York, 1965.

In our minds, Roger Brown is one of the most significant scholars of this century. The information we've provided in this chapter only scratches the surface of the status and solidarity norms. If you really want to explore these two norms in detail, we strongly urge that you read Part II of this book.

Wheeless, L. R. "Self-Disclosure and Interpersonal Solidarity: Measurement, Validation, and Relationships," *Human Communication Research*, 3, No. 1 (1976), 47–61.

While this discussion is somewhat advanced, Professor Wheeless does an excellent job of tying the self-disclosure and the solidarity concepts as the two interact in affecting relational development. Also, Professor Wheeless's article should give you some insight as to how communication scientists go about measuring such difficult-to-pin-down phenomena as self-disclosure and solidarity.

Chapter Twelve
Identities in Concert:
Intimate Communication
and Intimate Relations

SHOP TALK

Intimate communication Interpersonal communication behaviors characterized by a high degree of immediacy, expressiveness, and risk.

Intimate relationships Interpersonal relationships based on being common, rather than those solely based on common benefits.

Material selves Our physical selves, including our anatomy and appearance, as well as the objects with which we surround ourselves.

Immaterial selves Human factors that are not visible, like attitudes, beliefs, values, and past history.

Interactional synchrony Term used to describe nonverbal communication behavior and depict situations where people synchronize their body rhythms and patterns of communicating.

Autonomous partners Relational partners who continuously assist one another in maximizing their capacities for awareness, expressing authentic emotions, and intimacy.

In Chapter 9 we suggested that when stripped to the barest of essentials, interpersonal communication concerns the meeting and merger of human identities. We also overviewed this process, stating that it was facilitated by time, need compatibility, and purposeful self-disclosures. In Chapter 10 we concentrated on the factors that affect and work for or against successful first encounters. And in Chapter 11 we discussed the nature of interpersonal communication once people move beyond the encounter stage of a potential relationship.

At this point, we want to concentrate on intimate communication and intimate relations, which are not as easily discussed as the process by which people meet, become acquainted, and achieve some level of friendship. We will discuss the nature of intimate communication and relationships, a number of the factors that may serve to promote them, and some of the commitments that people may make to each other as they try to achieve intimacy. Also, we will touch on some potential consequences of these commitments and then examine how we can put our knowledge of the communication transaction to use in the attempt to sustain and nourish intimacy. But before we do any of that, let's first look at the question of why.

WHY INTIMACY?

When you think about it, you'll note that the world is full of contradictions. For example, intimacy is both natural and necessary for our psychological development. The womb is intimate, the caress of a mother or father is intimate, and small children locked arm-in-arm on the way home from kindergarten are intimate. Indeed, we are born with the need for intimacy as well as the capacity to be intimate. But in spite of this, we soon learn from the people around us that human intimacy must be suppressed. Think about the lessons many of us are taught as children. It is okay to be intimate with our bodies until we reach a certain age; it is okay to be intimate with the bodies of others until we reach a certain age; and it is okay for little boys to hold hands or kiss their father on the lips until they reach a certain age. Victims of our environment, we are taught to suppress our capacity for intimacy and intimate communication until we reach an age when human intimacy once again becomes natural.

The trouble is that no one teaches us how to recapture what we've been taught to suppress. As a result, our image of what constitutes genuine intimacy and intimate communication between people frequently is off base. While we are not so bold as to think we can teach people how to re-find their capacity for intimacy and intimate communication, we can at least aid in the search by discussing the concepts as they relate to interpersonal communication.

INTIMATE COMMUNICATION

Few of our communication behaviors are genuinely intimate. Most communication behaviors fall into one of the three categories that we discussed in the last chapter, that is, rituals, activities, and pastimes. How, then, can we distinguish intimate communication from some of the forms we've already discussed? There are no set definitions of intimate communication. It is an elusive concept and is more frequently described than defined. Genuinely intimate communication appears to be void of the ritualistic or gamelike behaviors that humanistic psychologists like Eric Berne discuss. As Muriel James and Dorothy Jongeward point out, intimate communication "occurs in those rare moments of human contact that arouse feelings of tenderness, empathy, and affection . . . . Intimacy involves genuine caring."[1] The question is, how can we conclude that people genuinely care for each other? Can we find clues in their nonverbal and verbal communication behaviors indicating the extent to which they genuinely care for each other? In answer to our own question, yes!

[1]Muriel James and Dorothy Jongeward, *Born To Win: Transactional Analysis with Gestalt Experiments,* Addison-Wesley Publishing Company, Reading, Mass., p. 59.

IMMEDIACY

You will recall from Chapter 10 that immediacy referred to the physical and psychological distance separating people from each other. We implied that people who engaged in nonverbal communication behaviors designed to increase immediacy were more likely to open up with each other — communicate authentic pictures of themselves.

At this point, we would like to add that intimate communication is characterized by a high degree of immediacy. In effect, this means that people carrying on intimate communication position their bodies and even their eyes in ways to feel close to one another. It is well established that during intimate encounters communicators increase touching behavior and position themselves so that no more than eighteen inches of distance separates them. It also is well established that this actual physical distance can be reduced in a psychological sense by intense and sustained eye contact. At a minimum, then, the extent to which people genuinely care for each other is reflected in communication behaviors designed to reduce the physical and psychological distance separating them.

EXPRESSIVENESS

Genuine caring also is reflected in the degree to which communicators feel free to express authentic emotions. In a sense, the capacity to be intimate is the capacity to express what was easily communicated as a child.[2] As we pointed out in our discussion of self-disclosure, children are honest communicators. Rather than providing people with edited versions of their feelings, they communicate exactly what they are feeling. If they don't feel right about doing something they say no. If they are sad or feel hurt, they cry unashamedly. And if they are happy, the emotion is reflected unabashfully. But adults are cautious about overt expressions of authentic emotions. We always worry about the consequences of communicating what we feel well in advance of actually expressing what we feel. More often than not, these long-range forecasts about the consequences of communicating our feelings cause us to either suppress an authentic emotion or communicate a highly edited version of it.

We are not suggesting that intimate communication is synonomous with the expressions of emotion that children sometimes are unable to control, for

[2]James and Jongeward, p. 266.

example, extreme selfishness or anger. What we are suggesting is that intimate communication frequently takes the form of constructive and honestly expressed feelings like saying no without feeling guilty, crying without worrying about how we are being perceived, or sharing the joy we feel.

RISK

Perhaps the best indicant of intimate communication is the degree to which people take psychological risks in communicating with each other. The risks people take when engaged in ritualistic communication or passing the time by discussing innocuous subject matters are minimal at best. The element of risk involved in communicating the depth of intensity of our feelings for another person, though, is tremendous because there is no guarantee that our communications will be met with the desired response. Consider the amount of risk a person takes in expressing love as opposed to liking. We can express feelings of liking without batting an eye. To say that we love someone, though, is a different story altogether. The word *love* implies an emotion of extreme depth and intensity, that is, an emotion that we are cautious about expressing because of the risks involved.

Intimate communication, then, concerns genuine caring. The extent to which people genuinely care for each other is reflected in both their verbal and nonverbal communication behaviors. At a minimum, genuine caring is reflected in the physical and psychological distance separating people, their comfort in expressing authentic as opposed to edited emotions, and the psychological risks inherent in their messages.

Finally, we need to add that while intimate communication is necessary for the development of an intimate relationship, we need not have an intimate relationship with someone in order to communicate intimately. Intimate communication can be very fleeting and can occur between coworkers who momentarily share in a success or failure, two strangers who accidentally make eye contact during a play that has moved both deeply, or a small child with a joyful look at the adult who's selling balloons at an amusement park. Again we explain, intimate communication "occurs in those rare moments of human contact that arouse feelings of tenderness, empathy, and affection."[3] Remember, then, people have not necessarily achieved an intimate relationship simply because moments of intimate communication have transpired. Intimate communications and intimate relations may be highly interdependent, but they are not the same thing.

[3]James and Jongeward, p. 59.

INTIMATE RELATIONS: WHAT AND WHEN

You would think that describing what is meant by an intimate relationship would be much the same as trying to describe what is meant by "good" art. Yet, descriptions of intimate relationships as opposed to nonintimate relationships have been remarkably consistent over time. In the *Ethics,* Aristotle implied an intimate relationship was one characterized by "two bodies and one soul."[4] Much later in history, Michel de Montaigne suggested that people are intimate when the seam binding them disappears.[5] And, within the last fifteen years, Erik Erickson concluded that a person was ready for an intimate relationship when he or she was willing to merge his or her identity with another.[6]

A single word permeates most discussions of intimate relationships — oneness. Whereas acquaintances and friends base their relationships on common benefits, intimates also seem to base their relationship on being common, on having similar needs and identities. An intimate relationship, therefore, is one that not only serves to satisfy the mutual needs of the participants in a relationship but also is one in which the relational partners perceive their individual needs as one and the same.

Of course, neither intimacy nor mutual perceptions of oneness occur without reasons. On the contrary, intimacy and perceptions of oneness are not likely to occur unless people: (1) feel their needs are compatible and will continue to be satisfied; (2) perceive that they are psychologically close to one another; (3) feel comfortable in their abilities to accurately interpret and appropriately respond to each other's communication behavior; (4) mutually project that their relationship is capable of taking on a new and demanding dimension; and (5) have begun to assist each other in realizing their individual capacities to be intimate.

NEED COMPATIBILITY AND NEED SATISFACTION

Given what we have already said about the role need compatibility and need satisfaction play throughout the life of a relationship, we need not belabor the subject here. If people perceive that their needs are incompatible or that their relationship no longer satisfies the needs it once did, there is little reason to

[4]Aristotle, *Ethics,* trans. J. A. K. Thomson, Penguin, Baltimore, 1953, p. 274.
[5]Michel de Montaigne, "On Friendship" in *Essays,* trans. J. M. Cohen, Penguin, Baltimore, 1958, pp. 97–98.
[6]Erik Erickson, *Childhood and Society,* W. W. Norton and Company, New York, 1963, p. 128.

talk about the prospect of them becoming intimates. And that is really the point we want to make. Unless people share in the perception that their needs are compatible and that their relationship has and will continue to satisfy a majority of the needs that they experience, intimate communication and the development of an intimate relationship is not likely.

INTERPERSONAL SOLIDARITY

It would be absurd to talk about people fusing their identities — achieving oneness — without their first decreasing the psychological distance initially separating them. You may recall from the last chapter that interpersonal solidarity parallels the concept of immediacy and concerns the degree to which people perceive that they are psychologically close to one another. You also may recall that interpersonal solidarity increases as people penetrate and exchange the deeper-seated facets of their respective identities. Two points are significant in this regard. The first, and more obvious, is that an enduring intimate relationship most commonly is achieved after people have had sufficient time to explore and exchange the more significant facets of their identity systems, and thereby reduce the psychological distance that separated them in earlier stages of their involvement. The second point stems from our comments on self-disclosure. Put simply, it is not enough for one person to perceive that he or she is psychologically close to the other party in the relationship. If intimacy is the question at issue, this perception must be shared. However, people have no way of really knowing whether others in the relationship share this perception unless all parties have engaged in honest and constructive self-disclosures.

FIDELITY OF COMMUNICATION TRANSACTIONS

Closely aligned to the preceding discussion is the question of fidelity. If relational partners do not feel comfortable in their abilities to accurately interpret and appropriately respond to their communication behaviors, it is doubtful that they will want to escalate their involvement. As we have repeatedly emphasized, the fidelity with which people communicate will increase as the amount of uncertainty in their relationship decreases. Reciprocal disclosures, therefore, will increase the fidelity of their communication transactions. In turn, this increased fidelity will serve to increase the probability of intimate involvement.

EXPECTANCY FORMATION

Although we have talked about the preceding factors as if they were independent, they are not. Rather they are interdependent, and a change in one is likely to affect the others. It is the sum total of these factors that will weigh most heavily in the expectancies that we formulate about the future of a relationship.

To review, we tend to periodically evaluate our interpersonal commitments. On the basis of these evaluations, we may formulate, extend, or modify our expectancies about a relationship's current or future status. These expectancies will influence the ways in which we communicate with our partner(s). Depending on what we expect, we may engage in communication behaviors that are designed to lead to the dissolution of the relationship, sustain it at its present level of involvement, or move it forward.

If people believe that their needs are compatible and that they will continue to satisfy their mutual needs, perceive themselves to be psychologically close, and perceive a high degree of fidelity in their communication transactions with one another, they may develop a new set of expectancies about the potential of their involvement. Specifically, they may come to expect that their involvement is potentially intimate. Moreover, this expectancy is likely to motivate them to engage in communication behaviors that will either confirm or disprove this mutual expectancy.

INTIMACY CAPACITIES

While each of us is born with the capacity to be intimate, sometimes it is unnecessarily suppressed. Even when our capacity for intimacy has been excessively suppressed, however, we can recapture it if we and our relational partners are willing to work toward that end. The question is, How can we assist each other in either discovering or becoming more aware of our capacities to be intimate?

There are no cookbook strategies for people to follow in their attempts to become aware of their individual capacities to be intimate. In fact, as two people explore and exchange facets of their identities, they may become increasingly aware of their individual capacities to be intimate spontaneously. This is because the process of identity penetration and identity exchange frequently facilitates self-awareness as well as relational growth. For example, in trying to learn about the identity of another we may discover or rediscover dormant facets of our identity, including our capacity to be genuinely intimate.

Yet this process need not occur helter-skelter. It can be facilitated when people communicate face-to-face about their interests, their worries, incidents between them, and their authentic emotions. This is because such expressions are indicative of caring. When people can create a climate that is void of defensive communication postures and can assist each other in expressing thoughts and feelings representative of mutual cares, two things can happen. First, they may discover or become more aware of their individual capacities to be genuinely intimate. Second, they may discover or become more aware of their capacities to be intimate with each other. We believe both of these byproducts of purposeful communication are essential to decisions about escalating an interpersonal relationship.

BECOMING INTIMATES: COMMITMENT TALK

As you might imagine, communication between people tends to become more intimate as (1) they make favorable judgments about need compatibility and need satisfaction; (2) they reduce the psychological distance between them; (3) they increase communication fidelity; (4) they expect that their relationship may escalate; and (5) they begin to discover their individual and collective capacities to be intimate. This also is true with respect to the probability of people making commitments to each other that imply that their relationship has taken on new meaning.

Obviously, the kinds of commitments that people make in the attempt to become intimate vary. Nonetheless, it appears that the development of an intimate relationship frequently is facilitated by a series of hierarchical commitments that concern four levels of relational involvement. First level commitments concern the sharing of material and immaterial selves. Second level commitments concern communication behaviors that indicate that a relationship is primary. Third level commitments concern cohabitation, and fourth level commitments concern the sharing of the future.[7] While intimate communication can occur in the absence of these commitments, it is doubtful that people can achieve a genuinely intimate relationship without making some of them. Consequently, we need to examine each level as it relates to intimate communication and intimate relations.

LEVEL ONE: MATERIAL SELVES

When we talk about an individual's material self, we mean the objectifiable characteristics of the individual such as, customary actions, body type, eye,

[7]Murray Davis, *Intimate Relations,* The Free Press, New York, 1973, pp. 192–205.

hair, and skin color. When we talk about the individual's material self, we also are talking about the objects that generally are associated with the individual, such as, the individual's wordly possessions. Thus, our material self is public in nature, visible to those who attend to us.

The sharing of material selves occurs in many dimensions, any of which may serve to facilitate the perception of a singular identity between people. When two people share their bodies in love making, for instance, their physical union may imply an additional promise, namely, some spiritual union in which their identities will be fused. So common is this belief, in fact, that some people will often ignore the physical pleasure that they derive from making love to dwell on the implicit spiritual union that accompanies their temporary coupling.

Of course, we need not make love in the effort to share our material selves. Potential intimates may exchange locks of hair, for example. For the most part, such exchanges are symbolic of oneness. Murray Davis, a sociologist and the author of a book on intimate relations, describes examples of anatomical exchanges such as of blood or hair. Youngsters may prick their fingers and temporarily join them so that they can become blood brothers or sisters.[8] Whether these changes are literal or figurative makes little difference. These symbolic acts have a singular purpose — making two, unique identities more common.

Potential intimates also may share their material selves by synchronizing their behavior. This synchronization is usually most evident in their verbal and

[8]Davis, p. 172.

nonverbal communication behaviors. Words that we all use everyday may take on highly specialized meanings between potential intimates. In the extreme, moreover, potential intimates may go so far as to create words. Consider some of the words that evolved from the drug culture of the 1960s — words like *stoned, bummer,* and *speeding.* Since the use of drugs was socially unacceptable and punishable under the law, such words were created to communicate a special kind of intimacy, a special kind of shared identity predicated on the use of drugs.

Potential intimates also will synchronize their nonverbal communication behavior. This is particularly true with respect to body movements. Certain postures, hand gestures, and ways of walking commonly become synonomous with the potential intimate relationship. More interestingly, the nonverbal movements of one person may be mirrored by the other in a relationship that is becoming intimate. Research on something called *interactional synchrony* clearly demonstrates that communicators tune into each other's body rhythms and establish a rhythmic pattern of talking and listening.[9] There is reason to believe, moreover, that intimates assimilate each other's body rhythms and talk as well as listen in unison when in the company of other people.

Finally, the sharing of material selves is evident in the giving or receiving of what Davis calls "intimacy trophies."[10] Just about any possession can serve as an intimacy trophy. Some of the more common ones are high school or college rings, fraternity or sorority pins, and articles of clothing. Some of the less common ones are books, plants, paintings, sculptures, and pieces of creative writing. In effect, when we give an intimacy trophy to someone, we are saying, "Here — please take this part of my identity." When we accept an intimacy trophy, which is a symbolic representation of another's identity, our identities become more common.

The sharing of material selves frequently includes moments of intimate communication, that is, genuine caring. Whether intimate communication will become more frequent and thereby promote the development of a genuinely intimate relationship, however, will depend on how honest people have been in communicating and sharing authentic pictures of their material selves. Keep this in mind as we turn to a more significant form of sharing.

LEVEL ONE: IMMATERIAL SELVES

When we talk about an individual's immaterial self, we are talking about characteristics of the individual that can only be inferred, such as, attitudes,

[9]W. S. Condon and W. D. Ogston, "Sound Film Analysis of Normal and Pathological Behavior Patterns," *The Journal of Nervous and Mental Disease,* 143 (1966), 338–347.
[10]Davis, pp. 176–177.

beliefs, and values. When we talk about an individual's immaterial self, we also are referring to a person as the product of his or her history. Our immaterial selves are comprised of identity items that are both personal and intimate.

In the preceding three chapters we talked about people sharing their immaterial selves so that they might communicate more effectively with one another. As people approach intimacy, the information that they share also will serve this purpose. How, then, does the sharing of information between intimates differ from the sharing of information between acquaintances or friends? The distinction is a simple one. Whereas acquaintances and friends use the information that they have shared to satisfy mutual needs and increase the fidelity with which they communicate, intimates also use information about their immaterial selves to further fuse their identities.

Intimates not only share information about their attitudes and the like, but they also tend to adopt each other's psychological attributes, causing their attitudes and personal tastes to overlap. For example, intimates may use different words in reference to some object but express similar if not identical opinions. Because we are accustomed to intimates engaging in such behavior, we frequently will assume that the expressed opinion of one party in an intimate relationship is the opinion of the other.

Clues concerning the degree to which intimate identities overlap also can be obtained from nonverbal variables. The clothes that intimates wear, for example, are sometimes more of an expression of their combined tastes than their individual tastes. Furthermore, when intimates reside under the same roof, this conclusion is likely to hold true for the decor of their living environment.

Beyond the preceding, the autobiographies of true intimates also may serve to facilitate their feelings of oneness. When we know a great deal about another's past, including its painful as well as pleasurable moments, we can better empathize with this individual in the present. By empathizing, we mean trying to experience on an imaginary level what this individual experienced in reality. The closer our imaginary experiences are to the real experiences of an intimate, the closer our feelings of oneness are likely to be.

When intimates disclose and familiarize each other with their respective autobiographies, they make their pasts familiar to each other. Murray Davis, in quoting an article on marriage and reality, makes this point quite well:

> It is not only the ongoing experience of the two partners that is constantly shared and passed through the conversational apparatus. The same sharing extends into the past. The two distinct biographies, as subjectively apprehended by the two individuals who have lived through them, are overruled and re-interpreted in the course of their conversation . . . . The couple thus construct not only present reality but reconstruct past reality as well, fabricating a common memory that integrates the recollections of the two individual pasts.[11]

As you can see, the sharing of immaterial selves takes on an added dimension when applied to the subject of intimacy. While this sharing process is bound to increase the fidelity with which intimates communicate as well as satisfy their mutual needs, it also appears to facilitate the growth of a singular identity and the mutual perception of oneness.

LEVEL TWO: COMMITMENTS — PRIMACY

Once people have had sufficient time to evaluate the consequences of their identities beginning to merge, the relationship may begin to further escalate as a result of level two commitments, in which people consider their association to be primary. By primary, we mean the partners in the relationship consider their association more important than other relationships in which they are involved. Examples of primary relationships range from best friends to marital partners.

Because such associations are extremely important, they affect the ways in which people communicate regardless of the context in which they find themselves or the people with whom they come in contact. In a sense, people who have made level two commitments continuously weigh and evaluate the

---

[11]Peter Berger and Hansfried Kellner, "Marriage and the Construction of Reality," in M. Davis, *Intimate Relations*, p. 178.

consequences of their communication behavior. This holds true even when they are not together. Thus, people who have made level two commitments not only communicate in a manner that will serve to reaffirm continuously the primary nature of their association but also may communicate to others in a manner that will convey that they're involved in a primary relationship with another person.

LEVEL THREE: COMMITMENTS — COHABITATION

When people decide to live together, they agree to more than sharing the same roof over their heads. Living together means the sharing of time and possessions as well. Thus, third level commitments are not to be taken lightly. The decision to live with someone is a commitment of real magnitude.

In any case, cohabitation is likely to have a number of effects on the degree to which intimates become common. At the very least, cohabitation enables intimates to have similar experiences in space and time. Prior to living with each other, for example, intimates frequently must communicate their experiences — including what, when, and where — retrospectively. When under the same roof, however, intimates may find themselves experiencing identical phenomena — for example, conversing with friends — while occupying the same space and within the same period of time.

Beyond this, cohabitation enables intimates to further assess the degree to which they are common. Communication initially intensifies when people live together. One of the potential consequences of this intensification is that the material and immaterial selves of intimates will become much more definitive. Each intimate, therefore, will be placed in the position of being able to judge better the extent to which he or she is similar or dissimilar to the other in these two dimensions.

Finally, the social amenities present in the earlier stages of intimacy have a tendency to fall off once intimates begin living together. For example, the impeccable table manners once displayed by an intimate may vanish altogether following a third level commitment. By the same token, tasks that were completed jointly prior to living together — for example, cooking and washing dishes — may be assigned on the basis of traditionally defined roles ("I'll be the handyman; you be the cook and seamstress").

In the last analysis, then, third level commitments provide intimates with at least three opportunities. First, living together enables intimates to become more common. Second, living together enables intimates to better judge the degree to which they are, in fact, common. Thirdly, cohabitation enables intimates to evaluate more realistically the degree to which they are truly compatible.

LEVEL FOUR: COMMITMENTS — SHARED FUTURES

Up to this point, the commitments we've discussed could be made by friends as well as lovers. While friends conceivably could agree to share their futures, level four commitments more commonly are made between people who are romantically involved. And although people who are romantically involved may agree to live together, they may not agree to a binding commitment regarding their respective futures.

We have suggested that intimate communication involves risks. This is also true with respect to establishing an intimate relationship. It seems to us, moreover, that there is no greater risk that people can take in the attempt to achieve genuine intimacy than the risk people take in agreeing to share their futures, because there is no guarantee that what people feel and communicate to each other today will be the same tomorrow.

Beyond the risks involved, there also is the question of importance. To paraphrase another author, we can give nothing more precious to another human being than our future.[12] We think it wise, therefore, that it only be given when one fully realizes the risks involved and the amount of genuine care it implies.

THE POTENTIAL CONSEQUENCES OF INTIMACY

Thus far we have discussed the nature of intimate communication, the nature of intimate relationships, and four levels of commitment that people may make in the attempt to become more common. We realize that the description of intimate communication and intimate relations that we've provided may not conform to everyone's image of these two concepts. We realize also that the kinds of commitments people make in the effort to achieve genuine intimacy may deviate slightly or even substantially from those that we have presented. Regardless of how one describes intimate communication or the nature and development of intimate relations, however, one thing seems certain: human intimacy at any level is not without consequence to the parties involved.

PAIRING

When people commit themselves to become intimate, they may lose a portion of their individual identities. For example, earlier in this chapter we talked about intimates synchronizing their verbal and nonverbal communication

[12]Davis, p. 195.

behaviors, assimilating their respective attitudes, and assuming like if not identical lifestyles. What is likely to happen in such situations is that people who come in contact with the parties in the relationship will ignore their individual identities in favor of a pair identity. Intimate friends may be referred to by some name that identifies them as a pair. When people become paired in this fashion, moreover, invitations to one of the parties in the relationship are likely to mean that all parties in the relationship are invited.

The common identity established between intimates, therefore, has meaning for people outside the relationship. More than that, though, for people outside the intimate relationship, this common identity may supersede the individual identities. The intimates, then, are seen as a pair rather than as unique individuals.

ENRICHED IDENTITIES

Intimate identities are enriched identities. When we become intimate with someone, we assimilate that someone's life experience with our own. In a very real sense, moreover, this process of assimilation makes us even more unique than we were prior to achieving intimacy. Think about it. Prior to becoming intimate we have a singular identity. While we retain a large part of this singular identity following intimacy, we also acquire identity items that couldn't have been acquired otherwise. These identity items not only enrich our experience but also change us — make us somewhat different in our uniqueness. In becoming intimate, therefore, we lose one kind of individuality and gain another.

ESCALATED RESPONSIBILITIES

When two people make their identities common and others come to regard them as a pair, each is faced with a new and demanding set of responsibilities. Most of us have engaged in communication behaviors we regretted because they caused others to perceive us negatively. As long as this behavior only reflects negatively on our individual identities, we injure no one but ourselves. But when we are interpersonally involved, it also may reflect negatively on the other person. At the very least those with whom we are interpersonally involved may perceive that our behavior negatively reflects on them. And this seems to be particularly true with respect to intimates. For example, imagine an intimate couple attending a cocktail party where one of them indulges in a little too much alcohol and becomes the uninvited center of attention. Regardless of the reaction of those in attendance, this person's behavior may do one of two things: first, this person's behavior may cause people to make a real judgment about the intimate couple as a whole; second, this person's behavior may cause his or her intimate to imagine that others are making such a judgment. Whether real or imagined, however, the outcome is one and the same — this person's behavior reflects on his or her intimate. Thus, when we become intimate, we also become responsible for more than our individual actions. Put simply, we are responsible for the impact that our individual actions have on our intimate partners.

In addition to this kind of responsibility, genuine caring demands that we not only share in an intimate's success and joy, but that we also learn to share in an intimate's failure and sorrow. In a sense, genuine caring demands that we feel what an intimate feels, regardless of whether the feeling is pleasurable or painful. Taking on such an additional responsibility is not easy. It demands that we learn to listen rather than react, absorb rather than evaluate, and, on occasion, let our own feelings be subordinate to the feelings of our partners.

At this point, then, we hope that you share in our perception that intimacy is not without consequence. Our intent in the preceding discussion was not to warn you against becoming intimately involved with others. On the contrary, we encourage you to do so when appropriate. Just try to keep in mind what intimacy will demand from you and your intimate partners.

MAINTAINING INTIMACY

Thus far in our discussion of intimate communication, we have dwelled on its positive side. At this point, though, we would like to discuss the more volatile side of intimate communication and how it can be thwarted.

As we merge our identities with another person, our knowledge about that person expands. Not only do we come to know how best to please this person, but we also know what will hurt or even destroy this person in a psychological sense. The messages we transmit, consequently, can be either constructive or destructive. For the most part, this is not a problem. The mutual rewards that we obtain and the needs that we satisfy serve to thwart the kind of volatile communication that may destroy an intimate association. Beyond this, however, there are a number of things that we can do as individuals to further thwart destructive communication from occurring in our intimate relationships.

DEFENSIVE COMMUNICATION

Intimates can't help but know their partner's defense mechanisms and the behavior most likely to elicit them. This information can be put to constructive use in the attempt to thwart destructive communication. Put simply, intimates can avoid engaging in commmunication behavior that may elicit defensive communication. For example, if one intimate knows that the other becomes defensive when the topic of family comes up ("Well, that's just the behavior I would expect from your father"), he or she may want to avoid the topic in order to avoid a defensive response ("My father! What the hell has my father to do with it?").

In the effort to avoid destructive communication, intimates also must realize that criticism is not always intended to be an ego threat or indictment. Because of the intense nature of their involvement and the worth they place on each other, intimates may overreact to critical comments. In this case, a simple comment like "I don't care for that outfit" may be interpreted as "I don't care for you." Obviously, not caring for someone's outfit is not the same as not caring for that someone. If the statement is perceived in this latter sense, though, it is likely to elicit defensive communication ("You just don't seem to like anything about me"). Intimates, therefore, should avoid overreacting to critical comments and making statements that may elicit defensive communication.

ESCALATING

One of the more common misconceptions about communication is that if people communicate about a problem, the problem eventually will be resolved. Whether this is true or not depends on the nature of the problem, the parties in the relationship, and the situation in which they find themselves.

Intimates will argue and will experience conflict. As long as they argue and experience conflict over issues, intimates will be able to control the intensity of the argument or conflict. The trouble is that they may lose sight of issues and begin to attack identities. For example, one party may attack a sensitive facet of the other's identity. In turn, this attack may invite an even more destructive comment and escalate the argument or conflict. Rather than assisting the parties in resolving their differences, then, sustained communication could very well serve to embitter the parties. In such cases, intimates might do well to break off face-to-face communication and later reinstate it when calm and common sense have returned. Again, if they do not, they run the risk of escalating their differences to a highly destructive level.

COMPLIANCE

Sometimes we will comply with the wishes of another person because the person can administer punishments or withhold rewards from us. On occasion, one party will try to make another in the relationship conform to his or her desires by employing these methods. Changes in behavior that result from forced compliance are temporary changes. A person will comply with the requests of another only if the person controls all of the rewards and punishments. This is seldom the case among intimates. What is likely to happen, therefore, is that the tables will be turned on the person who initially employs the compliance model.

If one intimate perceives that the relationship is in need of certain changes, it is a reflection of his or her behavior as well as his or her partner's. Instead of trying to make his or her partner change through compliance, he or she would do well to discuss the perception with the relational partner. In this way, the problem that is causing the perception may be identified, and both partners may decide that one or both of them needs to change. This alternative is far more constructive than compliance, which is a coercive model of persuasion.

PRIVILEGES VS. RIGHTS

Another method of thwarting destructive communication is to remain mindful that intimacy is a privilege and not a right. Simply because we have been given access to a person's past, present, and future does not mean that we can demand at will entrance to another's spiritual and physical lair. That is a privilege that is extended by invitation. When we fail to appreciate and respect this fact, we have forgotten that our singular, intimate identity was achieved through reciprocal behavior.

ENCOURAGING GROWTH

Intimacy is not an end in itself, nor does it remain static. Instead, intimacy is dynamic. Just as two people assist each other in planting the seeds of intimacy, they must assist each other in nourishing its growth. Toward that end, intimates should continually assist each other in becoming autonomous people.[13] Autonomous people are those who are continuously discovering new facets of their capacities to be aware, spontaneous, and intimate.

AWARENESS

As we are using the word here, awareness concerns a person's capacity to confront the self, the environment, and others in the present. As James and Jongeward point out:

[13]James and Jongeward, pp. 263–274.

An aware person knows the inner world of feelings and fantasies and is not afraid of them . . . can stand by a lake, study a buttercup, feel the wind, and experience a sense of awe . . . [and] make genuine contact with the other person by learning the skills of both talking and listening.[14]

It seems to us that intimates are in the unique position of assisting each other in maximizing their respective capacities for awareness, because intimacy not only enables people to tune into others but also assists people in better tuning into themselves. In so doing intimates can thwart the possibility of their relationship stagnating.

SPONTANEITY

Intimates also are in a position to assist each other in becoming more spontaneous, that is, to be capable of expressing a full range of authentic emotions, purposefully and responsibly. People who are genuinely intimate should be able to make decisions about their relationship on the basis of what they genuinely feel. For example, if a person doesn't feel like complying with a request, a decision about the request should be asserted on the basis of the feeling. Moreover, the decision should be acted on without unnecessary feelings of remorse or worry. Of course, in order to reach such a point in a relationship, intimates must assist each other in discovering and understanding the roots of their authentic emotions.

INTIMACY

Earlier, we suggested that potential intimates can assist each other in discovering or becoming more aware of their individual and collective capacities to be intimate. This kind of assistance should continue throughout the life of their relationship. Autonomous people are not plagued by the hang-ups that so commonly prevent the communication of warmth, closeness, and affection. Neither are they afraid to encourage the communication of such emotions in those about whom they care. Even when intimates have achieved some level of comfort regarding intimacy, however, they should not become complacent. They will have to work to sustain that level of comfort or, better yet, improve upon it.

Obviously, there are other behaviors we can engage in to ensure the maintenance of our intimate relationships. In the next chapter, which con-

[14]James and Jongeward, p. 264

cerns the deterioration of relationships, we will talk about other behaviors that may assist us in maintaining both intimate and nonintimate relationships.

CHAPTER SUMMARY

In this chapter we demonstrated that while nonintimate relationships are relationships of common benefit, intimate relationships are relationships of common being. Toward that end, we discussed the nature of intimate communication as well as the nature of intimate relations, giving some antecedents of intimacy, namely, mutual need satisfaction, interpersonal solidarity, fidelity of communication, common expectancies about the future of a relationship, and discovering or becoming aware of our capacity to be intimate. We discussed commitments that may accompany the decision to become intimate. You'll recall that first level commitments concern the sharing of material and immaterial selves, second level commitments concern the notion of primacy, third level commitments concern cohabitation, and fourth level commitments concern the sharing of the future. We emphasized potential consequences of becoming intimate and the maintenance of intimate relationships. Remember that while we can communicate intimately without the benefit of an intimate relationship, intimate communication is necessary to both the development and maintenance of a genuinely intimate relationship.

THINK ABOUT IT

IN GENERAL

Complete the exercises given under Think About It: In General at the end of Chapter 1.

IN EDUCATION

If we assume intimate communication increases the fidelity with which people communicate, a case might be made for people attempting to communicate intimately in all environments. How might intimate communication affect the classroom if teachers both communicated intimately and encouraged students to do likewise? Concentrate on both positive and negative effects. Take a position regarding your own stand on the issue, and prepare to defend it in class.

IN THE ORGANIZATION

While we may think otherwise, coworkers frequently communicate about intimate matters that are both relevant and irrelevant to the work environment. Assume the role of a manager or supervisor. What complications, if any, do you see arising from this kind of communication between subordinates and managers, or between subordinates and their superiors? If you perceive complications arising, how would you approach the subject with coworkers, and what would you do as a communicator so as not to alienate coworkers?

IN YOUR RELATIONSHIPS

We have suggested that intimates should assist each other in becoming autonomous people. Generate a list of communication behaviors that you believe will assist people in becoming aware, spontaneous, and intimate. Following this, write a description of the kind of climate that allows relational partners to assist one another in becoming autonomous and will minimize defensive communication resulting from the expression of authentic emotions. Compare and discuss your list and description with those of other people in the class.

SUGGESTED READINGS

Davis, M. *Intimate Relations.* The Free Press, New York, 1973.
Much of what we discussed in this chapter is attributable to the insights supplied in this book. Chapter 6 of Davis's book, entitled "Couples," should prove a rich supplement to our information.

James, M. and D. Jongeward. *Born to Win: Transactional Analysis with Gestalt Experiments.* Addison-Wesley Publishing Company, Reading, Mass., 1975.
This book is based largely on the work of the late Eric Berne. James and Jongeward argue that people must become autonomous if they are to discover themselves and others. We think you will find this book a stimulating and valuable supplement.

Morris, D. *Intimate Behavior.* Random House, New York, 1971.
This book deals with the entire question of intimacy. Chapter 1, entitled "The Roots of Intimacy," provides the reader with an interesting perspective on the origins of intimacy in humans.

Chapter Thirteen
The Deterioration of Interpersonal Relationships:
Contributive and Preventive Communication

SHOP TALK

Stress Psychological and physical feelings resulting from our inabilities to cope with external and internal pressures.
Procedural conflict Disagreements concerning the steps that should be taken to reach a goal.
Substantive conflict Disagreements about goals.
Affective conflict Personal attacks concerning identities.
Differentiating Verbal and nonverbal communication behaviors designed to emphasize differences rather than commonalities between people.
Circumscribing Failing to deal directly with communications from our relational partners.
Win-lose settings Settings where people perceive that they have only two options: winning at the expense of another or losing at the expense of themselves.

Up to this point, we have concentrated on the growth of our interpersonal relationships. But one reality we all must face is that any relationship can come apart. Even two people who have assisted each other in the satisfaction of mutual needs, have enriched their respective identities, and have realized goals that could not have been realized outside the relationship may decide to call it quits. No doubt in some cases this is as it should be.

We can't help but wonder, though, how many people decide to call it quits because it is the path of least resistance, that is, the easiest and most expedient course of action to take. We also can't help but wonder how many of these relationships might not have terminated if the parties in the relationship had been willing to learn to cope with the sources of their difficulties, including the ways in which they communicate. While we cannot provide unequivocal answers to these highly speculative questions, at least we can provide you with information that is applicable to these questions and to your own relationships. Therefore, this chapter will concentrate on behaviors that you and your relational partners can employ to thwart deterioration.

GROWING APART

Husbands and wives, friends, lovers, and business associates do not realize suddenly that they are disenchanted with their situations. Interpersonal relationships both grow and deteriorate systematically.[1] By this we mean that relationships rarely just blow up without rhyme or reason. There seems to be a

---

[1]Irwin Altman and Dallas A. Taylor, *Social Penetration: The Development of Interpersonal Relationships*, Holt, Rinehart, and Winston, New York, 1973.

sequence and pattern of communication behavior that signal that a relationship is in trouble and the extent to which it is in trouble. Obviously, there is no single set of factors that characterizes deterioration in all interpersonal relationships. People grow apart at different rates and for different reasons.

NEED SATISFACTION

Many relationships begin to deteriorate as a function of people failing to satisfy each other's needs. It is important to recognize here that our interpersonal needs will be satisfied by our relational partners as long as we perceive that they are being satisfied and vice versa. Thus, a relational partner may behave toward us as he or she always has behaved, but we may perceive that his or her behavior no longer satisfies our interpersonal needs. Our perceptions, in other words, are what really count when we talk about a relationship no longer satisfying needs.

Reciprocity   As we have pointed out, our involvement with people begins to take shape as a function of mutual needs that we satisfy, time, and purposeful self-disclosures. As long as the partners in a relationship perceive that the behavior they engage in to satisfy one another's needs is reciprocated, their relationship will at the very least be maintained. But if this perception cannot be maintained, deterioration may begin.

One person, for example, may perceive that while he or she is continuing to satisfy the interpersonal needs of his or her partner, the relationship has become one-sided. If this perception is solidified and not revealed to the partner, it may become a tremendous source of frustration. Sooner or later the perception as well as the person's frustration will be reflected in his or her communication behavior. If the perception and the negative communication (for example, defensiveness) that is likely to result from it are not changed at this point, further complications may arise. This is particularly true if the other person in the relationship fails to see that he or she no longer is satisfying the needs of the relational partner. Thus, when one person or all of the parties in a relationship perceive that their need satisfying behavior is not being reciprocated, the perception should be revealed. Otherwise, the perception may be overlooked and deterioration may occur more rapidly.

Need Compatibility   Like everything else, needs are subject to change. Whereas a need like social inclusion may be of utmost importance during the first half of a person's life, a need like self-actualization may eventually take its place. The trouble is that people may experience different needs at different stages in their lives. And these needs are not always compatible with one another. To illustrate this point, let's consider two needs experienced by a married couple: the need for social inclusion and the need for self-actualization. Joseph always has experienced a strong need for social inclusion. Whatever the occasion, he enjoys surrounding himself and his wife with friends. On the other hand, Mary no longer feels a strong need to have friends around constantly. After twenty years of marriage and three children, she desires to learn more about herself — including her capabilities beyond housework. Vacation time rolls around and Joseph and Mary must decide where they would like to spend two weeks. Joseph suggests that they accompany friends on a Caribbean cruise. He thinks that shipboard parties and joint sightseeing would be fun. Mary objects. She has read about a seaside retreat where couples can vacation, learn something about themselves as individuals, and use this information to benefit their commitment to each other. She believes that she has outgrown the couple who would accompany them, and she needs more from this particular vacation than rest and recreation aboard a cruise ship. Joseph cannot understand Mary's need to visit a retreat. Mary cannot understand Joseph's need to surround himself with old friends while on vacation. Joseph and Mary begin to perceive that their needs are incompatible.

Again, it is the perception of the parties that may eventually cause them problems. Joseph's need for social inclusion does not have to be incompatible with Mary's need to self-actualize. If they were to commit themselves to a course of action designed to find a way to satisfy both of their needs, they probably could reconcile their differences. However, if they base their communication behavior on the mutual perception that their needs are, indeed, incompatible, they may experience real problems. Mary might begin to perceive that she has outgrown Joseph and communicate with him as if the perception were wholly true. Then again, Joseph may misperceive the reasons for Mary's desire to self-actualize. He might project that he is deficient in Mary's eyes, and this projection will affect the way in which he communicates with her.

Two perceptions, then, both of which concern needs, can increase the likelihood of relational deterioration. First, the perception that one's need satisfying behavior is not being reciprocated can be a source of decay. Second, the perception that one's needs are incompatible with those of a relational partner also can be a source of decay. It is important, therefore, that people share these perceptions with their relational partners. Otherwise, they will assume that the perceptions are valid and base their communication behaviors accordingly.

THE LOSS OF INTERPERSONAL ATTRACTION

A second potential source of relational decay is the loss of interpersonal attraction. You'll recall from Chapter 10 that there are three dimensions of interpersonal attraction: physical attraction, task attraction, and social attraction.

Physical Attraction Given the importance of physical attraction to the beginning phase of a relationship, it's probably a good bet that the loss of physical attraction is all too frequently a source of decay. And we suspect this is particularly true in situations where the people are physically intimate.

Fortunately, physical attraction is a perception that is comprised of other perceptions. Normally we find those people with whom we are interpersonally involved to be physically attractive in a figurative if not a literal sense. This perception is attributable to their many fine qualities as well as to their physical appearances. As long as this perception holds up, the parties should be able to weather an inevitable consequence of age, the physical deterioration of their bodies.

Of course, there are relationships founded solely on physical appearance — not a composite of perceptions leading to a single perception of physical attractiveness, but the kind of physical attraction that is sold by Hollywood and Madison Avenue. In such cases, the loss of physical attraction of one partner for the other would probably lead to the relationship's termination. Perhaps that is just, given two people who are foolish enough to believe that they can build a sound interpersonal commitment solely on the basis of their good looks.

Thus, from our vantage point, we recognize that the perception of physical attractiveness can be attributable to more than appearances. If we can remain cognizant of this fact, keeping in mind all of the things that help to create the perception of physical attraction, the deterioration of our appearances need not be a significant source of relational decay.

Social Attraction In Chapter 10, we said that human beings are stimulatropic. By this we meant that human beings need to be stimulated and purposely need to seek out new and unique sources of stimulation. We used this notion to explain better the process of first encounters.

This need to be stimulated also can be used to explain the loss of social attraction. Sometimes we will grow so accustomed to a person's sociability that we will become bored with the person. While our familiarity with the person may not elicit our contempt, it may very well cause us to judge the person as less socially attractive than we originally thought. Like any other perception, this one eventually will be reflected in our behavior toward the person, for instance, in the frequency with which we communicate. Unless

this person is oblivious of us, he or she will begin to realize this perception. And, interestingly enough, this person also may begin to perceive us as less attractive in a social dimension.

Of course, the upshot of all of this is that the principals involved will begin to seek out new sources of social stimulation, which means that they will see and communicate with each other less frequently. Since some form of social contact is necessary to sustain an interpersonal relationship, deterioration will begin.

The lack of stimulation is not the only factor that may contribute to the loss of social attraction. The people we become friendly with in a social dimension may change. For example, they may violate the confidence we place in them, acquire obnoxious qualities, or exclude us from their activities with other people. Putting these reasons aside, though, we think one of the primary reasons that causes us to perceive another as socially attractive is the fact that he or she stimulates us in some fashion. It stands to reason, then, that the loss of this stimulative quality may affect an additional loss, namely, social attraction.

Task Attraction Although there are a host of factors that may diminish one's task attraction for another, we would like to concentrate on one in particular: excessive competition. As a student, you are all too frequently asked to compete against your peers and friends for grades and for the respect of your teachers. This situation does not change when you assume an occupational role

in society. Competition is the sine qua non of capitalism and it permeates all the professions.

Although competition may foster real benefits for those who compete, excessive competition may destroy friendships in school or on the job.[2] Take the case of students enrolled in the premed program at a well-known university in the Midwest. You would think students in the program would assist each other and develop close ties because of their common goals and common tasks. But nothing could be further from the truth. Experiments in biological sciences, some of which take weeks to complete, must be kept under twenty-four-hour surveillance. Why? Some students have had their experiments sabotaged in the most crucial phase, forcing these students to begin again. Why? Because other students, worried about their chances of being accepted to a limited number of medical schools, believe sabotaging projects will give them an edge over other students.

Excessive competition stifles communication and gives rise to deception and a general lack of trust between people.[3] This holds true for people who have built relationships around their mutual perceptions of task attraction. When forced to compete excessively or when operating under the perception that they have no alternative but to compete, they will close the channels

[2]Morton Deutsch, "An Experimental Study of the Effects of Cooperation and Competition," *Human Relations,* 2 (1949), 191–232.

[3]A. Pepitone and R. Kleiner, "The Effects of Threat and Frustration on Group Cohesiveness," *Journal of Abnormal and Social Psychology,* 54 (1957), 192–199.

of communication between them and become suspicious of the other's motivation to communicate. We suspect this will diminish perceptions of task attractiveness and begin to destroy the foundations of their mutual commitment.

Before moving on, we should mention that many of our interpersonal relationships are based on positive perceptions of all three of the dimensions of interpersonal attraction. In the case of marital partners or lovers, for example, perceptions of physical attraction may give rise to their involvement, but perceptions of social and task attraction are what seal the bonds of it. It is doubtful, therefore, that a change in perception on a single dimension of attraction would signal a relationship's end. The point is that a change in perception on a single dimension of attraction may lead to changes in perceptions on other dimensions. And these changes may lead to deterioration. As we suggested in our discussion of needs, perceptual changes should be constructively communicated to our relational partners. We believe that this is true in terms of both the needs we experience and our perceptions of interpersonal attraction.

DISSIMILARITY

The third source of relational deterioration concerns perceptions of dissimilarity.[4] To begin with, perceptions of dissimilarity can be the consequence of a relational partner's failure to satisfy our needs, the belief that our needs are no longer compatible, or the loss of interpersonal attraction. Beyond these reasons, we may begin to perceive that we are dissimilar on the basis of changes in our attitudes, values, and lifestyles.

Attitudes and Values In our discussion of first encounters and the acquaintance process, we said that interpersonal involvement is most likely to occur between people who perceive that they share similar attitudes and values. We expanded this notion in our discussion of intimacy, pointing out that intimates may assimilate each other's attitudes and values.

Perceptions of similar attitudes and values are important throughout the life of a relationship. The longer people hold onto these perceptions, the longer their mutual commitment is likely to survive. Like needs, however, attitudes and values change. Sometimes attitudes and values change simply because of a change in environment. It's not uncommon for college students to experience significant changes in attitudes and values while away from home. As long as the people they were interpersonally involved with at home have undergone similar changes, there is no problem. But what if this is not the case? Consider

[4]Ted. L. Huston, ed., *The Foundations of Interpersonal Attraction*, Academic Press, New York, 1974, pp. 3–25.

"I'm not getting older—I'm getting better!"

high school lovers who separate when one takes a job in the local community and the other travels crosscountry to attend school. Automatically, the physical distance that separates them may serve as a source of relational decay. More importantly, the change in environment is likely to affect changes in the attitudes and values of the college student, but not in the student's relational partner. These changes may give rise to perceptions of dissimilarities and this may negatively affect their former relationship.

Lifestyles   Closely aligned, if not inseparable from changes in attitudes and values, are changes in lifestyles. Lifestyles in this country have changed radically in the past twenty years. Whereas questions of unmarried people living together were not publicly discussed, now such topics frequently appear in the columns of "Dear Abby." What has this to do with relational deterioration?

The key word is *change*. Just because one partner in a relationship may want to change lifestyles, it does not mean the other partner will be so inclined. Since a change in lifestyle or the desire to make such a change is normally an indication of a change in attitudes and values, either partner may begin to perceive the other as becoming dissimilar. Think about this in terms of the feminist movement. Not so long ago, men automatically assumed that women would take on the role of wife, mother, and homemaker following marriage.

Many relationships conformed to this premise, that is, until women began to demand and assert their constitutional rights. So what happens when the loving homemaker, who once appeared to hold onto attitudes identical to her husband's, suggests a change in lifestyle, specifically, role reversal between her and her husband? Unless they talk about it, uncover the reasons for the suggestion, and negotiate, they may begin to perceive dissimilarities between them that heretofore were never recognized. Moreover, these dissimilarities may become even more pronounced, and this may work against them.

The perception of dissimilarities, whether in attitudes and values or lifestyles, normally results from one person undergoing or desiring to undergo change while the other remains entrenched. If the parties cannot come to grips with their different desires, they may come to perceive each other as increasingly dissimilar. This shared perception will undermine their involvement.

STRESS AND CONFLICT

Usually, stress and conflict are regarded as the most important agents of relational decay. However, we prefer to think that our inabilities to cope with the aforementioned sources of relational decay cause stress and that conflict is the most common manifestation of stress. People are not in the habit of revealing every little annoyance and irritation about their partners. As things begin to add up, however, people may feel stress and resort to affective conflict as a means of coping with it. There are better ways to cope with stress (something we'll talk about later); however, let us examine the relationship between stress and interpersonal conflict.

Stress As is the case with so many of the concepts with which we deal, there is no universally accepted definition of stress. Some say it is an external force that produces strain, others say it is the absence of balance, and still others equate stress with fear or anxiety.[5]

For our purposes, we define stress as something you already know and have felt: tension. Tension is the product of feelings that we either cannot identify or cope with. Just to make sure that you know the difference between tension and relaxation, though, we would like you to engage in a simple behavior. First, clench your teeth and close your eyes as tightly as you can. Hold this

[5]Stanley Coren and Martin A. Schulman, "Effect of an External Stress on Commonality of Verbal Associates," *Psychological Reports,* 28 (1971), 328–330; Leon Vande Creek and John T. Watkins, "Responses to Incongruent Verbal and Nonverbal Emotional Cues," *The Journal of Communication,* 22 (1972), 311–316; Dougals T. Hall and Roger Mansfield, "Organizational and Individual Response to External Stress," *Administrative Science Quarterly,* 16 (Dec. 1971), 4, 547–553.

expression for a few seconds, unclench your teeth, rest your eyes, and then relax. Repeat this expression two or three times, making sure you concentrate on the difference between the feelings you experience when your face is tensed or relaxed.

Now that you know what stress is, or at the very least how it feels, what are its origins? In our minds, stress seems to be a by-product of pressures brought to bear on us by external sources and our commitments. In school, for example, teachers commonly will bring pressures to bear on us. One may say,

> As you will note from your syllabus this class entails some work. In order to achieve an A, you will need to read no less than four books from the attached reading list, write two term papers, typed and double-spaced, and demonstrate 90 percent mastery on all quizzes and major exams. In spite of the work load, I expect this class to have a good deal of fun.

Teachers, however, are not the only external sources of pressure or tension. Many of the people with whom we are interpersonally involved exert pressures on us. Parents may add to the tension that we feel while in school, good friends may increase tension by asking us to share in their problems, and those with whom we are romantically involved may create tension by their demands. Finally, we ourselves may add to the tension by the importance that we attach to our commitments or by overcommitting ourselves. Given our need to feel competent and responsible, we may take on extra duties at work or back ourselves into a corner because we haven't the time to accomplish all of our goals.

Contrary to popular thought, moderate amounts of tension may work to our advantage. This is because moderate amounts of tension usually motivate us to work in constructive ways to alleviate it. For example, an assigned paper or realistic deadline at work may cause you to feel moderate tension. You can alleviate tension in this situation simply by completing the paper or meeting the deadline on schedule or ahead of schedule.

Excessive tension, however, is not motivational. It is dysfunctional from both a physiological and psychological standpoint. On a physiological dimension, excessive tension has been linked to high blood pressure, heart attacks, and strokes. On a psychological dimension, research suggests that excessive tension may induce psychological withdrawal and may affect negatively one's listening abilities, coping behavior, and ability to perform normal tasks.[6]

---

[6]James H. Straughan and Henry W. Dufort, "Task Difficulty, Relaxation, and Anxiety Level During Verbal Learning and Recall," *Journal of Abnormal Psychology,* 74 (1969), 621–624.

Excessive stress, therefore, may affect our interpersonal relationships by the frequency and intensity of conflict that may result.

Conflict Before we do anything else, let us dispel a pervasive misconception about conflict. It is not necessarily bad. The consequences of conflict depend on its type and management. There are three types of conflict that we and our relational partners commonly face: procedural conflict, substantive conflict, and affective conflict.[7] *Procedural conflict* occurs when relational partners disagree about the steps they must take in the effort to reach some goal. Examples of procedural conflict range from parents disagreeing about the best way to save money for their child's education to newlyweds disagreeing about which room in their apartment should be decorated first. In other words, there is an agreed-on goal but there is disagreement about the method to reach the goal. *Substantive conflict* occurs when relational partners disagree about the goals themselves. In this case, the parents might disagree about whether a college degree is worthwhile, and the newlyweds might disagree about whether they should decorate their apartment or buy a new car. Both procedural and substantive conflict may serve highly useful purposes. Research suggests that intelligent disagreements over procedures, issues, and goals may result in a superior end product to one occurring without conflict. As long as people can confine their disagreements to such matters, therefore, conflict can work for instead of against the quality of their commitment.

Affective conflict occurs when people attack their partner's identity. We strongly believe that affective conflict is commonly the result of an individual's inability to cope with moderate to excessive tension. Under conditions of excessive tension, relational partners may attribute to each other the tension that they feel, and this may give rise to affective conflict. Consider two people who experience excessive tension because of demanding jobs. Following work, one of them returns home, pours a drink, and collapses on the couch. When the other walks through the door, he or she notices that the house is in a state of disarray and says, "Well, the least you could have done before I got home was straighten up the house," and the conflict begins.

"Me? I cleaned up your mess all last week. You'd think I haven't anything better to do."

"Hey! I didn't mean it that way . . . So climb off your high horse and get off my back. I'm tired too."

[7]Thomas Knutson, Velma Lashbrook, and Arthur Heemer, "The Dimensions of Small Group Conflict: A Factor Analytic Study," Paper presented to the annual meeting of the International Communication Association, Portland, 1976.

"Certainly not from cleaning up the house, much less your own mess."

"Look who's calling who a slob! The bathroom looked like a pig sty when you graciously let me use it this morning."

"Listen! If you don't want that overswollen head of yours a hat-size larger, you'd better mind your mouth."

This example shows that people may take out on each other the excessive tension resulting from their work. We call this form of blame and recrimination *selective attribution* in the identity section of the book and point to its potentially negative consequences. Here, we show that the relational partners' inability to identify the source of their tensions is responsible for their affective conflict. Tongue lashings and the affective conflict that follows may temporarily alleviate concerns and tensions, but it also may result in irreparable harm and become a source of relational decay. The extent to which it causes decay, however, depends on the nature and health of the relationship itself. We have said that conflict is potentially most damaging between intimates because of the knowledge that they share about the other's identity. Put simply, intimates are in a position to attack the most sensitive facets of their partner's identity. Frequent affective conflict between intimates may destroy the singular identity that they created. If the relationship is healthy and the relational partners perceive that the benefits of being in union are more rewarding than anything that may be gained outside the relationship, occasional affective conflicts will be weathered easily. In the final analysis, then, the extent to which affective conflict will be a source of deterioration depends on: (1) how well the relationship satisfies needs; (2) the fidelity with which people communicate — including the willingness to constructively disclose feelings; (3) how close psychologically they perceive themselves; and (4) their mutual expectancies about the current and future status of their mutual commitment. We'll have more to say about conflict and its management following a discussion of the communication behaviors that people exhibit as they try to disengage from a relationship.

HOW CAN I SAY IT GENTLY?

Up to this point we have discussed some of the potential sources of relational decay. Along the way, we have implied that people can deal with these sources of relational decay if they are able to recognize communication behaviors that are symptomatic of deterioration. Prior to discussing some of the strategies we can employ to guard against deterioration, let us examine some of the communication behaviors that signal that a relationship may be in trouble.

In Chapter 2 we said that human communication is disclosive and therefore people cannot hide what they are feeling from their partners. One partner can sense what the other is feeling. Those who desire to disengage from a relationship, intentionally or unintentionally, give their partners clues about their feelings by what they do and don't say. Mark Knapp, a leading scholar in the area of interpersonal communication, suggests that there is a pattern to these clues and that people move through five, distinct stages of interaction as a relationship begins to deteriorate and, ultimately, terminates. Knapp calls these stages differentiating, circumscribing, stagnating, avoiding, and terminating.[8]

DIFFERENTIATING

During the developmental phase of interpersonal relationships, many communication behaviors are targeted at establishing commonalities between the relational partners. Whether on the job or in social environments, for example, acquaintanceship usually grows out of common backgrounds or interests, friendship grows out of common attitudes or values, and intimacy grows out of the establishment of a common identity.

Differentiating, or divergence as Murray Davis calls it,[9] is the reverse of the preceding growth process. Instead of trying to establish commonalities by way

[8]Mark L. Knapp, *Social Intercourse: From Hello to Goodbye,* Allyn and Bacon, Boston, in press.
[9]Murray Davis, *Intimate Relations,* The Free Press, New York, 1973.

of communication, people who desire to disengage themselves from a commitment may try to differentiate themselves from a relational partner by way of communication. Remember our example of the married couple, Joseph and Mary, who were experiencing what they perceived to be incompatible needs? It could be said that Mary also was differentiating because she no longer shared Joseph's strong need for social inclusion. The same could be said for our example concerning lifestyles. The woman's desire to assume a role other than house person or homemaker could have been her way of expressing that she and her husband were growing apart.

Differentiating may occur on a verbal level or on a nonverbal level. To illustrate this point, imagine two intimates who customarily dress in a conservative and complementary fashion. Now imagine that one of these persons abondons his usual three-piece suit and wing-tips for tie-dyed jeans, sequin-yoked cowboy shirts, and sandals. How is this person's relational partner likely to react? Do you think the relational partner might intuit that this person has changed, that he is somehow different or wants to be different?

It is important to note that some verbal and nonverbal statements proclaiming that relational partners are not completely alike are not intended as differentiation. It depends on the frequency and intensity with which such proclamations are made.

CIRCUMSCRIBING

When differences rather than commonalities become the dominant characteristic of a relationship, people may begin to circumscribe each other. We can look at circumscribing in several ways. First, circumscribing can concern the degree to which one person responds in a relevant manner to the inquiries of another. For example, if a friend were to ask you, "Are you going to Jan's on Friday night?" and you were to respond, "The history test really has me bugged," you would not be responding relevantly to the friend's inquiry. If you habitually responded to this person in such a manner, you would be circumscribing; in effect, communicating that you do not want to deal with the person.

Circumscribing also can concern the degree to which one person is willing to disclose to another person. In this case, circumscribing again may take the form of irrelevant responses to inquiries. Instead of communicating, "I don't want to deal with the inquiry," these irrelevant responses are intended to communicate, "I don't care to share that piece of information with you."

Relationships cannot be maintained unless the relational partners attend and respond in a relevant manner to each other. It is doubtful that people could maintain their involvement without sharing information through purposeful self-disclosures. Thus, circumscribing will accelerate relational deterioration.

STAGNATING

Any relationship can temporarily stagnate. But in most cases, people find the energy to get the relationship moving again. The difference between a relationship that is in a state of temporary stagnation and one that may be deteriorating rapidly is that one or both of the parties in the deteriorating one may not be willing to expend the necessary energy to get things moving again. Normally, this unwillingness to improve the relationship is most evident in communication behavior.

While we are not accustomed to thinking about it in this way, interpersonal communication involves a tremendous expenditure of energy. This is particularly true if a relationship is on a downward slide. The partners will have to identify and agree on the source of their difficulties, decide if their difficulties can be reconciled, and plan some course of action that enables them to actually reconcile. This process is difficult enough for people who are willing to expend the energy, more so for people who are reluctant or do not want to expend such energies. This unwillingness is likely to generalize to their relational partner and if neither is willing to communicate, there is little hope for them.

AVOIDING

When people know they are in trouble and have failed to do anything about it, they are likely to feel uncomfortable when in each other's presence. As a result, one or both of them may try to avoid situations that require face-to-face communication. When they cannot escape communication, one or both of the parties may make excuses that will limit the length of the communication transaction.

When cohabitation is not a factor, one partner can avoid the other without much difficulty. Even if cohabitation is a factor, they may become adept at avoiding situations that may require communication. Familiar with each other's schedules, one person may plan around the other's schedule. In extreme cases, one may express his or her dissatisfaction by violating a routine or an agreed-to schedule by purposely arriving late or early.

Whatever diversionary tactic is used, the point remains the same. Relationships cannot be maintained unless people sustain contact and communicate. Purposeful avoidance behavior is easily recognized and its meaning is easily discerned. Thus, avoiding will signal that an involvement is near its end.

TERMINATING

In point of fact, breaking up is hard to do, particularly if only one party wants out. As a result, people who desire to disengage may develop communication strategies designed to minimize guilt and maximize the probability of disengagement.

Rare is the person who suddenly turns to a relational partner and flatly states that he or she wants out. Most people try to communicate their disenchantment gradually and implicitly. The behaviors we've discussed thus far, in fact, are designed to let one ease out of a commitment rather than do so in one bold move.

But what happens when one person fails to take the hint or tenaciously holds on, regardless of how bad it has gotten? Well, one of the fifty ways to leave one's lover is to make things so intolerable that he or she, rather than the person who originally wanted out, will demand the relationship's termination. For example, the person could become totally uncommunicative, purposely violate expectancies, fail to reciprocate, and use every innocent remark as an excuse for affective conflict. Such abuse, which we think is less than desirable is not likely to go unnoticed. No matter how tolerant a person is, he or she may reach the point where leave-taking is the only alternative.

A more kind but nonetheless manipulative strategy is the "It's best for us both" approach. In this case, people who desire to terminate a relationship try to convince a relational partner that their separation is mutually beneficial. While this very well may be true, this strategy still is self-serving.

So is there some way in which a relationship can be terminated considerately? It depends on the nature of the relationship and the partners. Obviously, simple acquaintances can terminate a relationship more easily than intimates. But what about a long-standing relationship where one person wants out desperately and the other does not? How are such commitments terminated without one person being hurt or creating an atmosphere that a friend described as "hate city" following his divorce? People should employ the same skills that they employed during the growth of their relationship when it is about to end. In the case of long-standing commitments, people who desire to disengage themselves should try to evaluate the consequences of their communicative acts on their relational partners as well as themselves and base their communication behavior accordingly.

Is it necessary, for example, to employ evaluative-laden communications near a relationship's end, control communication, or adopt an air of superiority? We think not. People are not compelled to be manipulative, condescending, or hostile once a relationship has run its course. They have a choice.

Our commitments are not terminated easily. As we have described the process, the termination of a relationship is the last in a sequence of events that signals deterioration. This sequence of events begins with differentiating and includes circumscribing, stagnating, and avoiding. While deterioration may indicate that relational involvement is near its end, this does not have to be the case. If people recognize and deal with the communication behaviors signaling deterioration, they may be able to avoid the painful process that we have described. Let us now turn our attention to behaviors that enable us to cope better with deterioration.

PREVENTING RELATIONAL DETERIORATION

Few things in life are as rewarding, as demanding and as difficult to maintain as our interpersonal relationships. Therefore, we would like to discuss some preventive measures that can thwart relational decay.

COPING WITH STRESS

Stress is a part of life. We feel it as a function of our jobs, the people who enter into and exit from our lives, and the demands we place on ourselves. As we stated earlier, stress is often the consequence of factors that pick away at the foundations of a relationship. Unless we learn to identify the sources of stress and effectively channel it, stress can give rise to affective or dysfunctional conflict, which may accelerate the rate of relational deterioration. By learning to identify and cope with stress we can prevent deterioration.

Identifying Stress In our earlier discussion, we said stress seems to be a by-product of pressures brought to bear on us by external sources and by our commitments. We also said that failure to identify the appropriate source of stress may result in affective conflict.

To begin with, stress is commonly the result of our occupational role. Although we may like being a student, a teacher, or a business person, we may experience excessive amounts of stress because of the demands that are inherent in our occupation. Analysts, for example, frequently need an analyst because their occupation demands that they share in the problems of their patients, and this causes them to experience stress. Also, we may experience stress because of the importance that we attach to our occupational role and to our goals. The more important we perceive our role, the more seriously we take ourselves; and the more burning our desire to succeed, the more likely is it that we will expend excessive energies or overcommit ourselves. Ultimately, we may realize we cannot accomplish all that we want to accomplish because of our own limitations and time. If we cannot learn to live with this fact, we may experience severe stress.

Another source of stress that is commonly overlooked is disenchantment with ourselves. Occasionally, people will engage in behaviors that cause negative perceptions of self. In effect, they get up in the morning, look into the mirror, and decide that they don't like what they see. While negative perceptions of self may result in anxiety, alienation, and depression, they also may give rise to excessive stress. People may decide to change and may make far-reaching intrapersonal commitments. If they are unable to effect these changes and live by these intrapersonal commitments, stress may result.

The final source of stress that we will discuss concerns our interpersonal commitments. To begin with, we may experience stress as a result of factors that are intrinsic to such commitments. We may genuinely believe that a relationship no longer satisfies the needs it once did; that needs which were formerly compatible are no longer so; that a relational partner is less interpersonally attractive; or that we have grown apart as a result of changes in attitudes and values. Failure to disclose such perceptions will do little to alter the behavior that follows. As a result, the people who have become disenchanted will continue to be frustrated, and these frustrations will begin to increase.

Stress also may be a consequence of factors that are extrinsic to our interpersonal commitments, but which have direct bearing on us and our partners. For example, one person in a relationship may not understand the excessive demands of the other person's job. While the job may cause this person to experience stress, the inability of the relational partner to understand this would serve to compound the amount of stress experienced.

Sometimes people will be affected by persons outside their relationship. As a case in point, consider a recently married couple. One individual desires to maintain contact with people he was interpersonally involved with prior to marriage, whereas the other desires that they make new friends jointly. Whatever course of action is taken, frustration is likely to result and, ultimately, stress may be experienced. For example, if the person abandons former friends who are highly valued, these friends may put strain on the relationship:

> "Hey Tom, a bunch of us are going to get together Friday for a little poker game. Why don't you come? It'll be just like old times."
>
> "I don't think so, Jim. Susan has made plans to visit this couple she met through work."
>
> "Cracking the whip again, huh? Just because you're married doesn't mean that you have to turn your back on the people you grew up with."

On the other hand, if contact with his former friends is sustained, the person's spouse may not understand and this would put strain on the relationship:

> "Do you mind if I go to a poker game Friday night?"
>
> "Don't you see enough of those people as it is?"
>
> "I haven't seen any of them since the reception — three months ago."
>
> "But you're married now and we need to make friends with other married couples — people who are my friends as well as yours."

In this instance, strain would be attributable to another kind of external source of strain. Unless the relational partners correctly identified this source of strain, they might begin to attribute any stress that they feel to each other rather than deal with the real source of the problem.

The first step in coping with stress is to correctly identify its source. After all, it may be a person's job that is causing a deterioration rather than the interpersonal relationship. Or it may be an outside party, like a meddling in-law. Finally, you may be experiencing stress by being reticent with your partner.

Reducing Stress We have already said that selective attribution and affective conflict are poor methods of reducing stress. Selective attribution results from failing to identify the source of stress, while affective conflict results from failing to understand and constructively coping with stress. So what alternatives are open to us?

One of the sadder commentaries on our times is that we do not know how to relax — to expel stress and tension. Even in a healthy relationship there may be stress and tension. We are much better interpersonal communicators when we are relaxed — we listen better, process information more accurately, and are better able to empathize. Therefore, we should try to relieve tension through relaxation. We can induce relaxation through exercise, learning to stretch tightly and relax our muscles, and through introspective processes like yoga and meditation.

The way in which we induce relaxation, though, is not nearly as important as its influence. When we identify the source of stress, we are in a much better position to cope with it because simple identification tends to reduce stress. For example, if you perceive that a relational partner is the major source of stress in your life, you could deal with this person much better once you are sure your perception is valid. This is because you would not only be able to better articulate your own feelings but also better understand the feelings of your partner. Because of this increased capacity for communication, you and your partner might be able to understand and cope with factors that otherwise would cause your association to deteriorate.

You also can thwart the destructive side of stress by not letting it build to intolerable levels. Sometimes we mistakenly assume that it is better to keep our disenchantment with a person hidden than to bring it out into the open. The trouble with this strategy is that this person will continue to commit the behavior that originally led to our disenchantment. As a result, our disenchantment may give rise to stress, the stress may reach intolerable limits, and we may verbally explode. Such verbal outbursts will do little more than undermine the relationship and advance its deterioration. As we see it, then, people should purposely and constructively disclose their disenchantment with a relational partner as soon as they are sure they have correctly identified their partner as the true source of their disenchantment. While conflict may result from such disclosures, it is not likely to be nearly as intense as conflict following a verbal eruption.

The final coping behavior we will talk about is functional conflict. Functional conflict occurs when people discuss the sources of their difficulties rather than the flaws in their respective identities. As you might guess, people must be skilled in the management of conflict if this final coping behavior is to work. As a result, we will give the subject matter separate treatment.

CONFLICT MANAGEMENT

As we stated earlier, conflict is not necessarily bad. When constructively managed, conflict between people can be beneficial to all of the parties involved. It may open their eyes to factors that they had failed to consider, point to weaknesses in their thinking, or make them aware of potential problems that heretofore had not come to light. Because most of us are not schooled in conflict management, however, we frequently find it difficult to confine conflict to the sources of deterioration. This not only interferes with our abilities to use conflict in a functional way but also may cause us to experience frustration and stress. Since we want to reduce frustration and stress through functional conflict, it is important for us to learn and practice certain behavior that will maximize the positive benefits of functional conflict and minimize the probability of affective conflict occurring.

Win-lose Settings Conflict need not be a competition in which one party will win and the other party will lose. Unfortunately, many of us approach conflict as if it were, in fact, a competition. This attitude may be reflected in our communication behaviors toward the people with whom we are involved. Bringing out the worst in us, competition tends to stifle authentic communication, to give rise to deceptive and manipulative strategies, and to create an atmosphere of distrust. Such behaviors hardly are conducive to the successful management of conflict or to the health of a relationship. If anything, such behaviors will invite little more than affective conflict.

It is important, therefore, that we do not create a win-lose setting when using conflict as a helping device. We should realize that one need not win at the expense of the other to resolve differences. There are constructive alternatives to this kind of competitive strategy, for instance, cooperation, negotiation, and compromise.

Cooperation, negotiation and compromise arise out of the realization that conflict is most constructive when we adopt a strategy in which our respective winnings will be maximized and our respective losses will be minimized. When we approach conflict with this attitude, behaviors associated with competition will not be a factor. In effect, then, this strategy also will minimize the probability of affective conflict growing out of procedural and substantive differences.

Communication Behavior Needless to say, the way we communicate during times of conflict can assist us in putting conflict to a good use, or it can be fuel for the fire. To begin with, there are some obvious things we can do as communicators to thwart the possibility of conflict getting out of hand. At a minimum, we should avoid ego-threatening communication behaviors, that is, behaviors that will elicit defensive communication postures. In turn, we should try to avoid overreacting to statements and becoming overly defensive. During times of conflict, we have a tendency to perceive that every comment made to us is an indictment against our personal worth. Unless we are completely sure of the meaning of our partner's communications, consequently, we may want to avoid responding altogether.

In addition, we should avoid communicating downward to people when trying to use conflict as a preventive device. The notion that you can win an argument by adopting an air of superiority and intimidating people appears to be currently popular. While you may win the battle by intimidating people, you may lose the war. Intimidation seldom endears one person to another. On the contrary, it is likely to instill an "I'll get back at you" attitude. Instead of assisting people in the resolution of their differences, intimidation may serve only to create affective conflict at some later date. The hostility that is likely to build up during the interim, moreover, may make you dysfunctional.

During functional conflict the intensity with which we communicate bears monitoring. In the heat of a discussion, we tend to lose track of both the content of our messages and the way in which they are delivered. For example, to state that former President Nixon took certain privileges with the Constitution is not the same as saying he raped the spirit and essence of what the Founding Fathers laid down. The latter is much more intense than the former. The content of our messages can be further intensified by the inflection of our voices and by our gestures. Communicating in a normal conversational tone with your hands folded in your lap is not the same as shouting and shaking your fists. When high verbal and noverbal intensity occurs in one relational partner, a similar response may be evoked in the other partner. And the conflict may be reduced to a shouting match instead of a constructive search for sources of relational decay.

Listening and Closemindedness Closely aligned to the preceding discussion are listening and closemindedness. During times of even the most constructive conflict, listening skills may be forgotten. How can we expect to resolve differences of opinion unless we hear and process information concerning the reasons for such differences? We can't. It is of utmost importance to us, then, to try to ferret out the meaning of people's messages prior to responding. Otherwise, we risk responding in an inappropriate and dysfunctional manner.

In addition to listening, we should try to keep an open mind during functional conflicts. Relational partners can ill afford to entrench themselves in a particular position and doggedly defend it when trying to identify and resolve differences. The sources of relational decay are seldom dichotomous. That is to say, they seldom can be reduced to black and white terms. The factors that cause a relationship to deteriorate and cause the relational parties to experience stress are colored in every imaginable hue during functional conflict, and all of these sources need to be revealed. If they are not, the true sources of conflict may never be identified. It is doubtful, then, that the conflicting parties can come to grips with their difficulties.

Conflict is an inevitable consequence of relational deterioration, but it also can assist relational partners in airing and dealing with their difficulties if they learn how to manage it. Otherwise, conflict will contribute to, rather than prevent, further relational deterioration.

THE NECESSITY OF CHANGE

The final preventive measure that we will discuss is the necessity of change. In our discussion of dissimilarities, we said that relationships may deteriorate because one person experiences or desires to experience change while the other does not. We also said that these changes or the desire to change may be reflected in a person's attitudes, values, and lifestyles. Actually, change is the rule rather than the exception in interpersonal relationships. People change as they grow in age, maturity, and experience. We have no right, in fact, to ask them to stay the same. One of the obvious implications of this is that our relationships will change as the people within these relationships change. We may become friends with a former acquaintance, an intimate with a former friend, and lose contact altogether with someone who once shared our identity. Thus, changes in the people we come to know and in our relationships are bittersweet.

The point we want to make, however, is that change is not only inevitable, but necessary. Relationships that are void of change are ones that are stagnating. And stagnation, as we've already pointed out, is a sign of deterioration. It is important, therefore, that you not only try to understand change in those with whom you're involved, but try to be receptive to behaviors aimed at changing you. Unwillingness to change, albeit on your part or that of a business partner or friend, will seal the fate of the relationship.

CHAPTER SUMMARY

If you have ever witnessed or experienced a long-standing relationship as it begins to deteriorate and, finally, terminate, you know how painful it can be. In some cases, the pain present at a relationship's termination is of less consequence than the pain that would have been experienced had it been continued. It is apropos to ask again the questions that initiated this chapter. How many people disengage from one another because it is expedient? How many associations might not have terminated if the parties had been willing to learn to communicate the source of their difficulties?

We don't have all of the answers to these questions, but we sincerely hope that information in this chapter will assist you in thwarting the deterioration of your own relationships, or at least in making intelligent decisions about terminating them. Remember, there are sources of relational decay, there are communication behaviors that are symptomatic of relational decay, and there are preventive measures you and your relational partners can use to thwart relational decay.

THINK ABOUT IT

IN GENERAL

Complete the exercises given under Think About It: In General at the end of Chapter 1.

IN EDUCATION

We have suggested that excessive competition can be a highly destructive influence on interpersonal relationships between acquaintances, friends, and intimates. What communication behaviors in the classroom are most likely to generate excessive competition? What kinds of communication skills are most likely to facilitate cooperation? Finally, how can students use communication to minimize the negative effects of excessive competition when a teacher has created a learning environment in which students are forced to compete for grades and the like?

IN THE ORGANIZATION

1. Organizational leadership styles can serve to increase or decrease subordinate competition. Excessive competition among subordinates tends to cause distrust, infrequent and unauthentic communication, and even backstabbing. In terms of communication skills, generate a list of leadership behaviors that you think would serve to facilitate cooperation among subordinates, and ones that you think would serve to promote excessive competition. Discuss these kinds of behaviors in class; then generate a class list of behaviors designed to facilitate cooperation in organizational settings.
2. One of the more harsh realities of the business world is that people may come to work and find that they no longer have jobs. Assume the role of a supervisor who must tell not only a coworker but friend that his or her position has been terminated. What communication skills are necessary in this situation if you are to avoid eliciting a defensive communication and to maintain friendship with this person?

IN YOUR RELATIONSHIPS

1. In class, generate a list of communication behaviors that are exemplary of circumscribing. Following this, generate a list of communication behaviors that you might employ in the effort to bring a relationship back on course once you've noticed that a relational partner engages in circumscribing.
2. We've suggested that people should employ the same communication skills at a relationship's end as they employed during the relationship's growth. What are these skills and do you perceive such a suggestion as realistic? Why or why not?

SUGGESTED READINGS

Filley, A. C. *Interpersonal Conflict Resolution*. Scott Foresman and Company, Glenview, Ill., 1975.

By design, our treatment of the origins of conflict, its management, and resolution was limited. We recommend this book for those of you who would like to learn more about the resolution of conflict on the job, in social settings, and within your own relationships.

Knapp, M. *Social Intercourse: From Hello to Goodbye*. Allyn and Bacon, Boston, in press.

This book's primary purpose is to provide in-depth information about the growth and deterioration of relationships. You will find the chapters devoted to relational deterioration a worthwhile supplement to our information.

Chapter Fourteen
Interpersonal Communication in an Uncertain Future

Accelerated change The notion that changes in our lives are speeding up to the point that societal instability is becoming the rule rather than the exception.

Occupational diversity The notion that people should learn skills that will enable them to adopt to changes in their occupation without total reschooling.

Information management The ability to discriminate between important and nonessential messages whether at school, at work, or at home.

Information overload Being confronted with more information than can be handled psychologically.

Forecasting Attempting to predict tomorrow's events and mapping out a set of contingency plans to cope with the predicted events.

As recently as fifty years ago, people could go to bed at night and feel safe in the conviction that the world would look much the same the following morning. The expectation was for fathers to go to work, members of the family unit to maintain close interpersonal ties, sons and daughters to watch over their parents as they grew older, and long-time friends and neighbors to live nearby. We were a nation of close-knit families, and geographic stability was the rule rather than the exception. Parents could fully expect to see at first hand their children grow, marry, and rear offspring. People born in towns like Newcastle, Pennsylvania, could fully expect to live out their lives in close proximity to their geographic origins. Indeed, life was predictable.

Revolutions of one kind or another, however, have changed all that. In the past three quarters of this century, our concepts of identity and relational units have been changed by economic, technological, and psychological revolutions. The economic revolution grew out of what historians call the Great Depression, the technological revolution grew out of wars both hot and cold, and the psychological revolution grew out of a period of national introspection that is still with us.

But the changes we have gone through in this century are only previews of the changes yet to come — changes that will continue to affect our individual identities as well as our occupational, social, and relational roles. These changes not only will influence the accuracy with which we can predict the events of tomorrow, but also will influence the needs we experience and the ways in which we communicate to satisfy those needs. In this final chapter, therefore, we would like to discuss some of the changes that may occur in our interpersonal relationships and interpersonal communication behaviors in the not so distant future and to speculate on some of the strategies that may assist us in coping with these changes.

Are we really losing our sense of permanence in the world?

A NATION OF ACQUAINTANCES

One of the things Alvin Toffler writes about in his best-selling *Future Shock* is that America has become a "throw away society."[1] We buy and use products fully expecting them to serve only a temporary function. Most of us buy a car fully knowing our enchantment with it will be brief, purchase an article of clothing fully expecting its stylishness to be short-lived, and enthusiastically participate in fads, which are by definition only temporary.

In effect, we have lost contact with the idea of permanence and the idea that things are made to last. This is certainly true of the products we buy, and there is evidence that suggests it may become true with respect to our interpersonal relationships. To some extent, this may be the result of external pressures. For example, an employer may ask us to relocate, we may have an economic setback, or we may require an environmental change for reasons of health. To some extent, though, this also may be the result of personal choice. Whether our loss of contact with the idea of permanence is attributable to external pressures or to personal choice, this loss will affect the nature of interpersonal

[1]Alvin Toffler, *Future Shock,* Random House, New York, 1970, pp. 45–64.

relationships and interpersonal communication. Thus, to begin our discussion of interpersonal communication in an uncertain future, we would like to examine some of the sources of the loss of permanence, and then speculate on their potential impact.

THE DEATH OF ROOTS

In our opening remarks we said that this was once a nation of close-knit families and that geographic stability was the rule rather than the exception. These two factors gave rise to neighborhoods in which there were a sense of community and durable interpersonal relationships. People had immediate access to the identities of the neighborhood, friendships kindled in youth were likely to last a lifetime, and communication was largely face-to-face.

This all began to change during the economic and physical droughts of the 1930s. Whole families were forced to abandon both friends and the home-steads of their forebears. While these families found new homes, the chances to reestablish geographic roots all but disappeared with World War II at what Peter Drucker called the beginning of "the largest mass migration in our history."[2] There is little evidence to suggest that we have become less migratory since that time. Toffler graphically illustrates this when he states:

> Between March 1967 and March 1968 — in a single year — 36,600,000 Americans (not counting children less than one year old) changed their place of residence. This is more than the total population of Cambodia, Ghana, Guatemala, Honduras, Iraq, Israel, Mongolia, Nicaragua, and Tunisia combined.[3]

During the 1930s, people moved because it was an economic necessity — a matter of survival. As Steinbeck so vividly points out in *The Grapes of Wrath*, the migration of the 1930s was a reluctant one. While this continues to be true among the rural poor in America, those of us who have assumed occupational roles characterized by a high degree of geographic mobility appear to have adopted almost cavalier attitudes toward moving. Executives at IBM, for example, suggest that the company letterhead really stands for "I've been moved."[4]

It's not uncommon now for people to move for environmental rather than economic reasons. By environment, we mean both the physical environment and psychological environment where one works. For those who grew up in

[2]Peter Drucker, *America's Next Twenty Years*, Harper & Row, New York, 1968, p. 92.
[3]Alvin Toffler, p. 68.
[4]Alvin Toffler, p. 68.

metropolitan areas, this usually means that they continue to move further and further away from their familial and geographic roots.

So what are we saying? Since we are no longer a nation of close-knit families and there is geographic instability, our ideas of permanence and our interpersonal relationships and communication behavior have been affected. The question that needs to be addressed is: How did this come to be?

OCCUPATIONAL INSTABILITY

A little over one hundred years ago, we had livery stables rather than garages, blacksmiths rather than mechanics, and hitching posts rather than parking meters. Henry Ford not only changed all that, but in the process, created vocations that would have had no meaning whatsoever to eighteenth-century America.

The technological innovations of the latter half of this century have had a similar effect. Advances in technology like microcircuitry have given rise to an avalanche of highly specialized vocations. While these technological innovations have served to create specialized vocations, they also have eliminated the relevance of one-time useful and constructive occupations. Whereas camera lenses were once ground by precision craftsmen, they are now ground by an automaton working in conjunction with a computer.

Further advances in technology will undoubtedly give rise to more and more specialized vocations. At the same time, though, advances in technology may eliminate more vocations than it creates. Futurists like Toffler warn that the turnover in jobs resulting from both the creation and elimination of vocations will change the nature of interpersonal relationships within the organizational setting.

Toffler's warning is not without basis. In the 1960s alone, the average twenty-year-old male could expect to change jobs between six and seven times prior to retirement.[5] Assuming this figure will continue to increase, one cannot help but conclude that the number of permanent relationships that sometimes grow out of the organizational setting will decline.

The instability resulting from both the creation and elimination of vocations also may be a source of the loss of permanence. People may leave the organizational setting because their jobs are no longer relevant, or they may enter the organizational setting because they possess specialized skills. The temporal limitations of their jobs can't help but carry over to their communication behavior and their relationships with coworkers.

[5]U.S. Department of Commerce, *Population Characteristics*, Series P-20, #188.

ACCELERATED CHANGE

The increasing speed at which things change has taken away earlier feelings of stability and security. The person who presently goes to bed thinking that the world will remain the same is likely to have a rude awakening. The current rate of change is not about to slow down. On the contrary, the rate of change is accelerating at this very moment. We are not only talking here about technological change but also changes in our individual roles and relational units. Women are continuing to assume more important roles in business, government, education, and even religion. Men will have to continue to learn to share these former male-dominated provinces with women. Also they will have to learn to share in domestic roles. In the long run, this will affect increasingly both the nature of the relationships between men and women and the ways in which they communicate with each other.

The impact of accelerated change is evident in more than the changing roles of men and women. It is also evident in our changing attitudes toward marriage, toward the family unit, and toward heterosexuality. Within the relatively short span of fifteen years, the acceptance of unmarried couples living together has become commonplace, fewer and fewer married couples are having children, and widespread disdain for homosexuality has begun to wane. Perhaps we have come to accept the fact that times change and social mores reflect the times.

Accelerated change has become a fact of life. Therefore, to assume that the temporary nature of our technologies, our roles, and our attitudes toward sociological institutions like the family have whittled away at the concept of permanence does not seem unreasonable.

COMMITMENT

Whereas the 1950s were characterized by mass apathy, the 1960s were characterized by mass commitment. Whether the cause was civil rights, the actualization of human potential, or the war in Vietnam made little difference. People committed themselves totally and unequivocally to the cause in which they believed. These commitments were not without costs, for the murders of civil rights workers, strife on campuses, and chaos in the streets serve as bitter reminders.

We have reason to believe that the costs of total commitment in the 1960s have made us reluctant to commit ourselves totally in the 1970s, even in our relationships with people. Our students have told us that they believe the costs of total commitment to a relationship frequently exceed the rewards that can accrue from the relationship. As a result, many of them prefer temporary rather than long-standing relationships, particularly with members of the opposite sex. In effect, they truly believe relational partners should live one day at a time.

For all intents and purposes, the reluctance to commit oneself totally to another precludes the possibility of interpersonal relationships — as we now understand them — becoming intimate. You'll recall from the discussion of intimate relationships that one of the ways in which people achieve intimacy is by agreeing to a series of hierarchical commitments. Obviously, if we project that a relationship will be only temporary, we will not be motivated to communicate in a manner that will foster relational growth. Our reluctance to engage in total commitment will carry over to our self-disclosures and this will work against people sharing the more deep-seated facets of their respective identities.

If we are reluctant to commit ourselves at present, then what can we expect in the future? We think this reluctance may become even more pronounced as a result of geographic and occupational instability. If we customarily live and work in a given place for only short periods of time, we may avoid the painful process of having to say farewell by never saying much beyond hello. In other words, we may avoid the costs of commitments by simply not making them.

THE CONSEQUENCES OF IMPERMANENCE

As we see it, then, there are at least four sources of the loss of permanence: (1) the death of geographic roots, (2) occupational instability, (3) accelerated change, and (4) noncommitment. While we have discussed these four sources independently, there is little doubt that they have and will continue to have a collective impact on our interpersonal relationships and interpersonal communication behavior. Therefore, our discussion of their present and future impact will reflect this viewpoint.

The Depth of Relationships In the preceding chapters we said there were three levels of human relationships: an acquaintance level, a friendship level, and an intimate level. We also said that communication behavior changes as people move from one level to the next. Finally, we said that the probability of people penetrating beyond the superficial facets of their identities would be a function of the needs that they assist each other in satisfying, time, and purposeful self-disclosures.

The key word here is time. At present, we simply cannot expect relationships to grow unless the partners in the relationship are given sufficient time to explore their respective identities, establish need compatibility, and a pattern of communication with which they feel comfortable. The factors we've talked about thus far, however, suggest that there are real and imagined constraints on the amount of time people will spend together in the near future. Whether real or imagined, these constraints may influence the depth of their interpersonal relationships.

Assuming that the rate of relational growth remains constant, how can we expect people on the job to penetrate beyond the superficial facets of their identities if they believe their working relationship is only a temporary one? As it now stands, people frequently expect their relationships with coworkers to become more than that. This expectancy motivates them to communicate in a manner that will open the door to a relationship based on more than task attraction. But if people assume they will be working with someone on a temporary basis, the thought of making something more out of the relationship may never cross their minds. Even if it does, they may be reluctant to commit themselves to such a course of action because their projected separation may be painful, and their communication behavior will reflect this projection. Put simply, they will communicate with one another at a safe psychological distance.

The same can be said for family members who frequently must relocate with the breadwinner. What can they expect to gain by becoming involved with a community and its members or by committing themselves totally when they fully expect that their geographic roots will be temporary? Involvement and commitment might make it much more difficult to pull up their roots and leave. As a result, they may base their communication behaviors on this expectancy, and this may thwart effectively the possibility of them becoming more than acquaintances with the people they meet.

At a minimum, then, one potential consequence of the loss of permanence is that our relationships with the people we meet on the job and in our communities may become more shallow. Assuming that this does happen, our reluctance to try to decrease the psychological distance between ourselves and the people we meet also will diminish the fidelity with which we communicate. In turn, this may affect the quality of our work as well as the quality of life in general.

The Duration of Relationships Expectancies based on the idea of impermanence also may influence the duration of our interpersonal relationships. Even if we do establish friendships with people on the job, in the neighborhood, or in school, these friendships may be short-lived. We live in an age in which intercontinental communication is as easy as the nearest telephone or television set. But electronic communication is no substitute for face-to-face communication. This is particularly true when it comes to trying to maintain friendships.

Physical distance frequently gives rise to psychological distance. This may be more common in the future. To begin with, increased geographic instability will increase the probability of people being separated by vast physical distances. In addition, the psychological changes that occur in people will accelerate. The duration of a relationship between business associates, neighborhood friends, or former college roommates may be undermined by both the distance that separates them and the psychological changes that they undergo. In addition to influencing the depth of our relationships, therefore, the loss of permanence may work against the maintenance of relationships that have grown beyond the stage of acquaintanceship.

The Quantity of Relationships A century ago, people had relatively few interpersonal relationships. Yet these relationships were sustained over long periods of time and communication was frequent. At present, we have many more relationships than our predecessors. And by all indications, the number of relationships we will have in the future will increase as a function of geographic mobility and occupational instability.

Unlike the relationships of a century ago, however, the relationships of the future largely may be temporary. Further, they may be formulated with this expectancy in mind. Because people will expect their relationships to only serve a temporary function, attitudes toward the termination of relationships may begin to change drastically. In contrast to the present, for example, people may learn to terminate their relationships without experiencing psychological pain or guilt.

A third consequence of the loss of permanence, then, is that the number of relationships that we form will continue to increase. At the same time, the durability of these relationships may continue to decrease. While the quantity of our relationships may increase, therefore, there is no guarantee that the quality of these relationships will increase. This is because quality depends on the fidelity with which even temporary relational partners communicate.

Communication and Instant Intimacy The final topic we will discuss in relation to the loss of permanence concerns the human communication transaction itself. Up to this point, we have suggested that the fidelity with which people communicate will diminish with increased geographic mobility, occupational instability, accelerated change, and the rise of temporary relationships. In addition, the rate of self-disclosure and social penetration cannot be the same in the future as it is today. People of the future, accustomed to accelerated change and the temporary nature of their relationships, may try to adapt to the instability that characterizes their lives by engaging in *instant intimacy,* a term we used in Chapter 9. Instant intimacy, you'll recall, is a manipulative communication strategy by which people disclose deep-seated facets of their identities to achieve psychological or physical intimacy with someone in as brief a period as possible. People who employ such strategies are interested in an intimate relationship on a temporary basis rather than permanent one.

While this strategy may appear devious when placed in the context of contemporary interpersonal relationships, it may be necessary in the future. As a case in point, consider two people who are required to work jointly on a psychologically demanding task. If they know very little about each other, they will be unable to predict each other's communication behaviors or accurately interpret and appropriately respond to them. This lack of fidelity may undermine their ability to work jointly; this may add to the stress they feel as a result of the task's demands; this may delay completion of the task. On the other hand, if they overlooked the temporary nature of their relationship and mutually disclosed relevant intimate information about themselves, these problems might be thwarted.

The point is a simple one. In order to compensate for their transitory lifestyles and the temporary nature of their relationships, people of the future may engage in a highly accelerated form of self-disclosure and identity penetration. By doing so, they may be able to maintain a high degree of fidelity in their communication transactions, and thereby minimize any negative effects that may result from geographic mobility, occupational instability, accelerated change, and the reluctance to make long-range commitments. Of course, you may be wondering whether or not this accelerated form of self-diclosure is any different from instant intimacy, a term we introduced earlier. To our way of thinking, it is. Instant intimacy is a form of ingratiation and usually occurs between people who are physically attracted to one another. The kind of accelerated disclosure we are talking about here, however, should be targeted at accomplishing some mutual task in the work environment.

As you can see, then, our individual roles and relational units have undergone tremendous changes in a relatively short span of time. Close-knit families have all but disappeared, geographic instability has given new meaning to the idea of roots, technological innovations have undermined the security of vocations, and people appear to be more reluctant to make important commitments than perhaps at any other time in history. Whether these trends will become more pronounced is open to debate. There is evidence to suggest that we will become increasingly migratory, that our relationships will become increasingly temporary if not superficial, and that we are in danger of becoming a society of acquaintances.

But there is also evidence that is contrary to what futurists like Toffler would have us believe. For the first time since World War II, for example, the process of urbanization and the geographic mobility that has accompanied it is beginning to slacken. People are returning to their geographic origins as well as moving to smaller communities. There is also evidence to indicate that we have lost faith in products that serve only a temporary function. Be that as it may, we cannot afford to become complacent as we await tomorrow's events. We need to prepare ourselves for any contingency that may interfere or detract from our relationships with people. In concluding this chapter, consequently, we would like to speculate about some of the strategies that may assist us in coping with tomorrow's eventualities.

TODAY AND TOMORROW

If there is one thing we can say with absolute conviction, it is that we are in a period of transition and we are reassessing our individual identities and our relational units. The meanings of a masculine identity and of the feminine mystique are being redefined, and both males and females are reassessing every conceivable combination of relational unit. If anything, identities have become more diffused, and the roles people must assume in their relationships have become less stable.

It makes little sense to talk about coping strategies for the future if we cannot cope with present demands that are made on us. We believe as many futurists do that coping strategies for the present should be formulated with the future in mind. As a result, the strategies we will discuss reflect this belief. Let's now turn to strategies that will assist us in coping with present and future demands in professional, social, and relational settings.

DIVERSITY AS OPPOSED TO SPECIALIZATION

Historians very well may describe the sixties and the seventies as the age of specialization. And why not? General practitioners have been replaced by specialists in many areas, librarians have been replaced by information scientists, and the word *engineer* can mean anyone from the rugged individualist behind the controls of the Super Chief to one who has been trained to monitor the environment. Everyone has a specialty. But specialists should not become complacent because they have been so trained, for they very well may find their areas of specialization are no longer relevant. The first strategy that we would discuss, therefore, concerns the need for people to diversify — particularly with regard to their profession.

One of the things we emphasized in Chapter 13 was the necessity to be open and receptive to change. One expression of openness and receptivity to change is the ability to diversify. If specialists assume tunnel vision, it will carry over to their communication behaviors and their relationships in the organizational setting.

However, there is a more selfish reason for diversification. The individual who demonstrates a range of professional and interpersonal communication skills is likely to be less affected by technological innovation. On a professional dimension, for example, such individuals may not be forced to migrate because they can adapt to the new demands of a specific innovation. This is bound to have a positive effect, moreover, on the individual's relational partners. Rather than have to pull up their roots frequently and adjust to new environments, they may be able to establish enduring interpersonal ties as well as geographic roots. This will minimize the stress that inevitably accompanies relocation, and in turn this will improve the relational unit.

Diversification is important to more than the area of one's profession. Unlike the past, the present and future will continue to demand role diversification from people. Men and women who are locked into one particular role, whether in a social or relational setting, can expect frustration in the future. As it now stands, social as well as relational roles are being redefined almost constantly. The person who chooses a specific role today may find that the role will be redefined tomorrow. It is important, therefore, that people remain open to the diversified roles that the present and future increasingly will require.

PREPARING FOR TURNOVER

A second strategy that may assist us in preparing for the eventualities of tomorrow concerns preparing oneself and relational partners for turnover. Diversification may minimize the possibility of migration, but it cannot rule out that possibility.

Nothing can be quite as frustrating or as stress producing as a sudden and unexpected change in one's profession, social circle, or relational unit. In addition, sudden and unexpected change may be a source of affective conflict and destructive communication. The individual who is caught unaware by an employer's request that he or she relocate can't help but feel anxiety and tension. Relocation may mean a change in friends, in lifestyle, in school systems, and in working relationships. The anxiety and tension that this person feels may generalize to his or her relational partner and, unless they can deal with it constructively, it may prove to be a source of interpersonal upheaval. This need not be the case. Research suggests that people who anticipate and prepare themselves for sudden changes can cope with them nicely. Although their lives will be interrupted, negative repercussions will not occur.

By all means, then, people should prepare themselves for turnover on an individual basis and assist their relational partners in doing likewise. While sudden and unexpected change will not have an appreciable impact on the individual basis and assist their relational partners in doing likewise. While the individual with a spouse and children. The question that needs to be addressed is, What skills or behavior will assist people in preparing for turnover?

Openmindedness Throughout this book we stress the importance of open-mindedness. Up to this point, though, we have talked about openmindedness in terms of our encounters with people and the relational commitments that may follow. In addition to being openminded about people, however, the future will demand that we remain openminded about the changing values and social mores that will accompany it. People who want to grow with the times cannot afford to adopt rigid and unyielding attitudes toward values and social mores. This is not to say that people should never reject such changes, but that people should either accept or reject such changes after careful study of them. Careful study, in which the consequences of such changes are intelligently weighed and evaluated, demands a large measure of openmindedness.

Interpersonal Involvement Closely linked with openmindedness are our current and future attitudes toward the rate of interpersonal involvement. We suggested that our interpersonal entanglements may become increasingly temporary as a result of the transitory nature of the future. Does this mean that communication skills need not be as effective in the future as in the present? Does this mean that temporary relationships in the future will be less meaningful than the more enduring ones that are commonplace in the present?

We think that the communication skills demanded in the future will be far more taxing than those now required. Given the time constraints we will confront in the future, the potential for inaccurate interpretations of people's messages and identities will be quite high. It would seem, therefore, that the communication skills we now need to practice will have to become almost habitlike in tomorrow's world. Put simply, we will not be afforded the time to try to go back and start all over when our initial transactions with people are characterized by high degrees of error. Consequently, we must intensify our efforts to learn the communication skills currently taught and incorporate them into our customary ways of behaving.

There is no reason for an interpersonal relationship to be less meaningful because the parties are aware of its temporary nature. Such an awareness, in fact, places the parties in a position where they can come to grips with their real identities rather than the public ones people now communicate in their initial transactions. In the effort to take advantage of the position in which they've been placed, though, the skills we've stressed in this book will need to come to the forefront.

Information Management In the effort to maintain an open mind or realize the most from even a temporary relationship, however, we will have to manage the sources of stress that can undermine our communication skills.

One of the major sources of stress in contemporary society is information overload. Most of us are bombarded by far more messages than we can handle in a given day. If you have a full-time job and are a part-time student, for example, you must cope with innumerable messages on the job, as well as those supplied by your teachers and textbooks. If you are living with someone, the messages transmitted by your relational partner(s) compound this problem.

Because we can't possibly handle all of the information in our environment, we are sometimes guilty of something called supersimplifying. In effect, when we supersimplify we reduce complex issues and problems into simple ones and deal with them on that level. Obviously, supersimplifying may give rise to things like selective attribution, affective conflict, and communication denial. If we desire our interpersonal relationships to remain healthy, we can ill afford to engage in supersimplifying or the behavior it may lead to.

Since information overload is and will continue to be a source of stress and strain on our relationships, it is important for us to manage the amount of information and communication in our lives. Information management involves little more than making intelligent decisions about the most and least important messages that affect you and those with whom you are interpersonally involved. Most of us simply are not in the habit of managing important and unimportant messages. As a result, we pay more attention to gossip on the job than a memo concerning a policy decision, ignore the comments of a relational partner in favor of a television news commentator, or, in some cases, simplify the meaning of messages because our information processing abilities have worn down.

Continuous Education The last strategy we will discuss is the need for people now, and in the future, to embrace the idea of continuous education. Even the content of this book eventually may lose its relevance to you as a communicator. This is because knowledge claims about interpersonal relationships and interpersonal communication are constantly changing as a result of new thinking and new research findings.

We cannot afford to be content with what makes sense today; it may be nonsense tomorrow. Whatever the area, therefore, we must commit ourselves to a process of continuous education. In this way, we can take full advantage of knowledge claims as they are made rather than after they are made.

CHAPTER SUMMARY

We do not claim to have especially keen insights about the future, and we have included with our thoughts some of those of futurists like Arthur Clarke and Alvin Toffler. We presented a realistic picture of the changes that have occurred in interpersonal relationships and communication behavior, and we have suggested changes that may yet to come pass.

Simply because we have been a "throw away society" does not necessarily mean we will continue to be so. Simply because we've lost contact with the idea of permanence does not necessarily mean the idea is inoperative. One thing, however, does seem certain. The way that we relate and communicate with people today will, in part, shape the way that we relate and communicate with people in the future. In a very real sense, then, the uncertainty that characterizes future interpersonal communication can be dealt with here and now. Finally, we would like to comment on a current trend that holds both promise and dangers for the future.

During the sixties people seemed to be impetuously bent on discovering each other. While people also were concerned about discovering themselves in the same period, the search for "me" appears to have intensified in the latter half of this decade. Whereas both movements were initiated by college students and a few self-appointed gurus in the sixties, the current search for me appears to be spearheaded by the affluent and middle class, that is, people who have long left school and established themselves.

Organizations that currently offer people assistance in finding the real self or maximizing individual potential are having a monetary field day. The question is, Why? We speculate that an increasing number of people are in the position to confront their growth, rather than their deficiency, needs. Along the same lines, it appears that increasingly some people are less satisfied with themselves. Unable to pinpoint the source of their dissatisfaction, they turn to groups and organizations that parallel the encounter and T-groups of the sixties. Since we have contended that people must learn about themselves in the effort to become more effective interpersonal communicators, we are not about to condemn or malign this new period of national soul-searching. But

when we read articles about people continuously moving from group to group or continuously abandoning one form of philosophy in favor of another, we are reminded of the lessons learned by the characters in the *Wizard of Oz*. Each character already had what he or she had been looking for, but each had been looking for it in the wrong place. We think there is a lesson for all of us in that simple conclusion — whether it is applied to the present or the future.

THINK ABOUT IT

IN GENERAL

Complete the exercises given under Think About It: In General at the end of Chapter 1.

IN EDUCATION

We suggest that continuous education will assist people in preparing for turnover. We also suggest that interpersonal communication will be more taxing in the future than it is at present. In class, attempt to forecast (that is, predict) some of the factors that will make interpersonal communication more taxing in the future. Following this, generate a list of interpersonal communication skills that need to be taught now, and in the future, as people continue to educate themselves. Finally, discuss the methods by which these skills might be taught.

IN THE ORGANIZATION

We have implied that the major source of geographic instability in the future will be one's occupation. What is your current or intended occupation? Assume that you will have to relocate as a function of your occupation. What interpersonal communication skills do you plan to practice when reentering the work environment following relocation? Toward what purpose are these skills intended? Why?

IN YOUR RELATIONSHIPS

We have implied that the major source of geographic instability in the future affect a relational unit? How might one prepare the members of a relational unit for this kind of disruption? What kinds of interpersonal communication skills might assist the members of a relational unit in handling such disruptions? How might they be taught to the members of a relational unit?

SUGGESTED READINGS

Clarke, A. C. *Profiles of the Future.* Bantam Books, New York, 1958.
    Perhaps you know Arthur C. Clarke best for his screenplay and novel *2001: A Space Odyssey.* Clarke was making projections about the future long before he and Stanley Kubrick collaborated on this remarkable film. *Profiles of the Future* is fascinating. Many of Clarke's predictions have already come to pass.

    Lashbrook, W. B. and M. D. Scott. "Man-Machine Interface: The Message Strategy of the Future." In *Speech Communication: A Basic Anthology,* edited by Applbaum, Jensen, and Carrol. Macmillan Publishing Co., New York, 1975.
    This essay argues that the future will make extreme demands on the information-processing abilities of human beings and details strategies that

will assist people in coping with these demands. These strategies should prove to be a valuable supplement to those provided in this chapter.

Toffler, A. *Future Shock.* Random House, New York, 1970.

Anyone who cares to discuss intelligently the demands of the future should read this book. Toffler discusses the impact of the future on a full range of interpersonal settings, including the organization, social circles, and the family.

Epilogue

We opened this book with the tragic story of Christine Chubbuck, an intelligent and articulate young woman who committed suicide. We think it is fitting to end the book with Christine in mind because the world is replete with people like her.

It would be foolish to suggest that Christine's final and desperate attempt to draw attention to herself was solely the result of her inability to satisfy the needs that she and all of us have experienced. Christine was a very troubled and emotionally disturbed person. Her suicide testifies to this fact.

We can't help but wonder, however, whether Christine's fate might not have been thwarted had the people around her recognized and assisted her in satisfying her need to both give and receive affection. By the same token, we can't help but wonder whether Christine herself might not have changed the course of her life had she learned to express her own feelings and desires to her family and coworkers. We can't help but wonder — yet we will never know.

Be that as it may, Christine Chubbuck's death is not without meaning. There is a lesson in it for us all. Human beings are like the most delicate and difficult of flowers to grow. Too often we forget this fact. Too often we become callous because of the pressures that we feel and because of our preoccupation with looking out for number one. When we do, we run the risk of treating people as if they were consumable products with "no deposit-no return" tatooed across their foreheads.

We simply cannot afford to let ourselves become callous or indifferent toward the people with whom we live and work if for no other reason than a selfish one. The way we treat other people will go a long way in determining how they treat us. But more importantly, we cannot afford to be callous or indifferent because by doing so we negate all that is good about humankind.

Contrary to what some people would have us believe, there are no cookbook strategies that will make us more successful in communicating interpersonally. There are, however, a number of factors that may assist us in communicating interpersonally if we remain mindful of them. Those factors are really what this book has been about.

We realize the difficulties you face from one day to the next. We also realize how difficult it is to be mindful constantly of the needs of people around you and of the communication behaviors that you can engage in to assist these people in satisfying their needs. But in light of Christine Chubbuck and the people like her, we ask a single question: Are the difficulties that you face insurmountable?

SUBJECT INDEX

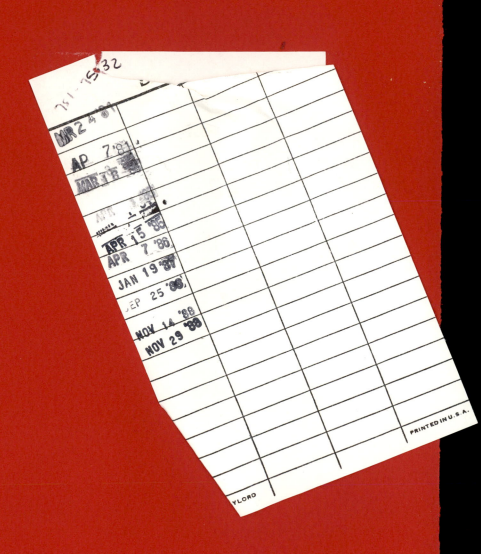